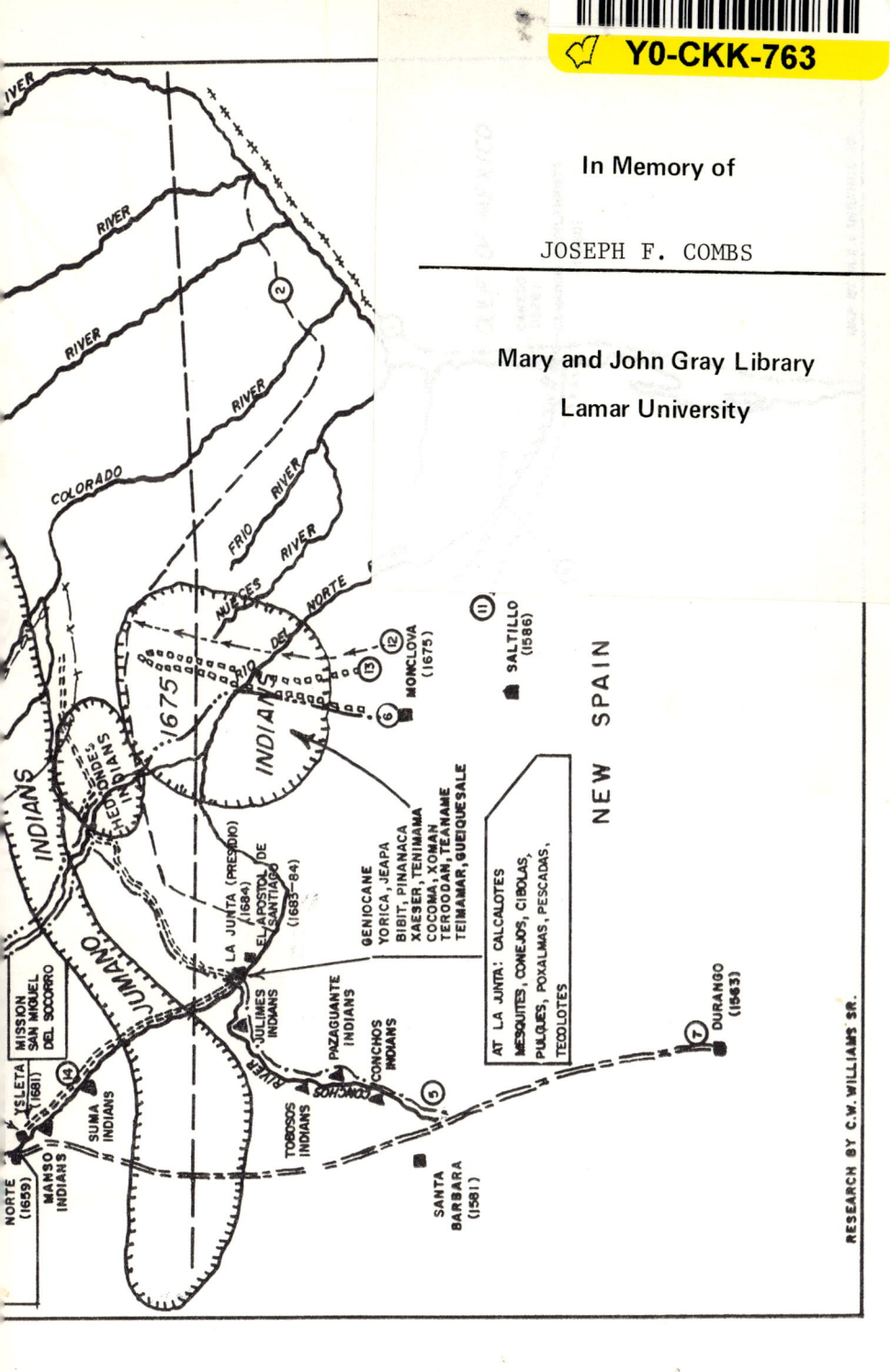

In Memory of

JOSEPH F. COMBS

Mary and John Gray Library
Lamar University

JOE F. COMBS
5635 DUFF AVENUE
BEAUMONT, TEXAS 77706

Never Again
Texas B. C. - 1821

Also by the author:
> *Ft. Stockton's First 100 Years*
> *Never Again: Texas 1821-1848, Vol. 2*
> *Never Again: Texas 1848-1861, Vol. 3*
>
> Articles:
>
> "Historian Thinks United States Must Flex International Muscles"
>
> "Historian Discusses Issues in Current Year Elections"

Never Again

Texas B. C. - 1821

Volume 1

by CLAYTON WILLIAMS

The Naylor Company
Book Publishers of the Southwest
San Antonio, Texas

Copyright ©, 1969 by The Naylor Company

This book or parts thereof may not be reproduced without written permission of the publisher except for customary privileges extended to the press and other reviewing agencies.

Library of Congress Catalog Card No. 68-29436

ALL RIGHTS RESERVED

Printed in the United States of America

SBN 8111-0275-0

Dedication

I wish to express my appreciation to my friends and my family for their assistance in completing this work.

Contents

List of Illustrations		ix
Chapter 1	B.C. — 1519	1
Chapter 2	Spanish Conquest and Exploration (1519-1535)	35
Chapter 3	Spanish Exploration and Settlements — Anglo Settlements, Indian Uprising in New Mexico — (1535-1683)	46
Chapter 4	Hazardous Times for the Spaniards — (1683-1728)	67
Chapter 5	Apaches Swarming in Northeast New Spain. The Comanches Moving in — (1728-1763)	91
Chapter 6	Synopsis of the American Revolution — (1774-1783)	113
Chapter 7	Depletion of Spanish Settlements in Texas — (1775-1800)	132
Chapter 8	Comanche War Trails to Mexico	151
Chapter 9	United States Expands Westward in Its Louisiana Purchase and Fights Britain as the Spaniards Attempt to Hold New Spain — (1800-1821)	168
Index		187

Illustrations

Picture section between pages xiv and 1

Page   1 Net from dry cave mouth of the Pecos. It is intact.
Trans-Pecos sandals of water grasses, the stalk, and fibre of Yuccas.

Medicine bag containing articles of mystical significance.
View of peyote photographed by W. D. Smithers of Alpine, Texas.

Page   2 Establishing the Virginia Colony, 1607.
Landing of the Pilgrims at Plymouth, Massachusetts, December 20, 1620.

Page   3 Settlement of Connecticut in 1636 and first meeting-house.

Comanche Indians: Horseback's Camp.

Page   4 Catlin, "North American Indians": illustration depicts a Comanche shooting arrows from the back of a running horse.

"Kiowa Archer" by Waldo Williams, Ft. Stockton, Texas.

Inside Illustrations

Page   3 Arrowheads as copied from the Texas Archaeological Society Bulletin, Vol. 25, 1954, Austin, Texas
Page 76 Ruins of Pecos — Catholic Church
Page 78 Ruins of Pecos — Astek Church
Page 80 Ruins of Pecos
Page 83 La Junta Region Map (1683-1760)
Page 102 Trans Pecos Spanish Explorations 1519 to 1684
Page 159 The Great Comanche War Trail Through Central Pecos County
Page 163 Comanche War Trails in Brewster County

Foreword

The object of this work is a study of the historical and political background of West Texas, including a region of semi-arid and arid lands within which are the foothills of the Rocky Mountains and the Rio Grande on the west, and the Pecos, Concho, Colorado, Guadalupe, Nueces and Devil's rivers within its eastern limits. Being an area of little rainfall, providing few places for man or beast to obtain drinking water, with scanty and tough vegetation, the problem of survival for the Indians and their descendants (the Mexicans), the early Spanish explorers, and the Anglo-Americans has long been severe.

It is not generally recognized that this particular country was explored by the Spaniards at earlier dates than was the case in the better-known areas of the eastern United States.

Also, this work is designed to pay tribute to the early settlers and pioneers of this region, whose hardships and efforts to survive must be recorded as achievements of an epic nature.

Publisher's Preface

During this early period of Texas history when records were sometimes kept in a desultory manner, with inadequate information or with a definite personal bias, many conflicting dates crept in; many divergent spellings of names and places occurred.

After careful scrutiny and diligent comparison of the data available in different sources, the author has used those dates and spellings which, in his opinion, checked out to be correct. The informed reader is urged to consider such variations, not as errors, but as differences of opinion.

Net from dry cave near mouth of the Pecos. It is intact.

Trans-Pecos sandals of water grasses, the stalk, and fibre of Yuccas.

Medicine bag containing articles of mystical significance.

View of peyote photographed by W. D. Smithers of Alpine, Texas.

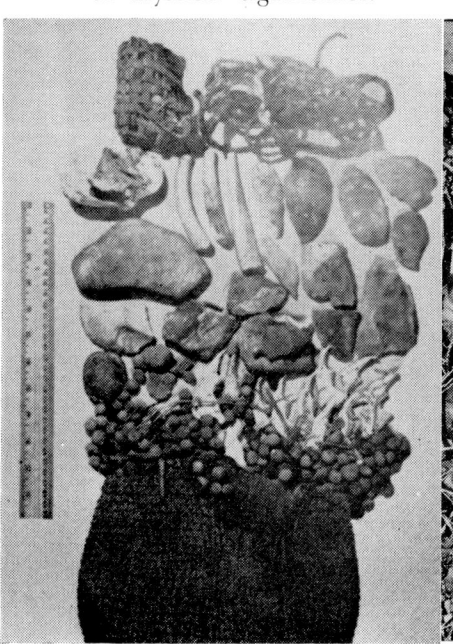 

Establishing the Virginia Colony, 1607.

Landing of the Pilgrims at Plymouth, Massachusetts, December 20, 1620.

Settlement of Connecticut in 1636 and first meeting-house.

Comanche Indians: Horseback's Camp.

Catlin, "North American Indians": illustration depicts a Comanche shooting arrows from the back of a running horse.

"Kiowa Archer" by Waldo Williams, Ft. Stockton, Texas.

Chapter 1

B.C. — 1519

As a relief from the present anxiety over new developments such as long-range missile bombs, man-on-the-moon projects, and the orbiting of astronauts in capsules, it might be somewhat reassuring to look back at past events involving sudden changes and dangerous vicissitudes which man had survived in West Texas, and particularly in Pecos County. For a long period, we have no written records by explorers and travelers. Information about the prehistoric eras comes only from the studies of scientists. About this earlier time, many questions come to mind to which the work of anthropologists and paleontologists may eventually find the answer.

Evidence of the prehistoric fang-toothed tiger, dinosaur, mammoth, horse, camel,[1] and the Midland Woman[2] in West Texas date back more than twelve thousand years.

The remains of the Midland Woman, with fauna of the Pleistocene Age found six miles south of Midland, Texas are now recognized as being the oldest recovered skeleton in the New World, dating back prior to the Folsom artifacts of 10,000 years ago. Associated with this discovery were two species of fossil horse *(equus* and *Asinus conversidens)*, bison, peccary *(Platygonus alemanii)*, camel, antelope *(Capromeryx*, both large and small), mammoth, bird, turtle, sloth, cervid (deer or elk), rabbit, rodent *(Neotoma, Cynomys, Cricetidae)* and wolf *(Canis dirus)*.[3]

During the Pleistocene epoch of the last one million years on this continent, several violent climatic changes occurred. In the warm periods, the animals from temperate climates wandered north to Alaska. When the ice-sheets extended to New Mexico and Texas, most of such animals were exterminated.[4]

Dr. Dee Ann Story of the Balcones Research Center in Austin, Texas, recently told me that the research at the Amistad Dam region at the mouth of the Pecos and Devil's rivers, indicates that human habitation existed there some 15,000 years ago, with vegetation similar to that of the present day. Since that time, the elephant, camel, horse, and a very large bison roamed the region.

From the report assembled by Dee Ann Story and Vaughn M. Bryant, Jr., GS-667 *Preliminary Study of the Paleoecology of the Amistad Reservoir, June, 1966*, it appears that specimens dated about 8,200 B.C. contained the butchered remains of now-extinct species of bison, which had been driven over the canyon rim, then slaughtered and butchered in the rock shelter. Other specimens, dating back to about 900 B.C. contained a thick deposit of burned, cut, and broken bones of Bison bison.

Dr. Story said there was considerable speculation as to why the bison had been burned after having been driven over the bluff to land at the mouth of the cave inhabited by the Indians.

The above mentioned report indicates the presence there of the following arrow points and their probable

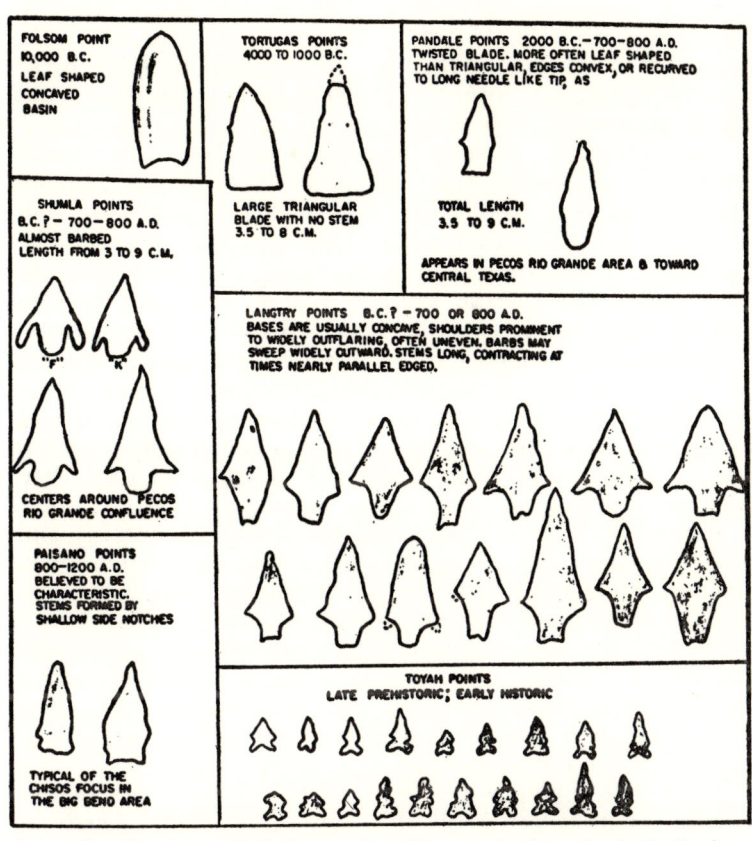

Arrowheads as copied from the Texas Archaeological Society Bulletin, Vol. 25, 1954, Austin, Texas.

dates: Plainview, Plainview-like, Plainview Golondrina, Folsom, Angostura, and Lerma — 8750 to 6820 B.C.; Gower-like, Early Barbed, Bifurcated Stem, Uvalde (?) — 7000 to 4000 B.C.; Nolan, Pandale — 4000 to 2500 B.C.; Langtry, Almagre, Valverde — 2500 to 200 B.C.; Montell, Castroville, Shumla, Marshall, Marcos — 1000 to 200 B.C.; Ensor, Frio, Paisano, Figueroa — 200 B.C. to 1000 A.D.; Clifton, Perdiz and others — 1000 A.D. to 1600 A.D.; and Metal points in 1600 A.D.

In sifting the decayed plant life of those intervening years, the scientists state that the West Texas climate varied from wet tropical to arid. For the past four centuries it has been that of a desert or semi-desert. The impressive magnitude and vastness of the deep canyons and rugged hills of the Langtry region, the great barrenness of the Big Bend Park topped by the Chisos Mountains and their assorted trees, the grandeur and stateliness of the Guadalupe Peak, and the loneliness of the country, far away from the noise of motors and the bustle of towns and cities, the serenity of this piece of nature causes one to wonder: What is God's real purpose in this destitute and forlorn country? But, shortly after the country is blessed with good rains and the Davis Mountains and other locations are as pretty and green as a front lawn, one can really appreciate its transformation in a few weeks from a desolate country to a scene of beauty. The golden sunsets of the semi-tropical sky begin with rich gold and red colors, fading, as the sun goes down behind the horizon, through shades of rose and pink to lavender, and projecting, as it does so, a variety of marvelous and changing colors on the margin of any nearby clouds.

The wide open spaces, now glistening with the rays of dazzling sun reflected off the light grays and browns of the plains vegetation, and with the various gray and purple tints on the ledges and gorges of the mesas and sierras, are periodically perfumed with the pungent scent of the black brush and blooms of the catclaw, and decorated with extravagantly colored blooms of various cacti. Although windblown, scorched, and cursed with dwarfed and thorny plants, this area is endowed with the most refreshing and invigorating early morning air on God's whole earth.

The late O. W. Williams,[5] in writing of the Chisos and other mountainous regions of the Big Bend, colorfully invested its plantlife with human traits, as:

> An hour's ride had carried us from the hills to a wide valley that lay between the mountain ranges. That hour transported us from one vegetable world to another, as if we were in the hands of the genie of some New World Aladdin's lamp. The sparse mountain oaks and junipers, with their stunted and dwarfed bodies, had disappeared, and we were now among the inhabitants of the valley — or "flat" as it is termed by our unpoetic frontiersmen — a floral people even more stunted and dwarfed and of forms infinitely more strange and grotesque than their kin of mountains. We had left a people of Quakers wearing the garments of peace and harmony; we had come among a people of war, frozen by some magic with sword in hand and armor buckled for the fray. Lance or sword or dagger peeped out from almost every bush, and where we saw a shrub without weapons in sight we scrutinized it with strong suspicion that somewhere in its drab or russett bosom there lurked some secret deadly missile ready to be thrust into the rash intruder.
>
> And here stands the gatún, the robber baron, with curved claws thrust out from his castle; claws that never loosen when once fastened, that grasp meat or raiment regardless of distinction, for everything is prey that comes his way.
>
> Over there is the tasajillo, an Italian brave, hiding under cover at the street corner, eager to thrust his stiletto into his unsuspecting victim, ready as he does so to draw back into obscurity.[6]

From the sand dunes east of the Pecos, across the salt grass "flats," over rock-capped mesas, and into the sierras, the shrubs were infested with small locusts, whose sudden flight startled man or beast with their warning rattle very like that of the deadly rattlesnake. In spite of the agile coach whip, the small lithe king snake, and the large bull snake, the rattlesnake was the recent, dominant reptile of the plains and sierra country.

The black-tailed deer ranged the mountainous country; the white-tailed deer, the foothills; and the antelope, the valleys and plains. At night the yip-yaps followed by the high pitched wail of the ever present coyotes gave cold chills to the timid. The two-toned low notes from the lobo caused anxiety and fear. Crouched in a springing position in the tall grass, the panther waved his tail in the air to entice a curious antelope within close distance, that the carnivore might make a dash for meat.

The Mexican eagle soared in the sky, rocketed downward to strike the back of a fleeing antelope or other animal, to sink his huge, powerful talons into its carcass and feast on its flesh. The buzzard, the scavenger of the west, sailed high into the wind while scouting for odorous remains of some animal. While cruising in the air, the hawk suddenly, and by some unknown instinct, plunged down on a hidden, frightened rabbit. Animal against animal of another species, human against human of another tribe, and snake against all life but its own, was the practice of nature in the far southwest. But on the plant life, directly or indirectly, all other life depended.

In this age of missiles and bombs, when our supplies could be immediately destroyed, we might have to revert to living on game and the vegetation of the country. One might wonder that anything could live on the scanty vegetation of the sunbaked earth. How could an animal exist in this region, much less a human being? Considering primitive man's food problem, one marvels that the Indian procured enough meat with arrows and lances. Pictures of the Folsom, Tortuga, Pandale, Shumla, Paisano,

Langtry, and Toyah points, reportedly found in this region of Texas, dating from 10,000 B.C. to historical times, could indicate that the design of the arrow was in direct relation to the size of the game.

Some of the finest and best preserved Indian artifacts, consisting of a bow, arrow, and food gathering net were recently found some thirty miles south of Marfa, Texas. Although estimated to be 1,000 years old, the mesquite, sixty-inch bow and arrows are well preserved. The net of yucca fiber supported by three sotol sticks, was possibly used to catch nuts, fruit of the prickly pear, or tuna as thrown by hand. It showed discoloration only in a few places. Although the bow was computed to have a substantial seventy-pound pull, comparable to that of the modern bow, Dr. Alfred E. Dittert, Jr., estimated that its range was little beyond thirty to forty yards considering the inefficiency and ballistically poor arrow point. This Indian's equipment is expected to be on display in the Santa Fe Museum.

Dr. George Hoffman, a physician of Fort Stockton, Texas, thinks that the spiraling ridged arrowhead (Pandale), was not constructed for the same purpose as spiraled rifling for guns, but to facilitate the extraction of the arrowhead from the flesh of game. There is some evidence of the Folsom Point in Pecos County. The atlatl, the fishermen's implement used to cast their darts in Lake Chapala, Mexico, is also found in this vicinity.[7] The dainty Livermore points, dated to be from the latter half of the thirteenth century, are found in the Comanche and Leon valleys of Pecos County and the Big Bend region. It took expert craftsmen to make these delicate points. Similar points are found in southeastern New Mexico.

How did the Indians make their arrow points? The dripping of cold water on heated flint is mentioned as a tedious way to break off chips. With modern tools or a sharp pointed instrument, Dr. George Hoffman completes an arrow head in about one hour. Blackhawk, a firm at Umitilla, Oregon, engaged in selling Indian artifacts and equipment and material along with instructions on how to make arrow points with modern equipment, states that the old Indian made his points by chipping or flaking with a deer horn tip or bone tool.

It is indicated that Indian craftsmen had workshops at various camp sites, where piles of flakes and chips of flint etc. are found in this Trans-Pecos region. The lower Cretaceous formation furnishes a series of various colored flints.[8]

Arrow shafts were made from the stems of the skunk bush, reeds, cane, chaparral, and the young shoots of the willow. The Comanches from the regions of the Red River brought with them the tough arrow shafts of the dogwood, and bows of the Osage Orange. Thwaites described the Apache arrow as being three feet long; the stem was of reed or cane, into which was inserted a piece of hard wood with a point of bone, iron, or flint. This arrow was shot with such force that it could pierce a man at a distance of three hundred paces.[9]

Travis Roberts of Marathon, Texas, said that the old-timers informed him that the Indians of West Texas used the limbs of Carrizo (Giantweed) and the Chittam bush (evergreen sumac) for the stem of the arrow shaft. Dr. Barton H. Warnock of Sul Ross State College at Alpine, Texas, in a letter on the subject, identified both of these plants, naming as one of them two large, woody grasses commonly called "carrizo." One variety of carrizo, he states, "is the *Phragmites communis,* which around Pecos, Texas, grows five to six feet tall with stems a bit larger than a pencil; the other variety, *Arundo donax,* grows abundantly around the Rio Grande, the young shoots of which could probably be used for shafts since the older stems are often used for fishing poles." The Chittam bush *(Rhus virens)* more correctly known as "Evergreen sumac," Warnock states, "is found throughout the Trans-Pecos in the Davis, Chisos and Guadalupe Mountains, being normally an evergreen shrub about three to six feet tall, with straight stems usable for arrowshafts."

Why did the Indian place the hardwood in the arrow shaft next to the point? Arrowheads were hard to come by. The purpose of the short length of hardwood probably was to withstand the impact of hitting and penetrating a victim and retaining the arrowhead for possible recovery from the dead victim, whereas the reed part of the shaft would not do so.

Available for bows were the limbs of the black locust, willow, wild mulberry, and the mesquite. The middle of the bows were strengthened by wrapping with the sinews or tendons of animals.

Lances were constructed to spear animals, fish, or other objects with what material they had, and conformed in length as to whether they were to be used on or off horseback. It is supposed that the large flint blades were attached by sinews or tendons to the body of the lance, but some Indians pointed the long, slim limb of the dogwood, and charred the sharp end with fire to harden it.

The Basket Makers lived primarily on the meat of rabbits. Cabeza de Vaca described the little boomerang which the Indians on the Devil's River used to kill rabbits in 1536. There the Indians brought him tunas, spiders, worms, and various insects to eat. Green mesquite beans mixed with earth were placed in an earthen hole, pounded to meal, combined with soil to make a certain mixture, then taken up and put in a basket to be saturated with water. It was tested for sweetness, and eaten if satisfactory. The tough seeds were spit out upon hides to be reworked and eaten after the same preparation. De Vaca said eating this mixture resulted in their stomachs being distended. These Indians used a large flint for a knife, sinews of the deer for the bow strings, and gourds for boiling water. The gourds were filled with water, heated by inserting hot stones, which were replaced to keep the water boiling.[10]

Found in many Indian graves are the teeth and bones of rabbits, portions of nets (assumed to have been used in trapping rabbits), along with baskets, sandals, mats, and numerous other articles made of the fibers of the yucca plants, identifying the lower Pecos region as having been inhabited by the Basket Makers and Rabbit Catchers.[11]

Plant fibers provided clothing, sandals, mats, and other materials. Spanish moss was made into cloth by weaving the strands. The down from the cattail made a soft lining for clothes and covers. Cattail stems and Bear grass blades were woven into the shoots of the willow to form baskets or mats.

The fiber from the long leaves of the Spanish dagger was used for clothing and footwear. The leaves were heated over a flame to soften the outer tissue, after which the fibers were stripped out and used to make twine, thread, sandals, or clothing. The Indians also made: needles of dagger points; brushes, mats, coarse twine, and strong rope from the leaves and fibers of the lechuguilla; basket strands from the young twigs of the red bud; decorative strands for baskets from the reddish-brown root bark of the skunk bush; baskets, mats, and shoes from tender limbs and shoots of the willow and other trees, or from the fibers of the yucca plant; and tough implements and needles from the dogwood.[12]

On the Conchos River in New Spain (Mexico), in 1582, Espejo found about one thousand Conchos Indians to be living on rabbits, hares, maize, gourds, melons, watermelons, fish, and mescales — the latter he explained were the leaves of the lechuguilla. They cooked the stocks of the lechuguilla and made a sweet preserve-like jam named "mascale." The Pazaguante Indians made him presents of feathers in different colors, some small cotton matas striped blue and white, and some mesquitama from the mesquite bean.[13]

The Pueblo Indians lived in mud-constructed or tule (bulrush) thatched huts, and cultivated maize, corn, beans, squash, melons, and gourds. The nomadic Indians lived in caves and various shelters of brush, animal hides, yucca mats or wickiups of the same material. Mrs. Charles Sherrill of Fort Stockton, Texas, states that at lone watering places, indications are that the Indians conveniently placed their camps a little distance from that water, so as not to interfere with the wild animals' source of water nor be molested by those animals when drinking. Game was abundant. Fish were generally plentiful in the few streams. In season, the fruits of the shrubs, trees, and cacti were eaten.

The nomadic tribes could always depend upon the sotol, saw yucca, and roots of the Bear grass. The Indian method of pit-oven cooking rendered some poisonous foods harmless and converted starchy foods to saccharine.[14] The cabbage part of the sotol and saw yucca was the principal year-round plant food. Sotol with meats and other foods was cooked for a large party in what is now called mescal pits. The average burned rock pile remaining today consists of a circular rim of rocks, one to two feet high, and six to twenty-five feet in circumference and sloping to the south. The rocks were placed on firewood, the wood lighted; food was put on the rocks after they were sufficiently hot; matted mud was placed over that, if water was handy; and the food was allowed to cook to the Indians' desire. Some authorities say that two days were taken to steam the pile.[15]

F. M. Buckelew related that when the sotol was "cooked they (the Lipan Indians) would remove the dirt and leaves, and take a hoe and rake the sotol out. When it had cooled, they would beat it up and make a thin sheet of it. They let this dry for several days and put it in a dry place for future use. It could be eaten raw, but their favorite way was to work it for some time in a wooden bowl, or until it resembled meal or flour; it was then mixed with water and made in small cakes and cooked in the ashes. This made a very good substitute for bread."[16]

Some of these large sotol pits are located where the mescal button, Devil's Root, or similar peyotes *(Lophophora Williamsii)* are scarce, and frequently where there is an abundance of sotol. The sotol pits on the T. W. Hillin ranch in Pecos County are in the shape of a quarter-moon with the opening on the south and the maximum build-up of rocks on its north side. Most of such sotol cooking places are in that shape, excepting seventeen on the Frank Hinde ranch, forty miles southeast of Fort Stockton. These were constructed in two rows of rocks, about fifteen feet long, running parallel a little west of due north. Each row of rocks is two or three feet wide, with one row two or three feet high, and the other somewhat lower. Among the rocks are found pieces of flint.

Close, and to one side of these two rows, is a hole in the ground about four feet square and lined inside with rocks. This is, I think, the true mescal pit. When mescal was cooked, it required only a little of that peyote to go a long way. Fowls, and heads of game wrapped in damp fiber matting when cooked within this underground oven were considered a delicacy.

Curious about the mescal pits, Jack Meeks brought Sam Haozous, the grandson of the Mimbreno Apache Chief, Mangus Colorado, to Pecos County. He got information from him and wrote it as follows:

> In preparing the mescal, the Apache first dug a hole in the ground approximately four feet deep and the width or circumference depending upon the number of families who were to cook mescal in that particular fire.
>
> After digging the pit, they covered the bottoms of the pits with much of the long grass that was in those days abundant in most of the western country. On top of the grass they placed firewood, and on top of the wood placed large rocks in a number to cover most of the pit. In preparing the fires, care was exercised in leaving an opening so that the same might be lighted at the bottom, evidently somewhat along the lines used by the charcoal burners of the Gulf Coast area.
>
> The grass, wood and rocks having been placed in the pit, the fires were lighted by some of the young boys.

After the wood and grass had burned, the boys would take large sticks and lift up the rocks so that they would fall as near the center of the pit as possible, then the young girls would place the mescal on top of the rocks. Next, the mescal was covered by a thick layer of grass, and on top of that, mud was used to make a covering to more or less seal the mescal on top of the heated rocks. According to Haozous, the rocks would remain hot for approximately two days. It usually required about one and one-half days to completely cook the mescal. After the mescal was done, the mud and grass were removed and the mescal taken out for use.

There were about six ways of preparing the mescal for use as food. One of the ways of preparing the mescal for food, was to pound, mash and squeeze out its juices into a container. This juice was sweet and used as a syrup with their bread.[17]

The Kiowa Indians brought back captives, plunder, and the mescal worship from the Rio Grande. In opposing the mescal rites of Indian tribes, the early Christian missionaries induced the United States government to prohibit the use of mescal. Lewin and Henning, in 1885, first described the mescal buttons some two or three centimeters in diameter as poisonous. John Mooney, an Indian agent, read a paper on mescal in 1894, and brought a supply of the buttons to the United States Bureau of Ethnology. Father Ortega named the plant Devil's Root. The Indians of Nayarit in the province of Jalisco regarded mescal as a food better than maize: as maize was food for the body, mescal was food of the soul, offered to the gods.[18]

The Indian peyote religion has spread to many of the Indians of the United States, and it is a most difficult task to convert those of that religion to Methodism, God, and Christ, according to the Reverend Steve Chibitty, a Comanche and pastor of the Oklahoma Methodist Indian Mission Church at Lawton. Humorously, he added, "I could much more easily convert a Baptist to Methodism and God."[19]

It is reported that only the Apache men took part in mescal ceremonies. Natividad was a Mexican boy friend of Guero Carransa, an Indian, in the vicinity of San Carlos, Mexico. Natividad learned to eat the powdered flour of the roasted sotol, and was told "how the mescal was roasted and hidden in a dry place to await the time of the mescal fiesta, when the wise men and warriors went away into the mountains to eat it, and dreamed dreams and had talks with the spirits while under the spell of the potent plant."[20] While becoming separated from Guero in trailing a wounded deer, Natividad saw some Indians in a cove of the high mountain, and secretly watched them.

Quite motionless, the Indians sat for a long time in a circle. Then, one of them got up, went to a nearby cave, and brought back a basket of willow bark in which were a number of round black objects. He offered these in turn to each Indian, who took a bit of it, and then placed it by his side. All of this procedure was in perfect silence, and monotonous to Natividad; so he slipped away. When he found Guero and told him about the sight, Guero was disturbed and cautioned him never to tell anyone at any time what he had seen for if he did the great spirit would be very angry with him and do him great harm.

In regard to the Indians' use of mescal as a stimulant, W. D. Smithers of Alpine, Texas, tells of witnessing a foot-race on February 23, 1927, of 89.4 miles, between San Antonio and Austin, Texas, by the Tarahumare Indians of Chihuahua, Mexico, who made the distance in 14 hours. Carrying along with them a small supply of pinole and mescal in a buckskin sack attached to a sash around their waists, they occasionally took these foods to aid them on their long hard run.

In the early 1940's, Smithers, living on the Rio Grande in the Big Bend, was informed of the capture of two of the Tarahumare Indians by the Border Patrol on this side of the river. Unable to understand either English or Spanish, they were taken to Ojinaga, where there was someone who could translate their language. It was then found that they had traveled the 225 miles east to find some mescal or peyote.[21]

A few years past, Baron Bruchlos, operator of the Cart Wheel on 64 East Seventh Street, New York City, had a quantity of peyote seized by Federal agents. His market for peyote was to beatniks and college students. Bruchlos stated he had contacted the Food and Drug Department, receiving their statement that peyote had no harmful effects. His containers of the molasses-colored drug bore seals of the Department of Agriculture, declaring that the contents were free of harmful insects. The agents and Bruchlos were both stalled, as the Federal charges were against peyote, and not Bruchlos. The peyote was obtained from cactus companies, and produced on Federally owned land leased by them in Texas; and the Agriculture Department's seal was on the capsuled product. To Bruchlos, the agents' act, as the Chinese say, "was altogether unexpected."[22]

The effects of mescal were studied by the late Dr. Valentine P. Wasson, a student of the mushroom family, who went to a Mexican-Indian village to examine the "sacred mushroom" which produced hallucinations. She stated:

> The mushroom is neither harmful nor habit-forming, but caused me to 'see' magnificent colors and patterns and a vision of a grand ball at the French Court of Louis XV.[23]

Although defined as a narcotic stimulant, if it is not harmful nor habit forming, why is it not cultivated, produced, and marketed to replace the habit forming narcotics? Dr. Charles Jones, a physician of Fort Stockton, Texas, answers the above question as follows: Narcotic drugs are used because of their ability to relieve pain. All have the side effect of causing a feeling of euphoria and tranquillity which is the cause of addiction. For that reason the colorful results of euphoria from mescal might come under that heading as it could affect some persons in that manner. Mescal could not replace the narcotic drugs being used, since it has no pain relieving ability.

One will be surprised at the food available behind the thorns, daggers and dirt. For instance, the Indians of the El Paso region took the heart of the lechuguilla *(agave wislizeni)* before it put forth its flowering stalk and, with its leaves trimmed off, baked and ate the head. In the area of Fort Stockton, the lechuguilla plants and their juices were considered poisonous. Tunas (fruit of the prickly pears) were peeled, squeezed, opened, and dried. The pulverized peeling and the dried pears were put into baskets to be eaten later.[24]

Sweet juicy blackberries of the bluewood, and stony, red, edible, pea-sized agarita berries were used in making jellies. The delicious fruit of pitihayas *(petaya)*, all covered with thorns, was ripe in July and August. Tubers of the water potatoes, found in the shallow ponds, were used as we use potatoes. The wild onion had a use similar to that of the cultivated onion of today.[25]

Bulbs of the wild hyacinth were roasted and eaten. Blossoms of the Spanish dagger were cooked and prepared like cabbage. Young stems and leaves of the wild spinach and the shoots of the pokeberry were cooked like greens. However, it was necessary to boil the latter for a time, pour off the first water and continue further boiling. Young leaves of the American lotus were used as we do spinach; the large tubers of it were baked, tasting much like sweet potatoes, and its round, brown nuts were roasted and eaten or stored for winter. The leaves and stems of watercress were cooked like spinach, or eaten raw.[26]

Dewberries, wild cherries, mulberries, and raspberries were available.[27] The wild raspberry of the Sacramento Mountains is reported to taste better than those cultivated. The wild gooseberry of that region must be cooked to be palatable. Pleasant tasting jellies and wines were made from the mustang and the purple-black mountain grapes. The dark olive-shaped fruit of the sparsely established Mexican persimmon was tasty after frost. Yellow plums on the Pecos River, also the fruit of the aromatic and ornamental anachuita,[28] and the pea-sized yellow fruit of the granjeno (chaparral) were good food. The ground plum tasted like green peas.[29]

Little tubers of the Indian breadroot were roasted or boiled. When raw, these roots made excellent salad. A sugarlike substance was obtained from the flowers of the butterfly bush.[30] The beans and pods of the screw bean were boiled in water to make molasses. The peculiar tasting ant honey, with an aroma similar to the syrup of squills, was available over the regions of the Rocky Mountains, West Texas, and Mexico. The ant colony, organized and regimented with policemen, honey-bearers, and workers, toiled from dark to daylight in gathering honey from the sugar saps issuing from the several points on the nectar-producing galls of the scrub oak limbs and from the leaves of the other nectar-producing plants. The honey-bearers transported eight and ten times their own weight of honey to the vertical entrance of their intricate system of underground palisades and storage rooms.[31]

In the fall, the piñón nuts of the mountainous regions were available. The edible acorn of the plains' shinnery was roasted or ground in the metates to be stored. The Mescaleros ate the fresh, sweetish inner bark of the pine, after pounding to pulp and baking. The fruit of the petaya, with its skin removed and the seeds taken out while it slowly boiled, was then cooled; portions were wrapped in corn shucks for preservation and later consumption. These tamales were reported to keep without spoiling for several months. The red doughnut-like fruit of the *mamillaria grahami* and the *cereus gregii,* and the berries of the juniper were eaten. Both the Lipans and the Mescaleros used the aroma of the *hedeoma reverchoni* for headaches, while rubbing its twigs and foliage together.[32]

In addition to food in the vegetable kingdom, wild game,

reptiles, and fish were eaten. Questionable, but reported, is the Indians' method of picking up drugged fish after throwing a stiff, toxic paste of the seeds of the Mexican buckeye into the water.[33] More customarily, the fish were seined with nets, shot with arrows, speared, or caught with small hooks.

As herds of buffalo were east of the Pecos River, but only a very few west of the Pecos, it was necessary for the Indians of West Texas to travel to the region east of the Pecos River for their buffalo meat, make jerky of it or salt it at the salt lakes in the present Crane County or southwest of the Guadalupe Mountains, to preserve it. Jerky, strips of meat dehydrated by being exposed to the sun and wind, (the Indians' most practical method for preserving meat), was and still is used for that purpose where refrigeration is unavailable. The early stockmen, trappers and others of Pecos County, Texas, used the jerky from deer and antelope as late as 1904. Even in the town of Fort Stockton, Texas, when the first butcher-shop opened up in the early 1900's, freshly butchered meat was screened away from the flies, cut up and sold on demand at ten cents per pound. Before it had a chance to spoil, the remainder was made up into jerky, which sold at twenty to twenty-five cents per pound.

Although the squaw was expected to butcher the carcass, liver was so favorite a morsel that the warrior cut it out, seasoned it with the gall bladder, and ate it and the marrow guts raw. The butchering was similar to that of the beaver trappers. The carcass lay on its belly with legs supporting each side, as a traverse cut was made from the nape of the neck along the spine to the tail. The skin was separated and pulled down each side to the ground and used as a receptacle for the dissected portions. The shoulder was then removed, and the hump-ribs cut off with a tomahawk, both being placed upon the skin followed by the "boudins," stomach, and tongue. The tongue and head were considered among the dainties.[34]

The brains were used to soften skins; horns made spoons and drinking vessels; shoulder bones, implements to dig and plow; tendons were used for threads and bow-strings; hoofs, for gluing arrows; wool, for garters, belts and ornaments; and the skin, for harnesses, lassos, shields, tents, shirts, leggings, shoes, and blankets.[35] The Plains Indians were reported by Vicente de Zaldiver Mendoza to have an amazing method of curing and coloring hides. In a village of five hundred tents covered with red or white buffalo hides, it was found that the hides were impervious to water, and would not harden after a wetting.

"The Indians of Central Mexico," says M. D. (Chico) Brown of Fort Stockton, Texas, who spent some time in that region, "scoff at the Texan's method of barbecuing meat. Those Indians use the pit-oven method to cook their meat by putting a good bed of coals in the bottom of the pit, placing meat wrapped in wet tow-sacks and tied to leaves of the Agave plant to keep the meat off the coals, and then covering the pit with something on which more coals are placed. Within twelve or fifteen hours, depending on the heat applied, they have the finest of cooked meat."

In adopting one type of the Indians' method of curing hides, the buffalo hunter stretched, dried, scraped off the flesh and fatty tissue, smeared the hairy side with a paste of wet ashes, rolled it up, and let it soak in water for several days. Then it was scraped of its hair; its inside plastered with animal brains; again soaked in water for a few days; stretched over rocks or a crude framework and knives run over it to squeeze out the water and remove loose material; then stretched to dry; and finally, rubbed and treated with tallow as a softener and preservative. Canagra (*Rumex hymenosepalum*) with roots in the shape of sweet potatoes contains about twenty per cent tannin. These roots were used by Indians and Mexicans for tanning. [36]

Stews or meats were seasoned with the ground leaves and stems of the Mexican tea plant, young green pods of the butterfly bush, the berries of the chilipitin plant, the ground meal of the cattail tule, the dry leaves of the shrubby sage, wild spinach, American lotus, pokeberry, the tubers of the Indian breadroot, and mesquite beans.[37]

For preserving meat and seasoning foods, the Indians

obtained salt from the salt lakes in the present Culberson and Crane counties, resulting in trails across the country. The Old Salt Trail, from the Presidio (La Junta) region on the Rio Grande from where the Cibolas (Indians who killed the buffalo) came up the Alamito Creek, passed by Kokernot Springs, Leoncita Springs, and Leon Springs, and went down Diamond Y Draw to the Salt Crossing on the Pecos River to get to the Cordova Lake in Crane County. This trail was still in use by the Mexicans just prior to and after the Civil War. That route from Leon Springs down to Presidio was taken over by the white man. As late as 1884, the Indian travois trail made by dragging their salted meat from the Cordova Lake to Comanche Springs (Fort Stockton) — could still be seen.

Flour or meal for bread was made from corn, the ground and dried roots of the Indian breadroot, root stalks of the cattail, shelled mesquite beans, screw beans, horse beans, and principally from the bulb of the sotol plant after it had been dried or cooked in the mescal oven, its pulp beaten up, ground, rolled into sheets, and allowed to dehydrate.[38]

Corn and maize, grown in "temporales," made flour for the Indians. The green or blue kernels were cherished by the Indians to the extent that, in honor of its crop, they put on a celebration, known by its name. The white man has never taken over that celebration; all that we have now is a dance, "Put your Little Foot," adopted from the Mexicans' "Maize Azul" (Blue Corn).

Grasses, grass seeds, and the roots of weeds and plants supplied the Indians with a variety of food. The multi-seeded leaves of the "Chamiza" plant on the Pecos River were palatable and full of protein. The early Tobosos Indians on the Conchos River in Mexico either derived their name from the Tobosos grass or the grass got its name from them, likely because they used and ate that grass. The choice of the grass seeds eaten by the Indians of West Texas is now thought by some authorities to have been the Eastern Gamma *(Tripsicum Dectyloidies)*, found especially in the mountainous regions and close by old Indian camps. This is a bunch grass with tasty seeds, which stock eagerly search for and eat in preference to other grasses of the region — so reported Wilson Smith and W. D. McBryde of Fort Stockton, Texas.

Liquors were made from a number of cacti and yuccas. The upper part of the peyote, mescal, or devil's root, after cooking, was chewed, or from it was obtained pulque to be made by distilling into the drink, mescal. Mescal was also made from roots of the lechuguilla. Alcohol was made from the prickly pear. Pulque, stronger than whisky, was made from the century plant. The top of the plant was cut off where the bud comes out; the inside of the plant was hollowed out to hold the liquid which ordinarily fed the stalk and flowers, and from this hollow, the agua miel (honey water) was collected. When this fermented it was called pulque. Upon being distilled, it became colorless and was known as tequila.

Petaya fruit was placed in large containers, its own weight causing the juice to settle out, which was poured off to ferment. The Mescaleros made liquor from the inner bark of the pine. Liquor so-called sotol, was made from the dasylirion, by baking, and allowing it to ferment. Perhaps, some amount of aguardiente was made along the Rio Grande from the intoxicating sugar cane rum.

The Mescaleros made tulipe or tesvino as a drink, adding *lotus wrightii* to make them "more drunk," *cassia corvesii* to "make noise," and *canotia holocanthe* to "make taste better."[39]

Ground mesquite beans, when mixed with water and allowed to ferment, made a weak beer.[40] Mustang grapes and agarita berries made wine.[41] The bean of the mountain laurel was used in portion to add exhilaration to liquor. The bean itself is deadly poison.[42] As early as 1536, the Indians often became intoxicated on the juices of several plants and were affected by the smoke of another plant, similar to the effects of marihuana.

By trial and error, the Indians had many plant usages for medicinal purposes. As an antidote for rattlesnake bites, an ointment made from snake herb was applied after the firm, sharp point of the Spanish dagger had been jabbed deeply into the wound to cause bleeding. A poultice of the mashed roots of the milk weed or the blazing star was applied to a snake bite, with an additional amount of substance given internally.[43]

The late Frank Hinde had an amusing story, relative to snakes, concerning the use of the rattlesnake's insides for medicinal purposes. His uncle, Jim Lacky, sent him out to a goat camp in southern Pecos County in the early 1900's to learn something about the stock business when he was just a lad. The goats were kidding and he was camped in a more or less permanent camp with the Mexican who was in charge of the goats. After finding a rattlesnake and pinning its head to the ground with a forked stick, he and the Mexican joined forces to sew up its mouth in the anticipation of some fun.

About sun-down, along came an Indian practitioner of herb cures, greeted them, unhooked his burro team and hobbled them out, and set his camp adjacent to that of Frank's and the Mexican's. The conversation thereafter brought up the subject of a lump on the Mexican's stomach, which was giving him so much trouble he would be compelled to go to town to see a doctor. The Indian told them he could cure the lump and went out to find some of his medicine. As this was their opportunity to pull a trick on the Indian with their harmless snake, the Mexican tied the rattlesnake in the lower end of the Indian's bedding, and got plenty of firewood to put on the fire to lighten up the surrounding region to be able to see the Indian's reaction when he went to bed. Darkness came, the fire was lighted to a high pitch, when the Indian stuck his feet down into the bed, slowly withdrew them, reached out for a candle and lighted it, lifted up the covers and with little concern grabbed the snake by the neck, just behind the head. Their anticipated fun was spoiled. They barely saved the snake from execution by showing the Indian that its mouth was sewed up, causing him considerable amusement about its helpless condition.

Afterward, the Indian made a deal to cure the lump on the Mexican's stomach for a consideration of $5.00 paid in advance, caught another rattlesnake, and mixed a concoction of the bile and blood of the two snakes for the Mexican to drink. The requirement for drinking this mixture caused a heated argument and nearly a fight with the Mexican as he wasn't at all disposed to drink that stuff. Finally, the Mexican agreed to drink half of it if the Indian would drink the other half. This was done, and within a few days the Mexican's lump disappeared.

Blazing star was chewed for coughs and sore throats. A tea from the leaves of the Jupiter's staff was used to treat colds, catarrh, and dysentery. Cough syrup was made from one tablespoon of chilipitin berries brewed in water, strained, and sweetened with the syrup of mescal, honey from the honey ant, the sugary substance from the butterfly bush, or fruit juices. Cough syrups and poultices were made from the leaves of the century plant.[44]

To relieve chills and fever, the bark of the red bud, the roots of the dogwood, the inner bark of the Mexican persimmon, the plants of the mountain pink collected while still in bloom, dried, and soaked in wine, were all used.[45] Frank Hinde stated that the milky substance of the odd shaped cactus (*strombocactus disciformis*), with the appearance of a pineapple with no leaves on top, was rubbed on the body of Mexicans to stop a fever.

Various teas were used as medicines. For relief of stomach ache, a tea of mesquite leaves, or leaves of the wild spinach was brewed; a tea of senna leaves for worms; of leaves and the bark of the goatbush for dysentery; of roots of queen's delight as an emetic; of horehound and gum of the mesquite for checking diarrhea; and of branches of the horse bean for diabetics. A tea of the dried roots of the dewberry was taken to check hemorrhages.[46]

Some of the Indians' cures for diarrhea were brought to Fort Stockton with the advent of Old Butcher Knife, an Indian woman, who with her husband had walked from Raton, New Mexico, to Fort Stockton about 1900 to work on the Rooney Farm. Afterward, she and her husband moved to Leon Farms, where he became an invalid and she made their living by making and selling various eatables, such as tamales, tortillas, and cheese. While following this occupation, she went to the Rooney & Butz store to trade, was tricked by its clerk, Ed Fromme, and took revenge by going to her cart, getting a butcher knife and chasing him through the various departments. She then got the name of Old Butcher Knife. But there was never a more friendly and accommodating person than Old Butcher Knife.

Joe Cordero tells that one of his children when very young was deathly ill with diarrhea. His wife was weeping in despair as the doctor had done all that he could do, and gave them only hours until the child would die. In that crisis, Old Butcher Knife drove up to sell her tamales. Upon being told the trouble, she advised them to wait her return with some herbs for medication. She then made a broth of the herbs and managed to get the child to drink it, following which the child soon recovered.

Milkweed (*Asclepias*), the milky juice of which is often recommended as an ointment to kill warts, is also used at present by Charley Stone of Fort Stockton, Texas, to remove from his face what he thought were a few skin cancers. After two weeks' application of this juice, one sore had disappeared and another was fading away. This cure was recommended to him by an old Mexican and probably originated with the Indians.

The Indians learned by trial and error, but our State Health Department advises us to treat unknown plants with caution and to teach children the same, as the content of mountain laurels, azaleas, water hemlocks, buttercups, and various other plants is poisonous. The foliage and acorns from oak trees and the twigs and foliage from wild and cultivated cherries can be deadly. The leaf blade of the rhubarb in your garden contains oxalic acid which crystalizes in the kidneys, causing severe damage. Either the leaf or one small red bean of the mountain laurel is sufficient to kill a child. The brew of mistletoe berries is deadly. Foliage and vines of the potato and tomato plants contain poisons, causing digestive upset and nervous disorder. A single leaf of the ornamental oleander bush, although containing a deadly heart stimulant similar to the drug digitalis, is so powerful that it can kill a child. People have died who have merely eaten steaks speared on oleander twigs and roasted over a fire.[47] We know that the native larkspur is deadly to livestock, as are some plants and shrubs with yellow blooms. The unripe berries of the black nightshade are very poisonous. For additional information, refer to Texas A&M University B-1028-*TEXAS PLANTS POISONOUS TO LIVESTOCK*.

In continuing the listing of the Indians' use of herbs, the roots of the granjeno were eaten as a blood tonic. Mosquitos were repelled with the oil from the leaves of lemon verbena. Ointment, made from the pokeberry plant, was used for ringworm, rheumatism, and eye inflamation. For jaundice, liniments made from the oil obtained from the seeds of the goatbush were applied. External parasites were discouraged when the Indians applied the powdered seeds of the larkspur to their bodies. A lotion of creosote leaves and twigs boiled in water was effective in the treatment of cuts, bruises, and sores.[48] The creosote plant has a preservative chemical, first discovered and extracted in the Big Bend of Texas during World War Two. This chemical is effective in the almost indefinite preservation of fats, cottonseed oils, milks, and other oils or fats. But, because of lack of interest this process has not been commercially utilized.

Dr. Barton H. Warnock of Sul Ross College states: "Several years ago lechuguilla was used as an experimental plant to get a super chemical closely related to cortisone . . . It has other possibilities too. One of the by-products reached were hormones that showed the possibility of producing fat on cattle. The 'pill,' used in birth control, also could be developed from these hormones. In fact the plant has interesting possibilities."

Even the goatbush is gathered in wholesale quantities for medicinal purposes. A tea made from the wax plant was used in the treatment of certain venereal diseases. The wax plant also has purgative properties. For skin diseases, the roots of the queen's delight and pale dock were used.[49] But perhaps best of all for skin diseases was soap.

Suds were obtained from roots of the Bear grass and the wild tuberose, from the oil from powdered seeds of the mustard plant, the berries of the wild china tree, and from the short trunk of the lechuguilla. The china berries took only several hours of soaking in water to make suds and soap, whereas, the cut-up pieces of the roots of the wild tuberose took several days. Japonin, especially good for shampoos and for removing dirt from woolen goods, is now obtained from Bear grass to form emulsions and soapy lathers.[50]

In this timberless country any kind of available wood such as rats' nests, brush, buffalo chips, and limbs from the scant timber in the mountains was used for firewood material. The best available firewood was the mesquite root. This was too much trouble and work for the Indian to dig out, it being much easier for them to move to a new camp site. Only the Pueblo Indians utilized those roots.

Emergency water could be found in the water or barrel cactus. The top of the stem or barrel was cut off, the heart of the plant mashed into a pulp, and drinkable, clear liquid would accumulate.[51]

The last Indians to inhabit this country were the Mescalero Apaches, deriving their name from their use of mescal, noted for their making of special baskets, no longer made by them, described as follows:

> This coiled basketry is marked by thin, flat and loose coils with coarse, irregular stitching and bold designs featuring large single stars, terraced pyramids, diamonds and squares. As the stiching is done with split yucca leaves and yucca root bark which are bleached, partially bleached or left natural, these baskets have a mottled surface of soft greens, yellows, creams and browns. The most common basket is a large tray-like bowl.[52]

Remarkably, the San Carlos Indian basket woven with the fibers of the Spanish daggers, was made tight enough to hold water; and liquid food was cooked in them by means of hot rocks.[53]

One of the outstanding achievements of the early Indians was their proficiency in use of dyes. The yellow substance between the bark and the inner stem of the agarita bush, when boiled in water made a yellow dye. Red dyes were made from the juice of the tiny red or inkberry, from the roots of the mountain mahogany mixed with juniper ashes, from the powdered bark of the alder, from the roots of the Indian tea plant, and from the thick red roots of the wild honeysuckle. Stems of the skunk bush furnished dyes for ornamenting the coils of basket designs. A scarlet dye was obtained from the roots of the dogwood. Prickly pear juice was frequently applied to tanned skins to color them.[54]

Discovery of colors and dyes naturally leads to painting. One of the often mentioned Indian paints is commonly called ochre, a native earthy mixture of silica and alumina, colored by oxide of iron, with occasionally a little calcareous matter and magnesia. Nodules of limonite (hydrated ferric oxide) are found at the contact of the Kiamichi and Comanche Peak geological formations where they outcrop at the west end of the Seven Mile Mesa and the Oate's hills, both within the vicinity of Fort Stockton. The hard surface of these nodules was broken and the soft inside material was easily pulverized to furnish a yellow or brown substance. The cinnabar of the Big Bend, when similarly treated, furnished the base for a red paint. For their other colored paints: black was made from a combination of charcoal and grease; yellow, from ochreous sandstone; white, from kaolin, gypson, or lime; green, from copper oxide.[55]

The Indians left their marks in so many caves and on bluffs that it is needless to mention more than a few of them. Decorating a cave south of Black Gap on the Hallie Stillwell ranch in Brewster County are paintings of scenery, coyotes, rattlesnakes, deer, and other animals. Close-by on the side of a bluff are pictures of five bears, holding up their front paws. On the side of another bluff in the Big Bend and close to a spring by the name of Comanche, O. W. Williams wrote of the picture of an angry buffalo.

Myers Spring, some thirty miles northwest from the mouth of the Pecos, was once called Painted Springs because of the painting of soldiers, a stagecoach, etc. Across from it and toward the mouth of the Pecos was the Painted Cave. Some twenty-five miles east and a little north of El Paso, the Hueco Tanks, a one hundred and fifty foot granite formation standing above the plain, contain numerous Indian paintings and sculptures of deer, birds, animals, reptiles, Indians on foot and horseback, designs, and symbols in red and brown colors. Hot Springs, at the mouth of Tornillo Creek on the Rio Grande, is the site of Indian pictographs on the foot of nearby cliffs. Eagle Nest Canyon, east of Langtry, is a well known archaeological site.

Clay urns, bowls, and water containers were made through the use of basket forms inside which clay was patted in and baked, later burning away the basket material to leave the utensil. The Warm Springs Apaches made water containers or jugs out of reeds, covered both inside and outside with the gum of the piñón. The outside rind of the barrel cactus formed a water container. Empty gourds provided cups, cooking pots, or storage vessels for materials, foods, and seeds when the gourds were corked with a portion of the yucca. The skin, bladder, stomach, and entrails of an animal, when cleaned and treated, were used to hold and transport water or food.

Evidence of the Indians' camps and campfires is scattered over the country on the banks of the rivers, creeks, springs, water holes, and arid regions. Remains of camps sometimes lie over the remains of older camps, indicating a favorite site over a long period, and where both large and small arrowheads are found.

The boy scout method of starting a fire is patterned

after that of the Indian. Two sticks were used: one, round and of the thickness of an arrow shaft, and larger at one end than the other; the other flat, about six inches long, one-half inch thick and one inch wide, and having several countersunk holes about one-fourth inch deep. Dry cedar bark, rubbed by hand to shreds, was placed over the flat stick and sunken holes. Over this, the large end of the round stick was rapidly twirled, back and forth, with the hands pressing down and often repositioning the hands to the top of the stick. With considerable energy, and practice, the Indian would get a few tiny sparks to burn the bark within fifteen minutes.[56] In this Apache country, the sharp point of the chaparro (evergreen oak tree) prieto (dark color) was whirled in the pit of the dried bloom stalk of the sotol.[57]

Few white men understood the smoke signal puffs of the Apaches. A continuous smoke upon a hilltop indicated preparations were being made to oppose a nearby enemy. A similar signal from the foot of a hill meant that a search was to be made by other members of the tribe. Halfway up the hill, the signal located their position, that friends might approach. Several small signals on the plain indicated the senders wished to talk to their enemies. An answer was delivered in a like manner. In addition to this meager information, W. P. Clark of the United States Army in *The Indian Sign Language* published by L. R. Hamersly & Company of Philadelphia, in 1885, gives considerably more data.

Warriors of the Apaches and Comanches were buried along the side of a hill — the higher their rank, the higher their place. The squaws were buried at the foot of the hill.

The prehistoric Indian inhabited a cave for a time; and when returning after a long absence, it would be rehabilitated with a covering of dirt and leaves. This action over the years would fill the cave, at which time it would be used as a burying ground. They, like other

Indians, had their trinkets and a few other earthly possessions buried with them.

The Comanche and the Pecos Indians are reported to have been buried in a sitting position, the Comanche with a wrapping of chamois or buffalo robe, and his war implements at his side.[58]

Although the creosote plant's preservative chemical has just recently been discovered, its leaves were used by the Indians to pack and preserve their stored foods.[59]

No doubt, the rubber quality of the guayule plant was brought to the attention of the white man by the Indian. It is the only indigenous source of rubber in the United States. Using the roots and plant leaves, a small factory operated in Marathon, Texas, for a short time (1905-1914; 1925-1930). As it is a perennial and of slow growth, the supply was soon diminished and the factory closed. From substances of the wax plant are extracted purgative medicines, and wax for phonograph records, celluloid articles, varnish, floor wax, electrical insulations, and candles.

The acceleration in the development of the primitive medicinal and food values of the vegetation of this region got under way with the advent of the white man. The Spaniards captured Mexico City in 1519; Cabeza de Vaca with his several companions wandered through West Texas in 1535-1536; Coronado's party explored portions of the present New Mexico, Arizona, Texas, Oklahoma, Kansas and Colorado as DeSoto's and Moscoso's Spaniards traveled through the regions of the Mississippi and Texas in 1539-40; Espejo and a few Spaniards came down the Conchos River of New Spain, went up the Rio Grande and across to the Pecos River and down it to cross the region of West Texas in returning in 1582-83; Juan Oñate established his Spanish settlement in the present New Mexico as Costaño de Sosa's colony with carts moved to the lower Rio Grande and went up the Pecos River to its source in 1589. These and other Spanish explorations occurred in the Southwest long before the establishment of the first permanent settlement of the Virginia Colony in 1607.

1 Matthews, W. H., *Texas Fossils, Guidebook 2:* Bureau of Economic Geology, The University of Texas, 1960. Fang-toothed tiger *(Dinobastis),* pp. 102, 103; horse *(pliohippus),* pp. 102, 103; mammoths, pp. 102, 104, 107; camels, p. 106; dinosaurs, pp. 89-100.

2 Wendorf, Krieger, and Albritton, *The Midland Discovery:* University of Texas Press, Austin, 1955.

3 *Ibid.,* Appendix 7.

4 *World Book Encyclopedia,* 1964-65-geology: Field Enterprise Educational Corp., Chicago.

5 Williams, Oscar Waldo, (1853-1946), born at Mt. Vernon, Kentucky, graduated with LL.B. degree from Harvard in 1876, came to Dallas in 1877, surveyed in the Panhandle of Texas for two years; thereafter he prospected in New Mexico until he moved to Dallas. In 1884, he came to Pecos County, Texas, serving as deputy county surveyor and county judge of Pecos County and carrying out surveying assignments for the University of Texas. In 1901 and 1902, he spent some time surveying in the Terlingua District of the Big Bend. Under such personal contact with the thorns and plants of West Texas, he picked up the story of "The Honca Accursed," and elegantly dressed it up as a classic.

6 Williams, O. W., "The Honca Accursed": written about 1902; later published in Raht, *Romance of the Davis Mountains,* 1919, Rathbook Company, El Paso, Texas.

7 The Cortez Society, *Documents and Narratives Concerning the Discovery and Conquest of Latin America,* No. 1, p. 23: New York, 1917.

8 *Texas Archeological and Paleontological Society,* Vol. III, pp. 7, 18: Abilene, Texas, 1931.

9 Thwaites, Reuben Gold, *Early Western Travels,* pp. 366, 367: The Arthur H. Clark Company, Cleveland, 1905.

10 Bandelier, A. F., *The Journey of Alvar Núñez Cabeza de Vaca,* pp. 144, 154, 124: A. S. Barnes & Company, New York, 1905.

11 *The Texas Geographic Magazine,* Summer, 1938, p. 12.

12 Schulz, Ellen D., *Texas Wild Flowers,* pp. 50, 26, 51, 59, 139, 286, 183, 204, 269: Laidlaw Brothers, Chicago, Ill., 1928.

13 Bolton, Herbert E., *Spanish Exploration in the Southwest,* p. 170: Charles Scribner's Sons, New York, 1916; Davis, W. W., *Spanish Conquest of New Mexico,* pp. 241, 245: Doylestown, Pa., 1869.

14 Hodge, Frederick Webb, *Handbook of American Indians. Part 2,* p. 176: Government Printing Office, Washington, 1907, Bureau of American Ethnology, A M Part.

15 *Ibid.*, Part 1, p. 846; Bartlett, John R., *Explorations and Incidents in Texas, New Mexico, California, Sonora, and Chihuahua*, Vol. 11, p. 291: D. Appleton & Co., 346 & 348 Broadway & 16, Little Britain, London, 1854.

16 Dennis, T. S. and Dennis, Mrs. T. S., *Life of F. M. Buckelew, the Indian Captive, as Related by Dennis*: Hunter's Printing House, Bandera, Texas, 1925.

17 Meeks, Jack, *Indian Fires in Pecos County*, manuscript at University of Texas (about 1927), a copy of which I have.

18 Ellis, Havelock, "A Study Of A Divine Plant," *Popular Science Monthly*, 1902.

19 Chibitty, Steve, in an address to the men and women of the Fort Stockton Methodist Church, January, 1963.

20 Williams, O. W., *By the Campfires in the Southwest*, brochure written sometime between 1900 and 1930.

21 As told to me on June 11, 1965, by W. D. Smithers of Alpine, Texas.

22 *New York Times*, June 23, 1960: "Peyote Peddler at Odds with U.S."

23 Wasson, Dr. Valentine, "Pediatrician, is Dead," article in *New York Herald Tribune*, 1-2-1959.

24 Schulz, Ellen D., as cited, pp. 59, 243.

25 Bandelier, A. F., as cited, p. 91; Schulz, as cited, pp. 218, 102, 28, 42, 44, 243.

26 Schulz, Ellen D., as cited, pp. 45, 70, 73, 74, 109.

27 *Ibid.*, p. 118; Information on the cherries and mulberries in the Glass Mountains was obtained from the late rancher, J. M. Montgomery, of Pecos County, Texas.

28 Information from H. E. Resley of Fort Stockton, Texas, as to raspberries and gooseberries.

29 Schulz, Ellen D., as cited, p. 66.

30 *Ibid.*, pp. 158, 299.

31 McCook, H. C., *The Honey Ants and the Occident Ants*, p. 36: Lippincott & Co., Philadelphia, 1882; Wheeler, *Ants*, pp. 361-377: The Columbia University Press, 1910.

32 Hrdlicka, Alas, *Bureau of American Ethnology, Bulletin 24*, pp. 23-25, 235, 259: Smithsonian Institution, Government Printing Office, Washington, 1908.

[33] Schulz, Ellen, as cited, p. 214.

[34] Ruxton, George F., *Life in the Far West*, p. 62: Harper & Brothers, New York, 1848.

[35] Bolton, Herbert, *Athanase de Mezieres and the Texas-Louisiana Frontier*, Vol. II, p. 280: The Arthur H. Clark Co., Cleveland, 1914.

[36] Osann, A., *Report on the Rocks of Trans-Pecos, Texas*, p. 166: Texas Bureau of Economic Geology, Austin, Texas.

[37] Schulz, Ellen D., as cited, pp. 299, 325, 26, 352, 70, 96, 73, 158, 135.

[38] Dennis, T. S., et ux, *Life of F. W. Buckelew, the Indian Captive, as Related by Dennis*.

[39] Hrdlicka, Alas, as cited, *Bulletin 24*, pp. 26, 27.

[40] Schulz, Ellen, as cited, p. 137.

[41] *Ibid.*, pp. 220, 102.

[42] *Ibid.*, p. 144.

[43] *Ibid.*, pp. 367, 406.

[44] *Ibid.*, pp. 406, 325, 358, 256, 299, 56.

[45] *Ibid.*, pp. 139, 286, 269, 285, 291.

[46] *Ibid.*, pp. 135, 70, 141, 184, 193, 345, 143, 118.

[47] *The Fort Stockton Pioneer*, Fort Stockton, Texas, June 10, 1965.

[48] Schulz, Ellen, as cited, pp. 66, 356, 73, 74, 184, 85, 180.

[49] *Ibid.*, pp. 184, 199, 193, 67, 59.

[50] *Ibid.*, pp. 51, 55, 111-112, 215, 59.

[51] *Ibid.*, p. 250.

[52] The Texas Memorial Museum, *Indian Baskets*, 1952.

[53] As told to me by H. E. Resley of Fort Stockton, Texas.

[54] Schulz, Ellen D., as cited, pp. 102, 73, 74, 122, 216, 331, 382, 183, 184, 269; Information on the dye from the mountain mahogany and powdered bark of the alder was given me by H. E. Resley of Fort Stockton, Texas.

[55] *Texas Archeological and Paleontological Society*, Vol. 3, p. 26: Abilene, Texas, 1931.

[56] Egan, Howard R., *Pioneering the West*, p. 246: Egan Estate, Skelton Publishing Co., Salt Lake, Utah, 1917.

57 Williams, O. W., *By the Campfires in the Southwest*, privately printed brochure. Chaparro prieto: According to Texas Western College *Monogram No. 10*, Vol. III, No. 2, S. D. Myres, p. 39 is Mimosa laxiflora as identified by Estado de Chihuahua (n.d.), 35. "It is a low shrub producing white flowers in dense racemes two to four centimeters long, and a long oblong, glabrous pod four to five centimeters long. I. Tidestrom and T. Kittell, *Flora of Arizona and New Mexico* (Washington, 1941), 152."

58 Richardson, Rupert N., *The Comanche Barrier to South Plains Settlement*, p. 42: Arthur H. Clark Company, Glendale, California, 1933.

59 Williams, O. W., *By the Campfires in the Southwest*.

Chapter 2

Spanish Conquest and Exploration (1519-1535)

The Indians are assumed to have entered America from northeastern Asia. The Great Spirit had instructed the wandering Aztecs to build a city where they first saw the sign of an eagle perched upon a prickly-pear stem holding a snake in its beak (these emblems later were adopted as the Mexican coat of arms). In their migration southward, they first observed that omen near Lake Tezcuco, and there they occupied Mexico City, one of the oldest metropolises in the new world. In living at this site for two hundred years prior to their subjugation by the Spanish forces, the Aztecs by means of their skill in mining and smelting precious metals, their craftsmanship, their ingenuity and dexterity in producing textiles from cotton and yucca plants, and their ferocity, had conquered most of the adjacent tribes from whom they collected a heavy tribute.

They had jewels, gold, silver, food and clothing, and other resources. With slave labor they constructed wide streets at right angles, and replaced mud and rush huts on that island in Lake Tezcuco (Mexico) with stone buildings, including a 170 foot high truncated pyramid, the latter located on the space now occupied by the Cathedral of Mexico.

After mounting the thirty vertical steps of the outside stairway of this pyramid, following the stairways and connecting corridors, one arrived at the spacious platform, large enough to hold five hundred men. Upon the eastern end of this platform stood two fifty-foot towers. One of these towers was dedicated to Huitzilopochtli, the god of war. The other tower was the sanctuary of Tlaloc, an Aztec Neptune or master of paradise.

A wall, sculptured with intertwined serpents and in the form of a square with temples annexed, surrounded this pyramid. The enclosure was large enough to contain a village of five hundred houses.

Converging on this immense structure from the mainland across the lake were four great streets and causeways, provided with a number of drawbridges.

Among the other lesser edifices adorning the city was one dedicated to the planet Venus, upon the altar of which prisoners were sacrificed when that planet showed in the heavens.

Large floating gardens, along with fruit trees, furnished a variety of food for the three hundred thousand inhabitants of that city. Great canoes passed among the private gardens, which were frequented by many kinds of birds. A museum or park displayed a number of wild animals, even the buffalo from the distant plains region.[1]

After the discovery of the West Indies by Columbus, Spain, with her great fleet, adventurous seamen, and immigrants, quickly occupied Cuba, captured Indian slaves, and imported Negro slaves.[2] Hernando Cortez was told of Juan Grijalva's recent discovery of the shore line of Mexico. After his wealthy brother-in-law outfitted Cortez with his portion of ten vessels, six hundred foot soldiers, eighteen horses, artillery, and supplies, he left Cuba (November, 1518) for Mexico and landed (March, 1519) near the site of Vera Cruz. Burning their ships, marooning themselves in a land from which there could be no retreat, they built their headquarters at the site of Vera Cruz. Upon his promise of conquest and a share in the spoils, they elected Cortez leader. It was to the advantage of the Spanish that the Indian priests had earlier forecast the coming of a White God.

Amazed at seeing the white men bringing with them horses, cannon, the arquebus, ammunition, and metal armor, a few of the Indians joined Cortez's forces to march inland and had their first serious encounter with the Indians of Tlaxcala, who were equipped with defensive "loose garments like doublets made of quilted cotton,"[3] impenetrable by arrows or darts and scarcely able to be pierced with a sword. Even with their heads protected by mounted heads of animals, and possessing bows and arrows, darts, the atlatl, wooden swords fitted with ground stone knives, slings, lances, and clubs, the Tlaxcala could not hold out against the cannon, horses and arquebuses of the Spaniards.

Thereafter, the Caciques of Tlaxcala entered into an alliance to aid the Spaniards in a war against Montezuma in Mexico City, bringing five beautiful maidens as gifts to Cortez and his captains. Although unable to induce the Indians to abandon idolatry and human sacrifice, Cortez was able to persuade them to worship the Spaniard's God. Within the Indian villages were seen lofty oratories covered with white plaster, large temples with idols, adjoining which were great piles of firewood for ceremonies in which cannibalism was practiced by the Indian priests.[4]

From Mexico City, Montezuma sent messengers with presents to Cortez. After an exchange of messages, the forces of Cortez cautiously marched into the beautiful city, to marvel at the causeways, drawbridges, imposing buildings, bright colored flowers, trees providing fruit and fragrance, and canoes gliding from the lake into gardens frequented by colorful birds.[5] In the court of the great temple, the highly polished stone pavement was so slippery as to endanger the footing of the Spaniards' horses. Montezuma established the Spaniards in elegant living quarters with food and servants, then discreetly sent a reconnoitering detail to the Spanish camp at Vera Cruz. A messenger from the detail brought back the head of a dead Spaniard, thus proving that these so-called gods invading the country were not immortal. On learning of this act, Cortez had Montezuma placed in irons, and caused him to order the surrender of the guilty persons and ransom his life but not his freedom with payment of gold, silver, and jewels.

While Montezuma was under guard, the Spaniards discovered and took possession of his hidden treasure vault. Looting was a sanctioned practice of the time. Exploration was reduced to a paying basis and robbery to a science to be condoned as a reward for a daring conquest. Cortez delayed the distribution of the spoils and conveniently held no recollection of a debt to the other men who had financed his expedition, and displayed no indication of loyalty to Governor Velasquez of Cuba. Concerned at this, Governor Velasquez sent Narvaez to Mexico with a force to subdue Cortez. Upon receiving messages that Narvaez had landed and surmising his purpose, Cortez left two hundred men to hold Mexico City and marched to engage the Cuban. His forces and the Indian allies defeated Narvaez. On the promise of a share in the plunder, the remaining members of the Narvaez expedition joined Cortez.

Enroute back, Cortez learned of a savage revolt in Mexico City resulting in the murder of Montezuma and the loss of some of his men, and most of the treasure, as they retreated from the city. The Spanish survivors of the Mexican revolt rejoined Cortez's forces, defeated the Mexicans on the plain of Otumba, subdued the adjoining provinces, fought their way down the causeways and built new crossings over the several destroyed drawbridges, and recaptured (August, 1521) the City of Mexico.

As a result, Spain laid claim to that region and its interior to the tip of Florida. Many years later, in Spain, when Cortez was poor and forgotten, he forced his way through a crowd and mounted the steps of the Emperor's carriage. In answer to the demand, "Who are you?" Cortez replied, "I am the man who has given you more provinces than your ancestors left you cities."

Previously, Alonso Alvarez de Pineda, whose four vessels left Cuba shortly after the departure of the Cortez forces, reached Vera Cruz, saw the sunken hulls of the Cortez fleet, exchanged messages with Cortez, and then sailed off to explore and map the Gulf of Mexico.[6]

While the Cortez forces were struggling to subjugate the Aztec Indians, Governor Francisco Garay of Jamaica sent three vessels, one hundred fifty men, seven horses, some artillery, brick masons, bricks, and lime under the command of Diego de Camargo to colonize. They landed at the mouth of the Rio Grande, were attacked by Indians, lost eighteen men, the three ships, all horses and accoutrement, then fled down the river, leaving the name Camargo to commemorate the site. The remnants of this expedition eventually made their way to join Cortez.[7]

For the next fifteen years, except for a settlement established at Pánuco (Tampico-1552) the Spaniards confined most of their explorations to the south and west of Mexico City. Unsuccessfully Sancho de Canedo attempted (1528) to colonize at the mouth of the Rio Grande, but the Indians were not there to feed them, so they returned to Mexico City.[8]

Panfilo de Narvaez, after being held prisoner by Cortez, was released and later granted the provinces from the palmas (Rio Grande) to the Cape of Florida! With several vessels and about six hundred men he sailed out from Cuba. Narvaez and a large portion of his forces debarked in the swamps of Florida. The commanders of the ships were to search for a suitable place along the coast, and those on land were to join them. The two groups never met again.

The Narvaez parties wandered among the swamps, trees, and hostile Indians, encountering frequent and severe attacks from the latter. They found a village in which were many boxes of merchandise from Castilla, containing corpses covered with painted deer hides, linen, feather headdresses and samples of gold. They were informed that these articles had come from a far-away province called Apalachen where there was much gold.

After losing many men from attacks and being in a starving condition, they converted the metal from spurs, stirrups and crossbows into tools, constructed five barges of wooden flues and deerskin, caulking the barges with palmetto oakum and tarring them with pitch.[9]

They sailed for seven days in waist-deep water among the inlets before reaching a strait between an island and the coast. At sea they coasted toward the River of Palms (Rio Grande) until their horse-leg water pouches rotted and they anchored near a small island in search of food and water. A violent storm held them there for six days, without an opportunity to get either food or water, resulting in the death of five men from drinking sea water.

After the storm subsided, the barges were guided to a location where an Indian canoe had been seen. Many Indians in canoes came, but left immediately without giving assistance. The Spaniards followed them to their lodges, where they were offered food and water. While eating, the Spaniards were attacked, and all of them wounded by stones and arrows during their retreat to their boats. In sailing down the coast, they encountered other Indians, who took their water containers and two Spaniards, leaving two Indians as hostages. The Indians returned with empty containers and without the two Spaniards, but demanded their two Indians. The Spaniards again took to the sea to avoid capture and obtained water from a stream which entered the Gulf.

In a disastrous wind and current, most of the boats were carried to sea. The unfortunate Narvaez, who had lost one eye in the Cortez attack in New Spain, succumbed. Remnants of two capsized boats managed to reach shore. The port of La Vaca, the site historians have selected as the location of the tragedy, bears the name of one of the survivors. The few men left, of 240 who set out in five barges, were captured, some killed, others put to hard labor by the Indians. Three survivors, after six years of misery among the Indians, managed to return to the Spanish settlement of Culiacan in New Spain. Among these three was Alvar Nunez (Cabeza) de Vaca, who returned to Spain and made a remarkable account for the king and church.

Historians conjecture many different routes for him. The late Robert Hill was convinced that the large spring mentioned by de Vaca, was that at New Braunfels. The late O. W. Williams limits de Vaca's course in West Texas to (1) a point south of the line from Galveston to Eagle Pass, where the prickly pear ripen in abundance for three months of the year; (2) the eastern limits of the growth of the piñón tree of Edwards County, the Pecos at Pontoon Crossing and the Guadalupe Mountains; (3) the shallow depth Rio Grande, where it could be crossed waist-deep; and (4) the banks where corn had been planted in "temporales" near Presidio and where the people had to go many leagues to get buffalo meat.

Many authorities agree with this general route of Cabeza de Vaca, and almost all of them concede that his travel westward began in the country south of the Galveston-Eagle Pass line.

In my attempt to trace de Vaca's route through West Texas, I place him first in the region of the lower Devil's River where the only food was provided by roots, sotol, and mescal, which de Vaca described as inflating and unhealthy and taking two days to roast. There the effects of the smoke from some plant caused the natives to abandon their newly-born children. Their diet consisted of an occasional deer, fish at rare intervals, spiders, ant eggs, worms, lizards, salamanders, deadly serpents, earth, wood, deer dung, the pulverized bones of fish, snakes and other animals. In the region of the lower Devil's River the mescal and sotol roots are available — the mescal for their dreams. The wood they ate was likely the guajilla,[10] the leaves and stems of which are relished by browsing animals.

De Vaca's men were in a land where the Indians used mats to sleep upon, and long flint knives of one and one-half palms length, (numbers of which have been found in West Texas). They crossed swift water on the Devil's River, where it was only waist deep. As they wandered from tribe to tribe and up the river they were among the tuna and piñón where the cones, like little eggs with thin husks, and the green seeds of the piñón were beaten, ground, made into balls and eaten. To the north were the mountains of West Texas.

They came to a village where tuna only was their food, traveled up the river for three days to arrive at a large village; and turned inland for more than fifty leagues (approximately three miles to one league), following the slopes of the mountains to arrive at forty dwellings.[11] I assumed that he wandered widely in traveling the sixty miles by way of Howard's Well, Cedar Spring and Live Oak Creek to the Pecos River.

In performing the duties of a medicine man, de Vaca took an arrow-point out of an Indian, close to the heart. The arrow had entered the Indian's back. The breast was cut open with a crude flint knife, the point removed and the cut sewed up with a bone needle and sinews of a deer. In spite of shock, the patient lived.

While traveling among thieving tribes of Indians who carried clubs three palms in length to kill rabbits, they were with the Basket Makers and Rabbit Catchers of West Texas, where loads of rabbits were given them. Houses were built of mats. They crossed the big river (the Pecos) coming from the north, and in moving up it, traversed about thirty leagues (actually less than that) of plains to meet other Indians who were seeking the services of de Vaca.

The Indians then guided them fifty leagues over desert and rugged mountainous country, where they suffered from lack of food and passed by a mountain seven leagues long, the stones of which were iron slags. The resemblance to iron slags in this region can be seen in the limonite and hematite nodules on the west end of Seven Mile Mesa, northeast of Fort Stockton, and in the Oates' Hills, southwest of Fort Stockton. Three hundred years later, Whiting, while making a reconnaissance for the United States Army, upon first seeing the Seven Mile Mesa, named it the Iron Mountain. Geologists are familiar with both places for their deposits of limonites and hematites, representing that which de Vaca could easily have called iron slags. I have previously mentioned the limonite, its inside yellow and brown material as used with snake oil to make paint.

From the vicinity of the present Fort Stockton, they passed through the Leoncita area and Kokernot Springs, and down to a very big river, with its waters reaching the chest. If I have properly surmised the route, they were then on the Terlingua Creek. This stream cannot be called a river, but in a few places it is waist deep. Next their women guides took Alonso del Castillo and Estevanico, the Negro, to "the river that flows between the mountains."[12]

This river is believed to have been the Rio Grande, for no other in this region is so marked as flowing between the mountains as the Rio Grande in the Big Bend. Escorted to the river between the mountains, de Vaca and his men were given beans, calabashes and squashes to eat and were furnished huts. Upon being asked why they did not raise maize, the natives replied that they were "afraid of losing the crops, since for two successive years it had not rained, and the seasons were so dry that the moles had eaten the corn, so that they did not dare to plant any more until it should have rained very hard."[13] The late Judge O. W. Williams wrote:

In the neighborhood of Presidio, corn has been planted since time immemorial in 'temporales,' that is, in sandy stretches near the river. It is not irrigated, but depends upon rain and sub-irrigation from the river to bring it to its fruitage. This is the only place in the country where I can learn of corn being planted in this way. Now the people at this point as described by de Vaca begged the Spaniards to tell the sky to rain so that they might plant their corn. Evidently, they must have planted in 'temporales' and not have used irrigation.[14]

Some authorities claim that the inhabitants of the Rio Grande below Paso del Norte at that time imported their corn grains for planting from the regions of the upper Rio Grande. Such might have been the case in times of extended drought.

Certainly belonging to an earlier era is the gourd dug up in a cave by S. D. Patillo of Fort Stockton, Texas, in 1948. While in the vicinity of Mesa de Angular near Lajitas on the Texas side of the Rio Grande, he investigated the grave of a basket weaver. Underneath the body was found a gourd, the neck of which was sealed with a yucca plant. Inside the gourd were found preserved grains of corn and beans. The body had first been covered with a matting of woven yucca fibers over which had been placed dirt, then rocks and finally cacti and thorns. The following year, Mr. Patillo was informed of the finding of another basket weaver's remains on the Sam Nail ranch, halfway between Lajitas and Marathon and near Santiago Peak in Brewster County, Texas. Ears of corn were also found with that body.

As Cabeza de Vaca had entered the Triangle of West Texas, west of the Pecos River at about the termination of the Basket Weaver and Rabbit Catcher Indian period, it is assumed that those Indians were cultivating corn in the Big Bend of Texas when he arrived.

De Vaca's party then walked up the Rio Grande for thirty-four days, receiving food and deer tallow from the

Indians until they met people living in permanent houses and subsisting on meal, squash, and beans. De Vaca is left here to make his way southwest and west to Culiacan.[15]

1 Biart, Lucien, *The Aztecs*, pp. 142, 145: McClung and Company, Chicago, 1886.

2 Johnson, Rossiter, *The Great Events by Famous Historians*, Vol. IX, p. 37: The National Alumni, 1905.

3 Cortez Society, *Documents and Narratives Concerning the Conquest of Latin America:* New York, 1917, No. 80, pp. 21, 22.

4 Keating, Maurice, Es., *The True History of the Conquest of Mexico, by Diaz and Castello*: London, 1800; Leonard, Irving A., *The Discovery and Conquest of Mexico*, pp. 154, 155: Farrar, Straus and Cudahy, 1956, New York.

5 Leonard, Irving A., as cited, pp. 157-191.

6 Castañeda, C. E., *Our Catholic Heritage*, Vol. 1, pp. 7-13: Jones Co., Austin, Texas, 1936.

7 Castañeda, C. E., as cited, pp. 16-18.

8 *Ibid.*, pp. 36, 37.

9 Bandelier, A. F., as cited, p. 38.

10 Texas A&M University, *Texas Plants Poisonous to Livestock* (3-1028), p. 5: Acacia herlandiere Guajillo causes poisoning to animals after an "excessive diet of the substance for 9 months or longer . . . guajillo is a valuable browse plant."

11 Bandelier, A. F., as cited, p. 138.

12 *Ibid.*, pp. 149, 150.

13 *Ibid.*, p. 152.

14 *Ibid.*, pp. 12, 13, 38, 49, 85, 95, 139, 142, 153, and 156; O. W. Williams, *Texas State Historical Issue* in July, 1899, "Route of Cabeza de Vaca," pp. 56-63.

15 Bandelier, A. F., as cited, pp. 156-231.

Chapter 3

Spanish Exploration and Settlements — Anglo Settlements, Indian uprising in New Mexico — (1535-1683)

De Vaca's report on metals, emeralds, turquoise and buffalo caused the reconnoitering party of Friar Marcos de Niza to go up from Culiacan (1539)[1] in northwestern Mexico into the regions of Arizona. Arriving in the proximity of Zuñi, Niza sent in advance Vaca's comrade, the Negro, Estevanico, and a few Indians to determine if the Zuñi Indians would be hostile. He soon learned that Estevanico and a few others had been killed. Intimidated by the Zuñi[2] Indians' act, he brought back a fabricated story of "Cibola," the Seven Cities of Gold.[3]

After Melchior Diaz affirmed the false report of Marcos

de Niza concerning the "Seven Cities of Cibola," Francisco Vasquez de Coronado,[4] the governor of the province of New Galicia in New Spain, organized a large expedition to investigate.

With three hunderd Spaniards, one thousand Indians and various supplies, cattle and sheep, Coronado (1540) moved up the west coast of Mexico from Compostela.[5] Although engaging in numerous Indian fights for a period of nearly two years, they explored the regions now consisting of Arizona, New Mexico, the Panhandle of Texas and of Oklahoma, and a portion of Colorado. They stormed the walls of Cibola (Kawikuh of the Zuñi Indians); they discovered the Tiguez,[6] (the pueblo Indian tribes of Taos), Picuria, Cicuya (the pueblo of the Pecos Indians), and the Grand Canyon of Colorado.

Near the banks of the Rio Grande, the lofty, often snow-covered Sandia overlooks the excavated ruins of Kuava, or Tiguez, one roof of which covered the immense five story structure containing two thousand two hundred rooms. The Coronado Museum, commemorating the discovery of this pueblo by Coronado, is located at the foot of the Sandia Mountain near Bernalillo.[7] Miles away the quaint, historic pueblo of Taos represents the habitation of innumerable generations, and remains populated by the Taos[8] Indians afford special interest and attraction to tourists.

East of Santa Fe, on a rock surrounded by a stone wall, the ruins of the square village of the Pecos Indians, Cicuye, are yet to be seen. The Spaniards described it as a four story building containing a central courtyard. Corridors encircled the first two stories by which one could reach the entire building. Having no doors nor stairs in the bottom story, moveable ladders were lifted up like drawbridges to allow access to upper stories.

Failing to find metal, gold, silver or jewels among the pueblos, the conquistadors searched the great plains for "Quivira," a mythical land of such riches as reported by their guide. Large herds of buffalo and packs of white wolves were seen, the latter being probably the white lobo, some of the last of which were exterminated thirty years ago in Pecos County and in eastern New Mexico.[9]

In the meantime, and resulting from Cabeza de Vaca's stories of possible riches in America, De Soto's Spanish expedition landed[10] (1539) on the Florida coast.[11] After exploring regions east of the Mississippi, they reached the river, where De Soto died. Luis de Moscoso then took command.[12] In the hope of contacting Coronado's forces, assumed to be in that region to the west, and in the effort to find more comfortable winter quarters, Moscoso led his followers west, possibly to the headwaters of the Brazos River.[13] In the spring they returned to the Mississippi, built boats, floated down the river into the Gulf of Mexico, ultimately to reach New Spain. Only three hundred of the original six hundred Spaniards survived those three hard years.[14]

Regardless of the hardships and apparent lack of success in some explorations, the Spaniards had capitalized on the conquest of Mexico City.

Two round plates the size of wagon wheels, worth over $40,000, had been given to Cortez. One, representing the sun, was made of gold, while the other, representing the moon, was made of silver. But the treasures found in Montezuma's hidden vault and decorating the palace of Quetzacoatl were really amazingly valuable. The east hall of that palace, the "Hall of Gold," decorated with delicately chased, finished gold, and the hall facing east ornamented with fittings of skilfully plated silver and seashells, together with presents sent to Cortez by Montezuma and the presents from other provinces, were estimated to have had a value of over $7,400,000.[15]

Mines and settlements were established at Durango[16] and Santa Barbara in 1563; and mining towns at Parral, San Bartolome and other places before 1580.[17] Forty million five hundred thousand dollars worth of gold and silver was coined by the Spaniards and Indians in New Spain between the years of 1521 and 1548. Spanish settlements had reached the head of the Conchos River where miners, priests and feudal stockmen occupied this avenue of approach to West

Texas and New Mexico. Before the first British colony was established in America, New Spain had produced approximately $300,000,000 in coins from gold and silver.[18]

On the eastern coast of North America, the Spaniards established themselves in St. Augustine, Florida, in 1565. But in those flowered lands the resistance of the Indians and other misfortunes had sealed the fate (1528) of most of the members of the Narvaez expedition, and had caused the members of Tristan de Luna's expedition (1561) to abandon their efforts. Similar conditions later provided a disastrous ending for Jean Ribaut's and Rene de Laudoniere's French Huguenots at the site of St. Augustine where the Spanish under Pedro Menendez de Aviles arrived (1565) to put most of them to death and established the oldest town in the United States.

As the Spaniards' search for riches in the southwest continued, Frays Francisco Lopez, Augustin Rodriguez, Juan de Santa Maria, accompanied by Francisco Sanchez and Hermando Gallegos, nine soldiers and sixteen Indian servants, left Santa Barbara (June 5, 1581), traveled down the course of the Conchos River to La Junta (Presidio) and up the Rio Grande. It was the second party of Spaniards to reach this junction, preceded only by Cabeza de Vaca's party. They journeyed up the Rio Grande, visited the Tigua pueblos near Bernalillo, the buffalo plains east of the Pecos River, the rock of Acoma[19] and the Zuñi Indians. While returning alone to New Spain, Father Santa Maria was murdered by the Indians. Subsequently, the soldiers returned to Nueva Vizcaya (Chihuahua and Sonora) leaving the other two missionaries to Christianize the Indians.[20]

A year later, to ascertain the fate of those two missionaries and to explore for minerals, Espejo's small party of one priest, fifteen soldiers and servants with 115 horses and pack mules, set out (November 10, 1582) from San Bartolome. In journeying down the Conchos River they passed through the grass hut villages of the Conchos,[21] Pazaguantes and Tobosos, finding bars of silver among the Pazaguantas.

At the junction of the Rio Grande and Conchos Rivers, (named La Junta by Espejo) and during twelve days of travel up the Rio Grande they journeyed through five pueblos and reported that more than ten thousand Jumanos Indians[22] lived in flat roofed houses along the river. Through an interpreter the Indians informed them that three Christians and a Negro had passed through there. This confirms that Cabeza de Vaca, two other Spaniards and the Negro, Estevanico, had been in that vicinity (Presidio-Paso del Norte).

In the area of El Paso they met two tribes, the Sumas[23] and the Mansos.[24] Upon arriving among the Tiguas, near the site of Albuquerque, they learned that Fathers Lopez and Rodriguez had been killed. They found rich ore in what is now western Arizona and mineral prospects near the Ubates on the Rio Grande.

Traveling east to explore the regions of the Tanos Indians, Espejo reported that within their large pueblos, one of which was Cicuye (Pecos), were more than forty thousand people. Refused admittance and food at one of the pueblos, Espejo's party rode on a distance of half a league to a river. (The Pecos River rises in the mountains a short distance east of Santa Fe and runs by the present towns of Pecos, Anton Chico, Santa Rosa, Roswell, and Carlsbad, New Mexico, and by Pecos City and Sheffield in Texas to enter the Rio Grande about forty-three miles above Del Rio.) Espejo later named this the Rio de las Vacas (Pecos) for they had seen many cows (buffalo) along its banks for nearly ninety miles. They traveled down the Pecos River one hundred twenty leagues and met three Jumano Indians, from whom Espejo learned that they were twelve days' journey distant from the mouth of the Conchos River on the Rio Grande (La Junta). They passed many watering places, creeks, and marshes before they arrived at the Conchos River.[25]

From the description of their route from the Pecos to the Conchos River, these several passages would fit: (1) Toyah Lake, Balmorhea Springs, Limpia, to Alamito Creek; (2)

Santa Rosa Springs, Monument Springs, Diamond Y Draw, Leon Springs, Leoncita Spring, Kokernot Spring, Alamito Creek; and (3) the marshes of lower Diamond Y Draw located near Buena Vista, to Leon Springs to follow the previous route mentioned. At one time Balmorhea Springs flowed through Toyah Lake into the Pecos River and the water flowing down Diamond Y Draw produced marshes near what later became the town of Buena Vista.

Enthused over the reports by explorers on the New Mexico region and having finally been awarded a contract for the conquest and settlement of New Mexico, Juan de Onate with men, families, wagons and carts and more than seven thousand head of stock, moved up from New Spain to San Geronimo on the Conchos River, marched directly across to Paso del Norte on the Rio Grande, arrived in a parched and dehydrated condition, and named the river El Paso del Rio Norte. Proceeding up the Rio Grande, and passing through the pueblos of the Tiguas Indians, they settled between the Chama River and the Rio Grande, where the Indians assisted in the building of their homes and supplied them with food. As soon as their houses were built and crops put in, they searched the mountains near Socorro, Puara, Tunque, and in the Puerto, Sienega, San Marcos, Galisteo, Pozes, Picoria and Jemez regions, finding granite, copper, lead, "magneta," sulphur, and turquoise.[26]

While Onate's settlement was being established, Gaspar Costaño de Sosa, lieutenant governor in Nuevo Leon, formed his mining camp of Nuevo Almaden, now Monclova, into a colony and then started north. With a Spanish charge against him of promiscuously enslaving Indians, and without any authorization, Sosa, with a wagon train and party of one hundred seventy men, women and children, oxen, supplies, plowshares and two brass cannons, crossed the Rio Grande below the mouth of Devil's River,[27] laboriously moved up that river to camp, and sent riders out to scout a passage northwest to the next watering, the Pecos River. During a difficult thirty days, they took the wagon train and two cannons across the deep canyons, and over the rugged mountains to the Pecos River.

Nine years before the first British colony was settled in Virginia, this first Spanish wagon train camped two days near the present town of Sheffield, Texas,[28] to rest after crossing from the Devil's to the Pecos River. While here, they are reported to have discarded some excess equipment. This might have included a number of small iron horse or ox collars, which were recently found in that vicinity. The party then traveled up the Pecos, defeated an Indian pueblo of the Pecos, and continued their conquest through the Tehua, Queres and Tiguas pueblos to Taos, before Sosa was arrested by a command sent up from New Spain.[29]

While Sosa's party was enroute up the desolate banks of the Pecos, Onate sent Sergeant Major Vincente de Zaldivar Mendoza with a mounted party of sixty soldiers from New Mexico to procure buffalo meat. They reached the village of "Pecos," left two priests there to preside, and then crossed the Pecos, meeting some Indians of the plains who guided them twenty-seven leagues to a large herd of buffalo. Enroute they were joined by many Indians who requested the Spaniards' military help against the "Xumanos." A party of these vaquero Indians were just returning from trading their meat, hides, tallow, lard, cotton and maize in the pueblos of New Mexico.

The vaqueros were reported generally to have been naked; some wore skins and a few wore blankets. The women wore some sort of chamois breeches and shoes or boots. In a rancheria were five hundred neat tents, round shaped like pavilions with fastenings of buttons and holes, covered with extremely well dressed hides of a red and yellow color. The curing of those hides was so extraordinary that water would not penetrate them, nor would the leather harden after being dried. Medium sized, well trained, woolly dogs with travois carried their meat or baggage or were saddled like pack mules. Flint or bone was used for arrow tips. The bows were described as being similar to the bows of the Turks.

Mendoza's party built large corrals for capturing the buffalo. However, the buffalo were unmanageable, stampeding through the lines of the herdsmen, killing a number of horses and injuring forty men. In spite of that difficulty, Mendoza reported that a large number of cattle were slaughtered, and eighty arrobas (two thousand pounds) of meat was taken.[30]

Before the Anglo-Americans built their first cabin on the Atlantic Coast, Onate, along with thirty men, had made his way west and south across the mountains and deserts from San Gabriel to discover the South Sea (Gulf of California) and back. On his return his party camped close to the two ancient pueblos of Zuñis, a portion of the famous "Seven Cities of Cibola." South of the town named Grants on Highway 66 and fifty miles southwest of the Santa Fe Railroad by way of the Zuñis Canyon, close by the ancient and deserted Zuñi Trail to the Rio Grande, along the escarpment of a juniper-dotted canyon and protected from the weather by a small protruding cap-rock with a lone pine doing sentry duty nearby, is "The Stone Autograph Album" or the "Inscription Rock." Upon this, Onate carefully placed the following data: "Passed by here the officer Don Juan de Onate to the discovery of the Sea of the South on the 16th of April, year 1605."[31]

Epidemics, small pox and frequent battles were eventually to depopulate some of these Indian villages. The most drastic abandonment was that of the Pecos Indians, a branch of the several Tano Tribes. Because of either the frequent Apache[32] and Comanche[33] attacks or a poisonous or contaminated water supply, the Pecos pueblo decreased to two thousand persons by 1680. The combined population of the Pecos and the Galisteo was 599 by 1760, and 104 by 1805. In 1838 the few remaining inhabitants moved west of Santa Fe to the Jemez pueblo.[34]

With peaceful co-habitation with some Indian tribes and fierce battles with others, Onate's settlement was well established in New Mexico before the first British American colonies were settled on the Atlantic Coast.[35]

The Spaniards settled and explored southwest North America earlier, and now the other Europeans were just beginning their settlement of the east coast. Following John Cabot's exploration of the northeastern coast of North America, Sir Francis Drake's voyage (1497) around the world,[36] Sir Walter Raleigh's futile attempt to settle the land flowing with milk and honey, and the cruises of Grosnold and Weymouth, the first British colony was established (May 13, 1607) on the lowly sandy beach at Jamestown, Virginia.[37]

Fort Nassau, now within the limits of Albany, was established by Dutch merchants of Amsterdam in 1615, as New York's first settlement. The Mayflower expedition by mistake (1620) landed at Plymouth, Massachusetts, instead of in Virginia. Half of the colony died during the first winter, and their graves were covered under newly planted crops to keep the hostile Indians from knowing the small numbers of the survivors. They celebrated the first "Thanksgiving Day" on the last Thursday in November, 1621, to rejoice in the harvest of their first crops.

New Hampshire was first settled (1623) by English fishermen and tradesmen at Little Harbor, now the site of Rye. New York's second settlement was made one year later (1624), when thirty Dutch families off the "New Netherlands" arrived at Manhattan. A few of the men and some families remained at Manhattan while others went up the Hudson River to settle at the site of Albany.

For the next nine years the British colonies, with frequent Indian troubles, were growing. In the southwest, Onate's followers had established villages up and down the Rio Grande. The village of Santa Fe[38] was occupied (May 16, 1624), and priests set themselves up in the adjoining Indian pueblos.

To Christianize Indians, Fathers Juan de Salas and Juan de Ortega, with a small party, marched out of Santa Fe (1632), down the Pecos River quite a distance and moved across the great plains of Texas to explore the regions of the Colorado River.[39] Upon their return, Father Ortega remained to work among the Indians,[40] thereafter establishing the second mission in Texas on the junction of two branches of the Conchos River, a tributary of the Colorado River, in Texas. On November 6, 1966, a State Marker in the southeast portion of San Angelo, Texas, was dedicated to Ortega's mission among the Jumanos Indians as being the second such mission established in Texas by the Spaniards. The first Spanish mission, as stated by Dr. Cleofas Calleros of El Paso, was placed near the site of the present Bay City, Texas, and properly documented in Vol. I of Castañeda's *Our Catholic Heritage in Texas*.

On the eastern coast, Connecticut was settled (1633) by Dutch emigrants at the site of Hartford. Two hundred English colonists, noted for religious tolerance, under Leonard Calvert, landed from the two vessels "Ark" and "Dove," in Maryland (March, 1634) between the Potomac River and Chesapeake Bay. Rhode Island received the discontented refugees from the theoretical communist settlement of the state of Massachusetts, as Roger Williams, with his emigrants, moved (June, 1636) to the site of Providence. The state of Delaware was settled (1638) by a company of Swedes at the site of Wilmington. Pennsylvania was first moved into (1643) by John Printz, Governor of New Sweden, and his followers, who built Fort "New Gottenberg" on Tinicum Island near Chester.

In the southwest, the Spaniards were troubled in the meantime with frequent Indian banditry and uprisings. Raids and counterraids were frequent. Because of this, missions were abandoned and afterwards re-occupied. From Santa Fe the ambitious Captains Hernando Martin and Diego Castillo, with some soldiers, followed (1650) much the same route as did de Salas in 1632. Arriving on the Colorado River in Texas, which they called the Nueces because of the nuts they found along its banks, and remaining in those regions for six months, they heard of a people called Tejas.

On the Conchos River in New Spain (Mexico), the Conchos Indians became troublesome and the Spanish carried on large-scale military operations (1652) against them.[41] Such trouble was not hard to understand. Priests went among the Indians establishing missions and preaching peace and good will to all men. The miners and stockmen established a traffic in Indian slaves. Diplomatically, such slaves were expected to be gotten from far-away lands, the result of which should not affect the peace of the Spanish settlements. This was not always done, resulting in serious opposition from those tribes upon which enslavement was practiced. Also, there were those roving bands of Indians who had always pillaged and raided.

In New Mexico, the Martin and Castillo reports of pearls on the Colorado resulted in Diego de Guadalajara's expedition from Santa Fe. With thirty soldiers, among whom was Juan Dominguez Mendoza, Guadalajara came east (1654) to the Pecos River, traveled down its banks for many miles, and crossed over the sandy and red plains to the regions of the Jumano Indians on the Colorado River, not far from the site of the present Brownwood, Texas. Pushing on thirty leagues past the region of the Jumanos, they engaged the Cuitaos[42] in a battle, after which they took home two hundred prisoners and many hides.[43]

On the Rio Grande, the first Spanish settlement at Paso del Norte (Juarez) reportedly was established around the mission of Nuestra Señora de Guadalupe del Paso, built where the Rio Grande takes an eastward course.[44] Although a few Spaniards lived at the place previously, it was reported by our guide on a tour of Juarez in 1966 that the mission was completed in 1659, a date in contradiction to that of some authorities. The tall, five-foot-thick walls, the timber work connected only with wooden pegs, the ornate and unique carving of the mahogany was done by the Mansos Indians, whose enthusiasm in their

Catholic religion influenced them to travel over two thousand miles on foot, requiring two years to make the round trip to cart back many tons of the mahogany from Southern Mexico for the building of this mission. Now, three hundred years later, the building is intact with its immense ceiling beams delicately carved and each weighing nearly a ton, and a mahogany door, which revolves on wooden axles, still in operation. This ancient structure, with its primitive watch tower, standing in the center of Juarez, Mexico, is overshadowed by the adjacent, modern splendor of the new Cathedral Guadalupe with its gold trimmings and glittering chandeliers.

The following year (1660) the state of North Carolina was settled by Virginia people on the Chowan River at Albermarle. Seventy-five years previously (1585), the English had made an unsuccessful attempt to colonize at Roanoke Island (1586), but the demoralized emigrants had returned to England with Sir Francis Drake.

In the southwest in the Coahuila province of New Spain, Indians made frequent raids. On a punitive expedition (1665) out of Saltillo, Mexico, the Spaniards under command of Ascue, with Indian allies, marched up to cross the Rio Grande near present Eagle Pass and traveled some one hundred fifty miles into Texas. Engaging the Cacaxtles, the Spaniards reported the killing of over one hundred of the enemy and the capture of an old woman, who by playing a flute, had encouraged the Indians to fight. Their Indian allies demanded possession of the old woman for the purpose of a cannibalistic feast. Being refused, they obtained a young relative of that woman and feasted on him.[45]

The Spaniards had temporarily settled on Parris Island from 1566 to 1588; the French subsequently had made an unsuccessful attempt to colonize that island. In 1670 the English established a somewhat permanent settlement on the west bank of the Ashley River on Albermarle Point, and moved later to the site of Charleston, in South Carolina.

Five years later (1675), Father Larios and his party as missionaries from New Spain crossed the Rio Grande between the site of Eagle Pass and Del Rio, and explored the regions in Texas to be known later as inhabited by the Lipans.[46] Larios brought back the names of the following tribes in that area: Geniocane, Yorica, Jeapa, Bibit, Pinanaca, Xaeser, Tenimama, Cocoma, Xoman, Teroodan, Tenimamar and Gueiquesale.[47]

For some time in New Mexico the pueblo Indians had tried to conform to the religious and governmental requirements of the Spaniards. God and the Great Father were one and the same to both the Indians and the Spaniards. All other matters of Spanish religion and civil authority clashed with those of the Indian tribal customs. The Indians attempted to serve and pay tribute to both.

Even as the ridiculous practice of burning witches at the stake was carried on in New England as late as 1675, the Spaniards captured forty-seven Indian leaders in the Santa Fe Province, and charged them with witchcraft and sorcery. Three were hanged and the others punished. Subsequently, for five years, those Indians secretly planned a revolt. Even the Apaches of the plains country and the Manso Indians of the Paso del Norte region joined in the plans.

August 9 to 13, 1680, were fateful days for two thousand five hundred Spaniards, many of whom were massacred in New Mexico. Only two out of twenty at Taos survived the attack of the Taos Indians and the Apaches. The six Tewa[48] pueblos revolted, killing priests and Spanish citizens, and carrying off women and children from Tesuque, Nambe, Pojoaque, San Juan, Santa Clara and San Ildefonso.[49] The Tano Indians exterminated the Spanish settlements at Galisteo,[50] Los Cerrillos,[51] and the pueblo of Pecos. Likewise the Spaniards of Cochiti,[52] Santo Domingo,[53] San Felipe,[54] Santa Anna,[55] and Sia[56] were slaughtered by the Queres[57] as were the Spaniards at the Jemez, Acoma, Zuñi, and Hopi pueblos by the natives.

The Spaniards had been "spread too thin." The site

of Isleta,[58] just south of Albuquerque, served as a refuge for fifteen hundred of the survivors, while Santa Fe held one thousand of those yet to be attacked. The majority of the Isleta Indians had not revolted nor taken part in the uprising. But fearful of such an eventuality, the fifteen hundred Spanish refugees at that place retreated southward, slowly and without sufficient food, to Socorro,[59] then to Fray Cristobal,[60] which place they reached on September 4.

Previously, on August 15, the actual siege of Santa Fe began. When those Spaniards were given the choice of withdrawing peacefully from the country or remaining to be destroyed, they decided upon neither. As the Indian negotiators "returned to their army, bells were rung and the chapel of San Miguel was set on fire."[61] The Spaniards' small force attacked the besieging Tano Indians, resulting in some casualties and the Indian retreat under the cover of darkness. The Tewa, Taos, and Picuris[62] warriors then joined the attack, destroying a number of houses and churches of the village, and cutting off the defenders' water supply from the river. After resisting two days of activities (August 20, 1680), the Spaniards attacked, killed three hundred Indians, shot fifty-seven captives, and recovered eighty head of cattle.

With further resistance futile, Otermin and nine hundred refugees, protected by only one hundred people capable of bearing arms, retreated through San Marcos, the deserted Santo Domingo, San Felipe, and reached Sandia[64] on August 26. Here they were forced to attack and break their way through a threatening band of Indians. In reaching Isleta, they found that even the Isleta Indians had deserted that pueblo following its abandonment by the previous refugees. At Fray Cristobal, Otermin's party joined the refugees from Isleta (September 13, 1680). Together, the two groups of 1,946 people, composed of only 155 men capable of carrying arms, 317 Indians from the pueblos of Sevilleta, Socorro, Alamillo and Senecu, and old men, women and children, arrived at La Salienta in the area of the site of El Paso. There was some protection for them in the two missions of La Soledad de los Janos, seventy leagues southwest of Paso del Norte and Nuestro Padre San Francisco de los Sumas, twelve leagues east of Paso del Norte.

By October 20 the three camps of Real de San Lorenzo, Real de San Pedro de Alcántara and Real del Santísimo Sacramento were established about two leagues apart on the right bank of the Rio Grande close to the future site of the mission of Guadalupe, which some authorities state was established later in 1683.[65] It took nine years for the conquistadors to establish themselves in New Mexico, but they lost no time in beginning.

In 1681, the mission of Corpus Christi de la Isleta, as reported by some authorities, was built and officially named in memory of the Isleta which many of the refugees had been forced to abandon. Nearby, the refugees quickly built new homes, close to protective walls. At Ysleta, Texas was in its beginning. A presidio or fort was also built near the Pueblo de los Mansos.[66] A little southeast of Ysleta, they placed Mission San Miguel del Socorro.

In the meantime, Otermin's expedition of 130 soldiers, 112 Indian allies, 40 additional persons, including several friars with 948 horses, had left El Paso (November 5, 1681), crossed the dry Jornado del Muerto, found the pueblo of Senecu deserted and destroyed, and saw the burned ruins of the church and friary at Socorro. They burned the pueblo of Socorro to prevent the enemy from occupying it. Continuing this scorched earth policy, they marched to and burned the villages of Alamillo and Sevilleta.

At Isleta, New Mexico, they found five hundred peaceful Indians. Only the church had been destroyed. From Isleta, Juan Dominguez de Mendoza, with seventy men, was sent to scout the pueblos of Alameda, Puaray, Sandia, San Felipe, Santo Domingo, and Cochiti. They found that Alameda had just been deserted by the Indians, fearful of punishment. At Puaray, Sandia, and San Felipe, the same situation prevailed. In those places, Mendoza's party destroyed the newly constructed Indian kivas.

Advancing to Cochiti, they found one thousand Indians assembled on a mesa a short distance away. With "trickery" these Indians agreed to peace and pledged their allegiance to the Spaniards but plotted a future convenient ambush and destruction of the Spaniards. Apprized of these plans, Mendoza retreated through San Felipe to Sandia, which he found burning. Otermin had advanced and extended his torch to Sandia, Alameda and Puaray. Then, finding few horses fit for use and only seventy men in fighting condition, Otermin picked up some of the friendly Isleta Indians and returned to El Paso, having burned a number of pueblos and re-established the Isleta Indians near El Paso.[67]

Real de San Lorenzo, reportedly twelve leagues south of the Presidio Paso del Norte, was raided by the Apaches and two hundred horses were carried off. Such depredations continued until October, when an expedition was sent against them, resulting in the capture of twenty-two, and the death of a number of Apaches.[68] In the following year the mission for the Sumas, named Guadalupe, was located in 1683 at a point eight leagues below Paso del Norte.[69]

---

[1] Culiacán: Capital of Mexican state of Sinaloa, situated along the Gulf of California.

[2] Zuñi: "The popular name of a pueblo tribe, constituting the Zuñian linguistic family, residing in a single permanent pueblo, known by the same name, on the N. bank of upper Zuñi, Valencia Co., N. Mex." Hodge, as cited — part N-Z, p. 1016.

[3] Bancroft, H. H., *History of the North Mexican States and Texas*, Vol. I, pp. 76, 77: The Bancroft Co., New York.

[4] Francisco Vázquez de Coronado (1510-1554), born in Salamanca, Spain, went to Mexico in 1535.

[5] Compostela: Capital of Nueva Galicia, Mexico.

[6] "Tigua (Spanish form of Ti'wan, pl. Tiwesh') Span., Tiguex, (Their own name). A group of Pueblo tribes comprising three geographic divi-

sions, one occupying Taos and Picuris (the most northerly of New Mexican pueblos) on the upper waters of the Rio Grande; another inhabiting Sandía and Isleta, N and S of Albuquerque, respectively; the third division living in the pueblo of Isleta del Sur, Texas, and the Senecu del Sur, Chihuahua, on the lower Rio Grande." *(Bureau of American Ethnology, Bulletin 30, Part 2, N-2, p. 747.)*

7 *The Santa Fe Magazine,* April, 1940, p. 11.

8 Taos: located on Highway 64, some seventy miles north and a little west of Santa Fe.

9 Bandelier, Adoff A., *The Journey of Coronado,* p. 62: A. S. Barnes & Co., New York, 1904; *West Texas Historical Association Year Book,* Vol. XX, October, 1944; Holden, W. C., *Coronado's Route Across the Staked Plains; Memoirs of Exploration in the Basin of the Mississippi,* Vol. I; Brown, J. V., *Quivira,* St. Paul, Minnesota, 1898.

10 Fernando de Soto, born 1496 in Spain, had been in expeditions to Peru and Nicaragua. Afterward, as governor of Cuba, he was given permission to conquer Florida.

11 Bourne, Edward G., *Narratives of the Career of De Soto,* Vol. I, pp. 5-12: Allerton Book Co., New York, 1904, and David Nutt, London, 1905.

12 Luis de Moscoso de Alvarado was with de Soto's expedition in 1537-1538, which passed through the present states of Florida, Georgia, the Carolinas, Tennessee, Alabama, Mississippi, Louisiana, and Arkansas: Webb et al., *The Handbook of Texas,* Vol. II, p. 240: Austin, 1952.

13 The Brazos River, the longest stream in Texas, has for its headwaters: the Double Mountain Fork, which rises in Roosevelt, Curry, and Quay counties, New Mexico, to continue through Bailey, Hale, Lubbock, Crosby, Garza, Kent, Fisher, and Stonewall counties in Texas; the Salt Fork, which rises in Crosby County, Texas, and runs through Garza, Kent, to unite with the Brazos in Stonewall County; and the Clear Fork, which rises in Scurry County and flows through Fisher, Jones, Shackelford, Throckmorton, and Stephens counties to join the Brazos in Young County.

14 Castañeda, C. E., as cited, Vol. I, pp. 123-138; Shea, John G., *Discovery and Exploration of the Mississippi,* pp. 2-17: Joel Munsel, Albany, 1903.

15 Anderson, Alex D., *The Silver Country of the Great Southwest,* pp. 31-33: Putnam Sons, 182 Fifth Ave., New York, 1877; Humbolt's *Researches in America,* p. 83; Bancroft H. H., *Native Races,* ii, 173; *The Memoirs of the Conquistador,* Bernal Díaz, i, 88, 90, 91, 277-299.

16 Durango, Mexico (also called Guadiana and Ciudad de Victoria), located five hundred miles northwest of Mexico City "is handsomely built, with a Cathedral, a former Jesuit College, and a mint. . . ." Collier & Son Co., *Collier's New Encyclopedia,* New York, 1921.

17 Santa Barbara. "Zacatecas was founded in 1548, Durango in 1563, and with the opening of mines in Santa Barbara, Parral, San Bartolomé, and other places in their vicinity, before 1580, the frontier of settlement reached the head of the Conchos River": Bolton, H. E., *Spanish Exploration in the Southwest.*

18 Humbolt, Alexander, *New Spain*, iii, 109, 413-420: Longman, Hurst, Rees and Brown, and Colburn, London, 1814; Bancroft, H. H., as cited, Vol. I, p. 366; Escalante, Carte, in Dec. Hist. Mex., series iii, Pareded, Noticias in Id., 213.

19 Acoma, located in an Indian reservation some twenty-seven miles southeast of Grants, New Mexico.

20 Bolton, H. E., *Spanish Exploration in the Southwest*, pp. 137-150.

21 Conchos Indians, a little-known tribe formerly living on a river of the same name in Chihuahua, Mexico: Hodge, *Bureau of American Ethnology* — American Indians, Washington, D.C., 1907.

22 Jumano: "A tribe of unknown affinity, first seen, although not mentioned by name, about the beginning of 1536 by Cabeza de Vaca and his companions in the vicinity of the junction of the Conchos with the Rio Grande": Hodge, as cited.

23 "Suma. A semi-nomadic tribe, one branch of which formerly occupied the region of the Casas Grandes in Chihuahua, Mexico, and the other the vicinity of El Paso": Hodge, as cited.

24 "Manso. A former semi-sedentary tribe on the Mexican frontier, near El Paso, Tex., who, before the coming of the Spaniards, had changed their former solid mode of building for habitations constructed of reeds and wood." Hodge, as cited.

25 Bolton, H. E., *Spanish Exploration In the Southwest*, pp. 163-190.

26 Davis, W. W. H., as cited, pp. 271-273; Castañeda, C. E., as cited, Vol. I, pp. 186-194.

27 Devil's River rises in the southern part of Crockett County, Tex., and flows south into Val Verde County, Tex., entering the Rio Grande northwest of Del Rio, Texas.

28 Sheffield, Pecos County, Texas, is located on the Pecos River in the eastern part of the county, seventy miles east of Fort Stockton, Tex.

29 Castañeda, C. E., as cited, Vol I, pp. 182-183; Bolton, H. E., *Spanish Exploration In the Southwest*, p. 200.

30 Hammond and Ray, *New Mexico*, pp. 45-58: *Quivira Society Publications*, Vol. VIII, 1938, Albuquerque; Bolton, H. E., *Spanish Exploration In the Southwest*, p. 200.

31 **Lummis**, Charles Fletcher *Mesa, Cañón and Pueblo*, p. 463: The

Century Co., New York and London, 1925; Lummis, Charles Fletcher, *Some Strange Corners of Our Country*, pp. 163-171, New York: The Century Co., 1903.

32 "Apache (probably from apachu, 'enemy,' the name for the Navaho, who were designated 'Apaches de Nabaju' by the early Spaniards in New Mexico)": Hodge, as cited.

33 "Comanche. One of the Southern tribes of the Shoshonean stock, and the only one of that group living on the Plains." Hodge, as cited.

34 Bandelier, Adoff A., *History of New Mexico*, Vol. I, p. 74; Bandelier, Adoff A., *Papers of the Archaeological Institute of America, Series IV, Part II*, pp. 128-138.

35 Bolton H. E., *Spanish Exploration In the Southwest*, pp. 253-265.

36 Trumbill, Henry, *History of the Discovery of America, of the Landing of our Forefathers at Plymouth*, etc., p. 11: Henry Trumbill, Norwich, Conn., 1810.

37 Lodge, Henry Cabot, *A Short History of the English Colonies in America*, p. 45: Harper Brothers, Franklin Square, New York, 1881.

38 Santa Fe, now the capital of New Mexico, was first visited by the Spaniards about 1542 when it was a pueblo: *Collier's New Encyclopedia*, New York, 1921.

39 Colorado River in Texas, rises north of Big Spring, passing through Mitchell, Coke, Runnels, McCulloch, San Saba, and Burnett counties to continue by Austin and enter the Gulf of Mexico south of Bay City.

40 Castañeda, C. E., as cited, Vol. I, p. 195. To commemorate the first effort to christianize Indians in Texas, Mrs. S. F. Hignett of San Angelo, Texas, Mrs. Cullen F. Thomas of Dallas, Texas, and Miss Gladys Walter in conjunction with the Daughters of Founders and Patriots of America plan to establish a marker in San Angelo, designating the region in which this event took place. Additional annotations for such were given to me as Hodge, Frederick F., *Land of Sunshine*, Vol. XIV, pp. 231, 234, 313: *West Texas Historical Review*, 1964.

41 Bancroft, H. H., as cited, Vol. I, pp. 354-362.

42 "Cuitoas. A tribe mentioned in connection with the Escanjaques (kansa). Their habitat and identity unknown." Hodge, as cited.

43 Castañeda, C. E. as cited, Vol. I, pp. 204-206; Bolton, H. E., *Spanish Exploration In the Southwest*, p. 314.

44 Castañeda, C. E., as cited, Vol. I, p. 212.

45 Coan, Charles, *History of New Mexico*, Vol. I, p. 212: American Historical Society Inc., Chicago and New York, 1925.

46 "Lipan (adapted from Ipa-n'de, apparently a personal name; n'de equal people). An Apache tribe, designating themselves Naizhan (ones, our kind) which at various periods of the 18th and 19th centuries roamed from the lower Rio Grande in New Mexico and Mexico eastward through Texas . . ." Hodge, as cited.

47 Castañeda, C. E., as cited, Vol. I, p. 215.

48 "Tewa equal Teva ('moccasins,' their Keresan name). A group of Pueblo tribes belonging to Tanoan linguistic family, now occupying the villages . . . lying in the valley of the Rio Grande." Hodge, as cited.

49 "Tesuque. (. . . The southernmost of the pueblos occupied by the Tewa situated 8 m. N. of Santa Fe. Nambe . . . A Tewa pueblo situated about 16 m. N. of Santa Fe . . . Pojoaque . . . situated on a tributary of the Rio Grande, about 18 m. N.W. of Santa Fe." Hodge, as cited.

50 "Galisteo — A former Tano pueblo 1½ m. N.E. of the present hamlet of that name, and about 22 miles S. of Santa Fe, N. Mex." Hodge, as cited.

51 Los Cerrillos — probably located in what is now known as the Cerrillo Mountains and the town of Cerrillos, some 25 miles south of Santa Fe. Perhaps it is the ruins of the San Marcos Pueblo.

52 "Cochiti (Ko-chi-ti') — A Keresan tribe and its pueblo on the W. bank of the Rio Grande, 27 m. S.W. of Santa Fe, N. Mex." Hodge, as cited.

53 Santo Domingo . . . A Keresan pueblo on the E. bank of the Rio Grande, about 18 m. above Bernalillo, N. central N. Mex." Hodge, as cited.

54 "San Felipe — A former pueblo of the Piro, on the Rio Grande, probably near the present San Marcial, Socorro Co., N. Mex." Hodge, as cited.

55 "Santa Ana . . . A Keresan pueblo on the N. bank of the Rio Jemez, a W. affluence of the Rio Grande, in central New Mexico. The original pueblo, according to Bandelier, stood near the Mesa del Cangelón, W. of the Rio Grande . . ." Hodge, as cited.

56 "Sia . . . A small Keresan tribe inhabiting a single pueblo on the N. bank of Jemez r., about 16 m. N.W. of Bernalillo, N. Mex." Hodge, as cited.

57 "Queres . . . A member of the Keresan family comprising several of the tribes along the Rio Grande other than the Laguna and Acoma a little distance to the West." Hodge, as cited.

58 "Isleta . . . A Tigua pueblo on the W. bank of the Rio Grande, about 12 m. S. of Albuquerque, N. Mex. . . ." Hodge, as cited.

59 "Socorro. A former pueblo of the Piro on the site of the present town of Socorro, on the Rio Grande in New Mexico." Hodge, as cited.

60 Hodge does not mention Fray Cristobal, but some forty miles south

of Socorro are the Fray Cristobal Mountains, which may be in the vicinity of the old Fray Cristobal.

61 Coan, Charles, as cited, Vol. I, p. 207.

62 "Picuris. A Tigua pueblo about 40 m. N. of Santa Fe . . . is said to have contained 3,000 inhabitants in 1860." Hodge, as cited.

63 "San Marcos . . . A ruined pueblo, 18 m. S.S.W. of Santa Fe, N. Mex. which, according to Vetancurt, was formerly occupied by Keresan Indians. Bandelier, however, makes the statement that the aboriginal occupants were Tano. . . ." Hodge, as cited.

64 Sandía (Span.: 'watermelon'). A Tigua pueblo on the E. bank of the Rio Grande, N. Mex., 12 m. N. of Albuquerque." Hodge, as cited.

65 Coan, Charles, as cited, Vol. I, pp. 201-209. I know too little about the location of early Spanish missions around Paso del Norte and refer you to El Paso *Herald Post*, October 7, 1964, and article by Dr. Cleofas Calleros, "Says Prof Adds Confusion to Errors," and same paper on Sept. 30, 1964 as to Dr. Eugene O. Porters, "Lower Valley Mission of San Elizario."

66 Castañeda, C. E., as cited, Vol. I, pp. 264-266 and Vol. III, pp. 198-202. Further reference is made to recent publication: Eckhart, George B., "Some Little Known Missions in Texas" in *The Master Key*, quarterly of the Southwest Museum Highland Park, Los Angeles, California, October-December issue, Vol. XXXVI, No. 4, pp. 127-136.

67 Coan, Charles, as cited, Vol. I, pp. 209-210.

68 *Ibid.*, p. 212.

69 Bancroft, H. H., as cited, Vol. I, p. 306; Castañeda, C. E., as cited, Vol. II, p. 312.

Chapter 4

Hazardous Times For The Spaniards (1683-1728)

The next forty-five years were difficult for the Spaniards. Indian revolts on the Rio Grande, a French attempt to settle in Texas, the Spaniards' establishment of missions in East Texas and their subsequent abandonment during the war with France, the reoccupation of New Mexico, the Apache raids into New Spain, the French traders' exploration of Texas, and the Spaniards' re-fortification and re-establishment of missions in Texas, all sufficed to keep them occupied. The remoteness of New Spain and slow communications from Europe had caused the Spaniards concern during the wars and political maneuvering of Europe in 1667-68 and 1672-78, but now during the "Last Turkish Invasion of Europe" in 1683-84, the Spanish monarchy was saved only by the intervention of England and Holland.

Living in dire circumstances, with little support from the Spaniards on the upper Conchos River in the province of Nueva Vizcaya, and expecting more trouble from Indians, the Spaniards at Paso del Norte eagerly assented to the plea of some friendly Jumano Indians living near La Junta (Presidio) on the Rio Grande, to meet with their various tribes east of the Colorado River. In command of that party was Juan Dominguez de Mendoza, a man of experience. He had made the trip with Guadalajara in 1654, across from Santa Fe to visit the Colorado.[1] He was a veteran of the retreat from New Mexico, and Otermin's futile expedition in New Mexico.

With Father Nicolas Lopez, a volunteer guard of thirty soldiers and two hundred Indian allies, Mendoza set out (1683) from the Mansos Indian mission of Real de San Lorenzo, marched down the Rio Grande through Suma villages subsisting chiefly on what he called "mescal," and bitterly complaining of their enemies to the northeast, the "Hapaches."[2]

In the vicinity of the site of La Junta (Presidio), they came (December 29, 1693) to the rancherias of the Julimes Indians,[3] who grew maize and wheat. This place was named Apostol Santiago by Mendoza's party. From Apostol Santiago the party proceeded up the Alamito Creek[4] to come to the extremity of a mesa which extends to the north. They moved through the hills of bare detached rocks, oaks, and cedars of the scenic Paisano Pass,[5] camped at the foot of a hill from which an arroyo flowed to the north, and named this site San Lorenzo (Kokernot Springs in Alpine, Texas) because of an immense grass fire, which they kept from enveloping them by building counter fires.

Five leagues to the north, along a dry arroyo dotted with some nut trees, Mendoza stopped at good water (Leoncita Springs)[6] naming it San Pedro de Alcantara. Because of the want of food by the Jumanos and their allied Indians, the party remained there a day so that the Indians could kill deer and other animals.

Continuing on, they made eight leagues to a dry camp

on the plains without water or wood. Four leagues farther on they arrived at a spring of alkaline but pleasant water around which were three small hills towards the west and a cliff on the north, fitting the description surrounding Leon Water Holes.[7] Three water holes, from which springs issued, is the description which the present generation recollects. The total distance reported by Mendoza from the Kokernot Spring to the Leon Water Holes is approximately correct. Around Leon Spring buffalo tracks were seen. They named this locality San Francisco Xavier.

Without giving a direction or distance from Leon Water Holes, Mendoza described their next camping place, which on January 11, 1684, they named San Juan del Rio. He wrote:

> It is in a beautiful plain. In its environs there are four high mesas; from the small one toward the north flows a spring; within three arquebus shots, apparently, there issue five other springs, all beautiful; and within the distance of half a league a most beautiful river is formed, although without any kind of a tree, it having only camalote patches.[8]

The description is that of the famous Comanche Springs,[9] long known as the third largest spring in the state of Texas. The camalote patches were likely the cattail, many of which were in that creek years ago. They evidently camped just south of the spring which did flow on the south side of the little hill upon which the present Catholic Church in Fort Stockton is located.

Later they marched down the Comanche Valley, passed by San Pedro Springs[10] to travel five leagues, camped without water, marched another six leagues, and came to mesquite trees and good pasturage near the muddy and alkaline waters of a river which apparently carried as much water as the Rio del Norte. They were then on the Salado (Pecos) River, where they hunted and killed six buffalo bulls, and discovered the salt lake located about a league on the northeast side of the river between some small hills in the present Crane County.

Three leagues down the river, Mendoza described a range of mountains four leagues east and across the river, from which extended a small mesa above which rose a little mesa. King Mountain and Castle Gap[11] to its west, located between the present Crane and McCamey, were then being viewed by Mendoza.

They traveled down the Salado River (Pecos) and because of burned vegetation, halted about a league from the ranchería of the Jediondo Indians.[12] Here, the Jediondos, some on horses and some afoot, came out to meet them. Among the Indians' possessions was a red and yellow cross constructed of substantial timbers. Especially interesting to the Spanish was the banner of white taffeta crossed with blue taffeta, undoubtedly a French flag. The French traders, with the fleur-de-lis, might even have been as far west as the Pecos before La Salle's ill-fated settlement on Matagorda Bay.[13] Jesuits and French traders were on the Upper Mississippi River and La Salle's party in 1682 had just explored the Mississippi to its mouth.

Although curious about the banner, Mendoza's party proceeded to the Jediondo ranchería of tule (cattail) huts, crossed the river, and pitched their camp at the foot of a great rock on a hill located nearby (adjacent to the present Bakersfield farming community). The name of San Ygnacio was applied to the locality, where they remained seven days to kill and feast on buffalo.

Having agreed with the Jediondo Indians to make war on the Apaches, the party marched off on January 24th. Some of the venturesome Jediondos joined them. Five leagues from the Jediondo ranchería, they made a camp without water and lost a portion of the horse herd that night to the Apaches. Enroute to the next camp at a spring, likely Grierson,[14] in a flat with good pasturage around it, they killed five buffalo. During two days of rest and hunting, they killed thirty-four buffalo, and were joined by the

"Twisted Bows" Indians. The name of San Honofre was applied to the place.

Ten leagues from Grierson Springs they camped at a spring on a branch of the Middle Concho,[15] named it San Marcos, and lost additional horses. After killing and butchering buffalo, they traveled down this branch four leagues, and camped in a gorge which had a good pool of water. Upon arriving at running water, enjoying fish, and seeing many groves of nut trees, lofty oaks, grape vines, and prickly pear patches, they camped on the Concho River, naming that place San Diego. Horse thieves got away with nine animals here. Again the Apaches were blamed.

Constantly on guard for Apaches and with an abundance of buffalo and game to appease their appetites, they traveled down the Concho to the Colorado, naming that location San Pedro.

At this point, Mendoza stated its location was about eight leagues farther down the Colorado than where Don Diego de Guadalajara had arrived in 1654. As Mendoza was with Guadalajara's party when they had traveled to the Colorado, this could have been a conjecture on Mendoza's part, but it is the best available evidence that the Guadalajara party had been on the Colorado.

Fourteen leagues past the Colorado they camped (May 1, 1684) and named the place San Isidro Labrador. Here the combined party killed 4,030 buffalo. They were attacked three times by the Apaches, one soldier receiving three arrow wounds and two Jediondo Indians being killed while hunting. They arranged to meet the Jumanos in 1685, and departed.

Returning to the Pecos and finding the Jediondos ranchería deserted, Mendoza's party marched up the Pecos to return on their same trail to Apostol Santiago (Presidio).[16]

As the floods of the Rio Grande often changed the terrain, and as the missions by names were occasionally moved from one location to another, there is a controversy among historians as to the original site of several of the old missions on this river. This work takes what information is easily available and recognizes that later some of the information may be found in error.

Evidently, several missions were established among the Indians at La Junta (Presidio) in 1683-84. On a state marker at Fort Leaton is inscribed:

> In this vicinity the missions of San Antonio de los Puliques, San Francisco de los Julimes, Santa María la Rendondo, San Pedro Alcántara, El Apóstol Santiago, and San Christóbal were first established in 1883-84, by Mendoza Fray López, for the Christianizing of the Apache, Natoges, Faraones, Pulques, Julimes, Jumanos, Sumas. . . Administered and controlled, in 1746, by the Custodia of New Mexico.

The large, fairly well preserved remains of a mission, representative of El Apostol Santiago, one of the oldest missions in the state of Texas, stands aloof in a desolate country a few miles east of Presidio. The tall, thick, adobe walls support a flat roof, consisting of huge tree trunks as rafters, over which is a latticework of small tree limbs covered with dirt. Enclosed within the structure is a large patio surrounded by a series of large and small rooms with connecting doors. The foundation still shows the past existence of a contiguous corral for holding livestock.

About two hundred miles up the Rio Grande were the Spanish settlements around El Paso. The population of the entire El Paso valley at this time (1684), according to a recent discovery by Rex E. Gerald, was reported to be five thousand persons, including five hundred Spaniards, mestizos, mulattoes, and Piro and Tigua Indians in the small settlements of the Mission Nuestra Señora Guadalupe and the Presidio (Fort) Nuestra Señora Pilar del Paso del Rio del Norte. Three miles north across the Rio Grande in the mountains, lived the Apaches.[17]

Perhaps encouraged by the Apaches, and resentful of the Spanish authorities in this region, the Manso, Suma, Jano, Julime, Concho, Apache, Jocome, Chinara, Salinero, and Dientes Negros tribes of the northeastern province of Nueva Vizcaya revolted. These were the serious conditions which the Mendoza and Lopez party encountered soon after their return to La Junta (Presidio). Evidently, Lopez, Mendoza and their followers hurriedly prepared the mission for shelter and defense.[18] The mission at the mouth of the Conchos River, La Junta, and the mission Guadalupe near Paso del Norte which had been founded for the Sumas during the previous year, were destroyed by the Sumas and Janos, who at the same time killed Father Beltran at Soledad.[19] For two years the Spaniards waged incessant warfare with these Indians.

Subsequently (August, 1684), Captain Roque de Madrid, with fifty Spanish and one hundred Indian allies made a "sortie" out from Paso del Norte in a campaign against the Apaches. Because of incessant depredations the refugee settlers from New Mexico were sorely pressed for food and clothing. Many deserted and moved back into New Spain. Their stock had to be continually guarded from Indian raids, and they suffered from the loss of their crops and irrigation ditches because of floods on the Rio Grande. Another expedition under Crusate sent out several years later (1688-89) fought the Queres and other tribes at Sia. From the reports, six hundred Indians were killed and seventy captured. The captured Indians, for the most part, were sold into ten years' slavery while the remainder, a few old Indian men, were shot on the plaza at Paso del Norte or burned in their dwellings.[20]

Another such campaign from Paso del Norte was planned in 1690 to punish the thieves and raiding parties, but it was postponed because of a Suma revolt at Paso del Norte's door step.[21]

It took only a few years for the Apaches to extend their raids in the southwest past the habitations of the Jumanos, Jediondos, Julimes and Suma Indians on the Pecos and Rio Grande. As early as 1690, just six years after Mendoza's experience with the Apaches on the Pecos and Conchos Rivers, the Apaches were seriously troubling the inhabitants of Chihuahua. The Apaches were good horse thieves, as experienced by Juan Dominguez Mendoza on the Colorado River, but the fierce Comanches were even better. Unintentionally, the Apaches were simply bringing "remudas" of horses back from Chihuahua to equip the advancing Comanches.

At the same time the French were moving into Spanish-claimed territory. With no knowledge of the tributaries of the Mississippi, the French claimed ownership to a part of West Texas from 1685 to 1690. After La Salle's exploration of the Great Lakes and the Mississippi, he got a commission to make a settlement on the Mississippi. By error, he and his forces landed at Matagorda[22] Bay, Texas. Two of his ships were wrecked and his remaining ship had sailed out of the Bay for France before La Salle discovered his plight.

Leaving part of his company, La Salle and forty men on foot commenced the long journey to Fort St. Louis.[23] Enroute, La Salle was murdered by one of his own men, near the Trinity River and the present Navasota, Texas. Only a few members of his party lived to reach Fort St. Louis. His settlement at Matagorda Bay was discovered by the Indians, who killed most of the inhabitants. The few survivors were eventually captured by the Indians. La Salle's lone ship, enroute to France, was captured by the Spanish off the coast of Santo Domingo, and from its occupants, the Spanish first learned of the French settlement on the Texas coast.

Mendoza's discovery of a French banner among the Jediondos on the Pecos northeast of the present site of Fort Stockton was circumstantial evidence of the French presence or at least of their trade relations with the Indians in West Texas, but the evidence of the French now on the Texas coast was substantiated by good witnesses from La Salle's captured ship.

With information moving slowly, it was later (1686) that Captain Alonso de Leon with a company of cavalry went out from the Kingdom of Leon, New Spain, along the coast of Texas to search for the French intruders. Again, a year later, he and his party traveled to the site of Laredo and down the Rio Grande to Canedo in a futile attempt to locate the French settlement.[24]

On de Leon's third searching trip (1688) he reached a point located some one hundred and fifty miles northwest of the site of San Antonio, where he arranged with the Indians to bring an old, naked, sunburned and painted Frenchman to him. From this old man, de Leon learned that La Salle's settlement had been located farther up the Gulf Coast than had previously been searched.

The fourth trip of de Leon's party, in planning to colonize Texas, left Coahuila, crossed the Rio Grande, Nueces, Frio, Colorado and Brazos rivers, finding the relics, deserted houses, and dead bodies of a number of the emigrants of Fort St. Louis on Matagorda Bay.[25] Onate's Spaniards in exploring far to the southeast of New Mexico had heard of the Tejas Indians of this region. But when de Leon encountered these friendly Indians on this trip, he honored them by naming the province Tejas (Texas).

De Leon, Father Massanet, and their party then established missions in east Texas among the Tejas Indians on the Neches River. One was the mission San Francisco de los Tejas, and thought by some to have been located in the northeastern part of Houston County and near the present town of Weches. One writer, William Moses Jones, locates its site as being six miles west of Alto in Cherokee County. The mission of Santisimo Nombre de María was established nearby. Following a trip by Governor Teran of Coahuila in 1690 to the missions to investigate French encroachment on Spanish territory, he recommended their abandonment because of their faraway and untenable position.[26]

Meanwhile, Diego de Vargas, at Paso del Norte, had waited several years before food, clothing and equipment could be procured for the recapture of New Mexico.[27]

Ruins of Pecos — Catholic Church

While biding his time for the conquest (1691), and inspired by the reports of quicksilver at Sierra Azul in New Mexico, Vargas sent out a scouting party across to the Hueco Mountains,[28] and into the "Sierra Negra" among the Mescalero Apaches. They found the route across to the Pecos River and discovered the Salt Lakes located southwest of Guadalupe Peak.[29]

The Spaniards at Paso del Norte then established the mission San Diego, two leagues from Socorro and seven leagues from Paso del Norte, where three hundred Christianized Sumas made their new homes.[30]

With forty to one hundred and fifty Spaniards and about one hundred Indian allies, Vargas moved over the Jornada del Muerto (August 16, 1692) and pushed through Las Peñuelas, to arrive at Fray Cristobal, located on the opposite side of the river from Senecu. In turn, they passed through the deserted pueblos of Alamilla, Las Barrancas, to Mexia, to establish their base of supplies and operations (September 13, 1692). The villages of Cochiti and Santo Domingo[31] were also found abandoned. At Cieneguilla, preparations were made to capture Santa Fe. They reached the abutments of Santa Fe, and following early morning prayers and after hours of negotiations and attempts to intimidate by displaying cannon and cutting off the defenders' water supply, the Indians were induced to allow the entry of the Vargas forces.[32]

With the Apaches thieving, raiding, and causing friction among the Pueblo tribes, many of the Pueblos welcomed some assistance. Also, other tribes were in constant fear of another Domingo de Crusate campaign and the resulting casualties.[33]

Vargas promised the Indians assistance against the Apaches, Pecos, Faraones, Queres of San Felipe, Santo Domingo, and Cochiti. With a number of new Indian allies, and joined by two troops of cavalry from Parral, Vargas marched to the Pecos village, found it deserted, returned to Santa Fe,[34] moved north from Santa Fe, and took peaceable possession of Tesuque, Cuyamungue,

Ruins of Pecos — Astek Church

Nambe, Pojoaque, Jacona, San Ildefonso, Santa Clara, San Juan, San Cristóbal, and San Lazaro. By October 5th, the Picuri pueblo was in their hands. Taos was found abandoned.[35] They passed through the deserted Galisteo, and San Marcos, to enter Cochiti peacefully.[36]

Vargas then moved down to his base, crossed over to and took possession of the deserted Sia. At the abandoned Jemez, they found three hundred hostile Indians in the adjacent hills who were easily won over by payment for corn and mutton. Going by way of Santa Ana, Vargas returned to Mexía for commissaries and fresh horses.[37]

Sending much of his equipment, worn-out horses, crippled soldiers, and some captives to Paso del Norte, Vargas, with eighty-nine soldiers and some Indians, passed the deserted village of Isleta, crossed the Rio Puerco, watered at the small pozo, and moved to see the smoke from Penol de Acoma, that fortress upon a solitary round mesa in the desert. Following hours of negotiations, the Indians of Penol de Acoma agreed to Spanish rule.[38]

Then the Vargas forces in segments crossed the lava beds, the Continental Divide, camped dry at Little Rock, arrived at the El Morro water hole, and upon reaching Ojo Pescada on November 9th, were met by a small number of Zuñi Indians with gifts of butchered sheep, watermelon and cakes. Close to the Zuñi pueblo, they met hostile Indians, and their cattle were stolen by the Apaches. Ignoring the theft, the Spaniards went peacefully to the top of the mesa, and the pueblo. The Apaches again stole some of their stock.

Leaving a detail to guard the mules and carts, Vargas with sixty-nine soldiers and many Indians, pushed toward the Hopi country, traveling four days and encountering only three springs for watering. Suddenly they were confronted by eight hundred Moqui Indians, but peace was made with them. Enroute to the pueblo of Jongopavi, Vargas examined the red soil for evidence of mercuric ore (quicksilver). The Vargas soldiers returned by way of Mexía, to Paso del Norte, to report the unusual circum-

Ruins of Pecos

stance of the reconquest of New Mexico without the firing of a shot.[39]

In the re-occupation of New Mexico by the Spaniards more than eight hundred persons — men, wives, children, servants, maidens and bachelors, together with friendly Indians, twelve wagons, mules, pack animals, horses, supplies, three carriages and some nine hundred head of cattle, all under guard along with two pieces of cannon, moved out of Paso del Norte toward their future home in Santa Fe.

Upon arriving in the vicinity of Santa Fe, the soldiers had a number of engagements with Indians, were forced to lay siege to obtain only a portion of Santa Fe and found very few Indians, other than the Pecos Indians, loyal to Spain and willing to spare extra food for the hungry Spaniards. Vargas, his soldiers and allied Indians, were for several years continuously on the march in putting down uprisings.

At this period, other problems were facing the Spaniards. The Comanche Indians, rapidly becoming the masters of the plains country, moved south from the Shoshone region. They were well established in the region of the Red and Arkansas rivers by 1700.[40] In 1717, the Utes, and Comanches attacked the Spanish settlement of Taos, New Mexico, took captives and retreated north. They were followed and defeated by the Spanish Captain Serna and his troops.[41]

The Apaches were conveniently moving southwest, keeping their ranges outside the reach of the Comanches, and penetrating New Mexico, Arizona, West Texas, and Mexico. South and west of the lower Rio Grande in Mexico, they had, prior to 1700, destroyed Santa Ana del Torreon, its four adjoining pueblos and Santa María de las Carretas and its three adjacent pueblos.[42]

The French traders were finding their way into Spanish territory from the Mississippi River in search of Indian trade and minerals. Pierre le Moyne d' Iberville built and colonized the present city of Biloxi, located about forty miles above the mouth of the Mississippi, Louis St. Denis and his French party traveled from Louisiana by way of the San Pedro Springs (San Antonio) to New Spain and back in 1705. The French merchants made the same trip in 1707.[43] Seven years later (1714), in an attempt to open more trading relations with the Indians, St. Denis took a party to the site of Natchitoches Island on the Red River and then traveled across Texas, fighting the Lipan Indians on the Rio San Marcos, passing San Pedro Springs, and arriving at the Spanish presidio of San Juan Bautista on the Rio Grande. There he was arrested on suspicion of his motives and sent to Mexico City to explain his reason for being in Texas, resulting in his advocation of Texas being occupied by the Spanish and his services being employed by the Spaniards in doing that very job.[44]

Following a petition by the natives from the region of the junction of the Rio Grande with the Rio Conchos (La Junta), and enthusiastic over the re-occupation of New Mexico and strengthening its lines of communication, Padres Gregorio and Juan Antonio Garcia, with a guard of thirty soldiers, re-established missions (1715) — along with eleven pueblos — in the La Junta (Presidio, Texas) area. They were: Santiago de la Ciénaga del Coyame; Nuestra Señora Begoña del Cuchillo Parado; Loreto, S. Juan Bautista; San Francisco de Asis de La Junta; Nuestra Señora de Arnazazu; Guadalupe; San Jose; San Antonio; and San Cristóbal.[45]

Shortly afterward, Captain Domingo Ramon, son of the commandante at San Juan Bautista, along with St. Denis and his wife, eight women, a number of friars, twenty-five cavalrymen, a thousand goats, a large number of pack animals and oxen, started from Saltillo, and made their way to San Juan Bautista, where Friars Hidalgo and Massanet joined the expedition.

After traveling over the San Marcos River, they met the Tejas Indians, who guided them across the Colorado and the Trinity to where they established (July 3, 1715) the mission San Francisco de los Neches, inland from the

MAP OF LA JUNTA REGION (1683-1760)

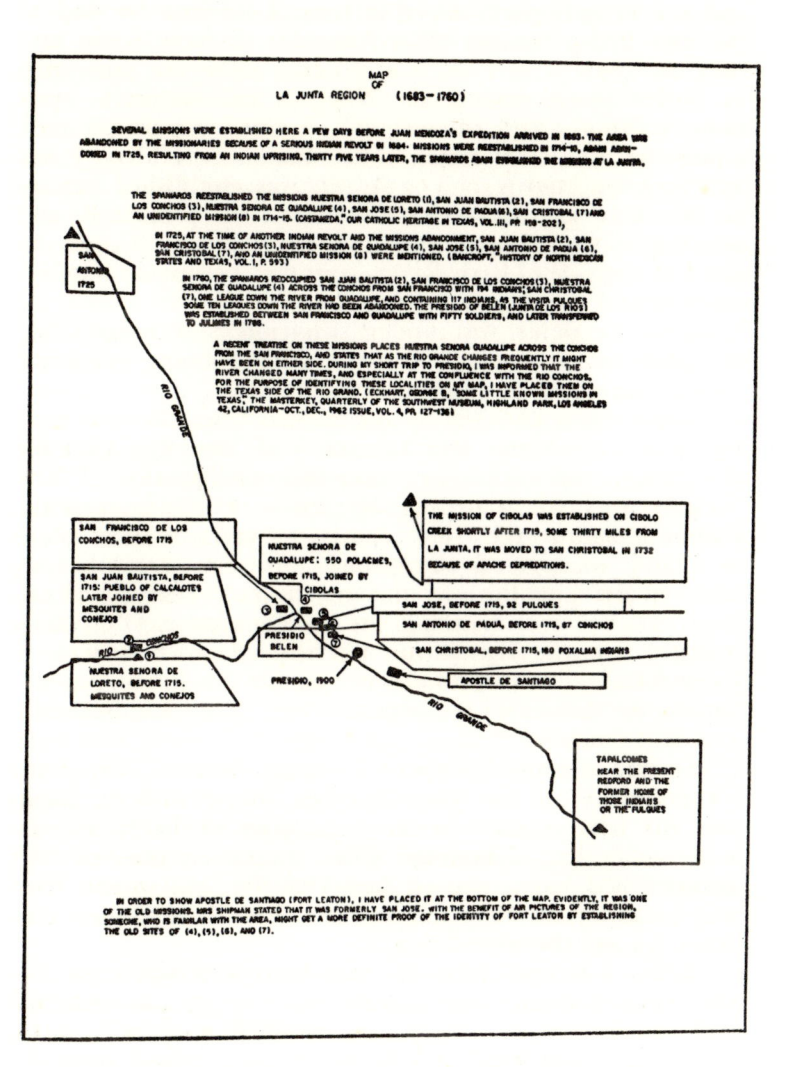

SEVERAL MISSIONS WERE ESTABLISHED HERE A FEW DAYS BEFORE JUAN MENDOZA'S EXPEDITION ARRIVED IN 1683. THE AREA WAS ABANDONED BY THE MISSIONARIES BECAUSE OF A SERIOUS INDIAN REVOLT IN 1684. MISSIONS WERE REESTABLISHED IN 1714-15, AGAIN ABANDONED IN 1725, RESULTING FROM AN INDIAN UPRISING. THIRTY FIVE YEARS LATER, THE SPANIARDS AGAIN ESTABLISHED THE MISSIONS AT LA JUNTA.

THE SPANIARDS REESTABLISHED THE MISSIONS NUESTRA SENORA DE LORETO (1), SAN JUAN BAUTISTA (2), SAN FRANCISCO DE LOS CONCHOS (3), NUESTRA SENORA DE GUADALUPE (4), SAN JOSE (5), SAN ANTONIO DE PADUA (6), SAN CRISTOBAL (7) AND AN UNIDENTIFIED MISSION (8) IN 1714-15. (CASTANEDA," OUR CATHOLIC HERITAGE IN TEXAS, VOL. III, PP. 198-202),

IN 1725, AT THE TIME OF ANOTHER INDIAN REVOLT AND THE MISSIONS ABANDONMENT, SAN JUAN BAUTISTA (2), SAN FRANCISCO DE LOS CONCHOS (3), NUESTRA SENORA DE GUADALUPE (4), SAN JOSE (5), SAN ANTONIO DE PADUA (6), SAN CRISTOBAL (7), AND AN UNIDENTIFIED MISSION (8) WERE MENTIONED. (BANCROFT," HISTORY OF NORTH MEXICAN STATES AND TEXAS, VOL. I, P. 593)

IN 1760, THE SPANIARDS REOCCUPIED SAN JUAN BAUTISTA (2), SAN FRANCISCO DE LOS CONCHOS (3), NUESTRA SENORA DE GUADALUPE (4) ACROSS THE CONCHOS FROM SAN FRANCISCO WITH 194 INDIANS; SAN CRISTOBAL (7), ONE LEAGUE DOWN THE RIVER FROM GUADALUPE, AND CONTAINING 117 INDIANS, 49 THE VISITA PULQUES, SOME TEN LEAGUES DOWN THE RIVER HAD BEEN ABANDONED. THE PRESIDIO OF BELEN (JUNTA DE LOS RIOS) WAS ESTABLISHED BETWEEN SAN FRANCISCO AND GUADALUPE WITH FIFTY SOLDIERS, AND LATER TRANSFERRED TO JULIMES IN 1788.

A RECENT TREATISE ON THESE MISSIONS PLACES NUESTRA SENORA GUADALUPE ACROSS THE CONCHOS FROM THE SAN FRANCISCO, AND STATES THAT AS THE RIO GRANDE CHANGES FREQUENTLY IT MIGHT HAVE BEEN ON EITHER SIDE. DURING MY SHORT TRIP TO PRESIDIO, I WAS INFORMED THAT THE RIVER CHANGED MANY TIMES, AND ESPECIALLY AT THE CONFLUENCE WITH THE RIO CONCHOS. FOR THE PURPOSE OF IDENTIFYING THESE LOCALITIES ON MY MAP, I HAVE PLACED THEM ON THE TEXAS SIDE OF THE RIO GRAND. (ECKHART, GEORGE B., "SOME LITTLE KNOWN MISSIONS IN TEXAS," THE MASTERKEY, QUARTERLY OF THE SOUTHWEST MUSEUM, HIGHLAND PARK, LOS ANGELES 42, CALIFORNIA-OCT., DEC., 1962 ISSUE, VOL. 4, PP. 127-136)

SAN ANTONIO 1725

RIO GRANDE

SAN FRANCISCO DE LOS CONCHOS, BEFORE 1715

SAN JUAN BAUTISTA, BEFORE 1715: PUEBLO OF CALCALOTE'S LATER JOINED BY MESQUITES AND CONEJOS

RIO CONCHOS

NUESTRA SENORA DE LORETO, BEFORE 1715. MESQUITES AND CONEJOS

NUESTRA SENORA DE GUADALUPE: 550 POLACMES, BEFORE 1715, JOINED BY CIBOLAS

PRESIDIO BELEN

PRESIDIO, 1900

THE MISSION OF CIBOLAS WAS ESTABLISHED ON CIBOLO CREEK SHORTLY AFTER 1715, SOME THIRTY MILES FROM LA JUNTA. IT WAS MOVED TO SAN CRISTOBAL IN 1732 BECAUSE OF APACHE DEPREDATIONS.

SAN JOSE, BEFORE 1715, 92 PULQUES

SAN ANTONIO DE PADUA, BEFORE 1715, 87 CONCHOS

SAN CHRISTOBAL, BEFORE 1715, 100 POXALMA INDIANS

APOSTLE DE SANTIAGO

RIO GRANDE

TAPALCOMES NEAR THE PRESENT REDFORD AND THE FORMER HOME OF THOSE INDIANS OR THE PULQUES

IN ORDER TO SHOW APOSTLE DE SANTIAGO (FORT LEATON), I HAVE PLACED IT AT THE BOTTOM OF THE MAP. EVIDENTLY, IT WAS ONE OF THE OLD MISSIONS. MRS SHIPMAN STATED THAT IT WAS FORMERLY SAN JOSE. WITH THE BENEFIT OF AIR PICTURES OF THE REGION, SOMEONE, WHO IS FAMILIAR WITH THE AREA, MIGHT GET A MORE DEFINITE PROOF OF THE IDENTITY OF FORT LEATON BY ESTABLISHING THE OLD SITES OF (4), (5), (6), AND (7).

Neches River and near to the abandoned Francisco de Tejas. The presidio Nuestra Señora de los Dolores de los Tejas was placed at the old mission San Francisco, not far from the present site of Nacogdoches. Mission San Jose was located west, among the Noachis and Nazones. The missions Dolores and San Miguel de Cuellar were located among the Aes and Adaes. The mission San Miguel de Linares, later known as Los Adaes, was established across the Sabine in Louisiana near the site of the present Robeline, Louisiana.[46] The French, fearing that the Spaniards would occupy the Red River country, occupied Natchitoches Island in the Red River.[47]

Louis St. Denis was under suspicion of duplicity by the Spaniards when he returned with Ramon bringing trade goods from Louisiana into Mexico. Arriving there at a time when the war between Spain and France was known, he was again arrested, tried in Mexico City and ordered to confinement in Guatemala in January, 1718.[48]

Early in 1718, Alarcón, governor of Coahuila, accompanied by Santo and a large party, moved out from Coahuila and established the presidio of San Antonio de Velero (Valero) at the site of San Antonio. After traveling over East Texas and seeing the missions close to French settlements on the Mississippi, and as England, France, and Holland had joined in an alliance against Spain in August, Alarcón recommended the abandonment of those missions.[49]

The French reinforced Louisiana with three hundred settlers and a large number of Negro slaves (1719), and took possession of the mission of San Miguel de los Adaes. Only the friar escaped to carry the news to the Spaniards in the other East Texas missions. Thereafter, the Spanish soldiers and missionaries of East Texas retired to San Antonio, making that site as the only Spanish settlement in Texas for the next two years.[50]

St. Denis escaped from the prison in New Spain (1719), and with his Spanish wife, made his way back to Natchitoches where he commanded that French post, and established Fort St. Louis de Carlorette, close to Natchitoches.[51]

In scouting French occupation west of the Mississippi (1720), Aguayo's expedition traveled from about the location of the present Eagle Pass, to San Pedro Springs (San Antonio); thence north to about the location of the Tuacana (Tawakoni) Indians, and east to Natchitoches.[52] Valverde's expedition moved out of Santa Fe, crossing the Pecos River and exploring the northwest tip of the present Panhandle of Texas,[53] while Villasur took his party from the Santa Fe area and crossed through the Panhandle of Texas, just above the Red River.[54]

Authorized to re-establish the Spanish missions in Texas, Marquis de San Miguel de Aguayo, governor and captain-general of Coahuila and Texas, established the mission of San Jose y San Miguel de Aguayo (1720) near the presidio of San Antonio.[55] In the meantime, the French sent M. Beranger by ship with men and supplies to investigate St. Bernard (Bay of Espíritu Santo) in anticipation of establishing a settlement there. He left a number of men at an unknown port who were never heard of afterward.[56]

Governor Aguayo, with five hundred men, crossed the Rio Grande and arrived at San Antonio on April 4th, to establish themselves firmly in Texas. After assigning fifty men to examine the area of Espíritu Santo Bay (Matagorda Bay) for signs of Frenchmen, his large party searched the Brazos River and marched on the Camino Real where he met St. Denis on the Neches River. Following a conference, St. Denis and his forces retreated back to Natchitoches, leaving Aguayo with plans to re-establish the Spanish missions in the Neches area.[57]

As navigation was not easy in those days, the vessel Marechal d'Esdres (French), containing a large number of troops and convicts had erroneously arrived in Galveston Bay. In an effort to avoid contagion from an epidemic on board ship, five officers landed with only eight days' provisions. The ship sailed away without them. For twenty months, that small party of five men wandered among the Indians before St. Denis rescued them in April, 1721.[58]

Meanwhile, the Spaniards were firmly establishing themselves in Texas. Aguayo refounded the six missions in east Texas,[59] and established: Fort St. Louis on Matagorda Bay, and an additional mission at San Antonio, the presidio Santa María de Loreta de la Bahía, on Matagorda Bay and the nearby mission of Espíritu Santo de Zuñiga at the site of La Salle's old fort;[60] and the mission of San Xavier de Naxera, close by that of San Jose in the San Antonio region in 1722.[61]

The Apaches had raided and stolen horses at San Antonio, and had recently murdered two frairs in East Texas, besides committing other depredations. Even after Aguayo's arrival, they ran off with eighty horses from the corral of the presidio of San Antonio. Captain Flores with thirty soldiers and thirty Indians, and only two pack loads of flour took the trail, following it to the site of what is now Brownwood, where a six-hour engagement took place with the Indians. Three Spaniards and one Indian were wounded before the Apaches retreated, leaving twenty Apache women and children as captives.[62]

Aguayo had been instructed to patronize the Apaches in an effort to induce those war-like Indians to settle in the missions,[63] but by 1724, the Apaches had become so troublesome up the Rio Grande that the six missions at La Junta (Presidio del Norte) had been abandoned. Local Indians took possession of the mission buildings and traded with the Apaches upon the grounds bordering Alamito Creek.[64] The Jumanos Indians had been pushed out, captured or exterminated by the Apaches in the region of West Texas. Even the Sumas and Julimes frequently raided the Spanish missions in and near El Paso (Paso del Norte), San Elizario and Ysleta.

Aguayo's re-establishment of the Spaniards in Texas had been at an expense of over $250,000. A hard rain during freezing weather in East Texas had caused many trees, loaded with ice, to fall. The freeze and the falling trees killed all but fifty of the five thousand horses they had taken along with their troops.[65]

Following Aguayo's return to Coahuila, some of the

Lipan Apaches around San Antonio expressed friendship; while others continued to commit depredations. At the presidio Espíritu Santo, Captain Ramon ruled with such cruelty and harsh treatment that the Indians killed him and abandoned the missions. After having been continually harassed by hostile Indians for four years, the mission of Espíritu Santo de Zuñiga and the presidio of La Bahía were moved (1726) from Matagorda Bay to the Guadalupe River near the site of Meyersville, among the friendly Tamiques, Aranamos, and Xaranames Indians, where they were to be frequently attacked by the dreaded Karankawas.[66]

Rivera, on an inspection tour in 1727, made the trip from the Rio Grande to San Pedro Springs (San Antonio) across to La Bahía and thence directly to Nachitoches. On Rivera's return to Mexico (1727-28), he suggested, for economical reasons, the suppression of the Tejas presidio and the reduction of forces at the other three presidios,[67] which resulted in the transfer of three of the East Texas Neches missions first to the river of San Javier (unidentified).

---

[1] Bancroft, H. H., as cited, Vol. I, p. 386.

[2] Bolton, H. E., *Spanish Exploration In The Southwest*, p. 320.

[3] "Julimenos. A former tribe in N.E. Mexico, probably of the Coahuiltecan linguistic family, which was gathered into the mission of San Francisco Vizarrón de los Pausanes, in Coahuila, in 1737. . . ." Hodge, as cited.

[4] Alamito Creek is an arroyo which rises close to Marfa, Presidio County, Texas, and runs south and then turns a little west as it is joined by the Ciénaga Creek to enter the Rio Grande, close to the present Presidio, Texas.

[5] Paisano Pass is located in the mountains about half-way between Marfa and Alpine, Texas, on highways 67 & 90.

[6] Leoncita Spring is situated on the eastern rim of the Davis Mts. about forty-five miles southwest of Fort Stockton, Texas, on the west side of Paisano or the upper Coyanosa Draw.

[7] Leon Water Holes, formerly springs, are located some seven miles west of Fort Stockton, Texas.

8 Bolton, H. E., *Spanish Exploration In The Southwest*, p. 328.

9 Comanche Springs, now dormant, are located in Fort Stockton, Texas.

10 San Pedro Springs, a number of springs located five to ten miles north of Fort Stockton, Texas.

11 King Mountain, a large table-topped mountain, is located between McCamey and Crane, Texas, having a small pass known as Castle Gap on its west end.

12 Located on the William Walter Phelps map of 1891, covering Blocks 11 and 12, of the H&GN Railroad Surveys in Pecos County, and in the handwriting of O. W. Williams is the following: "Old camp of Jediondo Indians (Mendoza 1684). This location appears in the present Crockett County, and opposite the Pecos County joint survey lines of section 11 and 12 in Block 12, H&GN Survey, and in the vicinity of the old Torres irrigation system of the 1870's."

13 Castañeda, C. E., as cited, Vol. I, p. 215.

14 Grierson Spring in Crockett County, Texas, is located fifteen or twenty miles southwest of the town of Big Lake.

15 Middle Concho commences in eastern Upton County as Centralia Draw and runs eastward through Reagan and Irion counties to the site of San Angelo, Texas.

16 Bolton, Herbert E., *Spanish Exploration In The Southwest*, pp. 320-343; O. W. Williams, "Mendoza," privately printed brochure.

17 El Paso *Herald Post*, Section B, September 5, 1966 — *1766 JUAREZ MAP FOUND IN LIBRARY OF CONGRESS*.

18 Coan, Charles, as cited, Vol. 1, p. 21.

19 Bancroft, H. H., as cited, Vol. I, p. 366; Bailey, J. B., *Diego de Vargas, Reconquest of New Mexico*, p. 9: University of New Mexico Press, 1940.

20 Bailey, J. B., as cited, p. 9.

21 Bancroft, H. H., as cited, Vol. I, pp. 371-372.

22 Matagorda Bay on the Gulf of Mexico, southeast of Victoria, and southwest of Bay City, Texas, has Port Lavaca for one of its principal ports.

23 "Fort St. Louis (Webb et al, *The Handbook of Texas*) was established by Rene Robert Cavelier, Sieur de la Salle, in February, 1685, in the Matagorda Bay area, the temporary fort . . . was moved March, 1685, to a permanent site on the Lavaca River, about five miles above the bay."

24 Wharton, Clarence, *Texas Under Many Flags*, Vol. I, p. 21: The American Historical Society, Inc., Chicago & New York, 1930.

25 *Ibid.*, pp. 22, 23.

26 Bolton, H. E., *Spanish Exploration In The Southwest*, pp. 346-350.

27 Bailey, Jessie B., as cited, pp. 12-14.

28 Hueco Mountains are located about twenty-five m. east of El Paso.

29 Guadalupe Peak close to the New Mexico and Texas line and north of Van Horn, Texas, is the highest point in Texas with an elevation of 8751 feet.

30 Bailey, Jessie B., as cited, p. 19.

31 *Ibid.*, pp. 25-33.

32 *Ibid.*, pp. 33-36.

33 *Ibid.*, pp. 82-106.

34 *Ibid.*, pp. 36-61.

35 *Ibid.*, pp. 61-68.

36 *Ibid.*, pp. 68-71.

37 *Ibid.*, pp. 71-74.

38 *Ibid.*, pp. 74-78.

39 *Ibid.*, pp. 78-82.

40 Wharton, Clarence, as cited, Vol. I, p. 90.

41 Richardson, Rupert N., as cited, p. 55.

42 Bancroft, H. H., as cited, Vol. I, p. 365.

43 Winsor, Justin, *The Mississippi Basin*, p. 92: Houghton, Mifflin and Company, The University Press, Cambridge, Boston & New York, 1895; Bancroft, as cited, Vol. I, p. 609.

44 Castañeda, C. E., as cited, Vol. II, Chapter 1, "French Settlements of Louisiana and Spain's Renewed Interest in Texas, 1693-1714," Austin, Texas, Von Beeckmann-Jones Co., 1936.

45 Bancroft, H. H., as cited, Vol. I, pp. 598-611, with footnotes.

46 *Ibid.*, Vol. I, pp. 611-615.

47 Winsor, Justin, as cited, pp. 95, 96.

48 Bancroft, H. H., as cited, Vol. I, p. 617.

49 *Ibid.,* pp. 617-668.

50 *Ibid.,* pp. 618-619.

51 *Ibid.,* Vol. I, pp. 617, 619; Winsor, Justin, as cited, pp. 95, 96.

52 Castañeda, C. E., as cited, Vol. II, Chapter 4, "The Aguayo Expedition and the Founding of San José Mission," pp. 110-148: Austin, Von Beeckmann-Jones Co., 1936.

53 Bancroft, H. H., as cited, Vol. I, pp. 619-622.

54 Castañeda, C. E., as cited, Vol. II, pp. 311-348.

55 Wharton, Clarence, as cited, Vol. I, p. 23.

56 Webb, W. P. *et al,* as cited, Vol. I, p. 148: "Beranger, Sieur."

57 Wharton, Clarence, as cited, Vol. I, p. 45.

58 Bancroft, H. H., as cited, Vol. I, pp. 619-622.

59 *Ibid.,* Vol. 1, p. 46; Bancroft, as cited, Vol. I, p. 622.

60 Oberste, William H., *Remember Goliad,* p. 4 (In Commemoration of the Bi-Centennial of la Bahía) — Copyright 1949, W. H. Oberste . . . No location given; *Peña's Diary of the Aguayo Expedition.*

61 Bancroft, H. H., as cited, Vol. I, p. 628.

62 Reeve, F. D., "The Apache Indians in Texas": *The Southwestern Historical Quarterly,* Vol. L, No. 2, Oct., 1946.

63 Castañeda, C. E., as cited, Vol. III, p. 191; Bancroft, Vol. I, p. 593 states that the reoccupation of the Junta missions was ordered in 1725, which were Santiago de la Ciénaga del Coyame, Nra. Sra. Begoña del Cuchillo Parado, Loreto, S. Juan Bautista, S. Francisco de Asís de la Junta, Nra. Sra. de Aranzazu, Guadalupe, San José, San Antonio, and S. Cristóbal.

64 Castañeda, C. E., as cited, p. 1.

65 Bancroft, H. H., as cited, Vol. I, pp. 622-629.

66 *Ibid.,* pp. 630-631.

67 *Ibid.,* p. 633.

Chapter 5

*Apaches Swarming in Northeast New Spain.
The Comanches Moving in — (1728-1763)*

During the following thirty-five years, the Spaniards made a feeble attempt to stem the flow of Apache raids by forming a treaty with them against the oncoming Comanches. They moved a number of missions closer to the presidios, and established two missions to pacify the Lipan Apaches.

In order to explore the advisability of placing presidios on the upper Rio Grande, an expedition under Captain José Berroteran started from the Presidio de Conchos on January 13, 1729, to investigate the source of Indian raids. They moved through Santiago Mapimí, Monclova, and San Juan Bautista on the Rio Grande, then proceeded up and along the west side of the Rio Grande to about the present location of Langtry, Texas, crossed to the northeast side of the river and made their way over some rough country to about the site of present Dryden. Upon encountering unfriendly Indians, they returned, retracing the route by which they had come.[1]

The following year — forty-six years prior to the American Revolution — the villa of San Fernando de Bexar (San Antonio) was founded with the settlement of fourteen or fifteen families, close to the presidio Valero. From an effort commenced in 1722 to arrange for the transfer of four hundred families from the Canary Islands, culminating in a cost of $70,000, it was found more expedient (1730) to settle families from elsewhere.[2]

As the Apaches took possession of the Trans-Pecos region, the Jumanos were either captured, killed or put to flight, becoming extinct in this region. The Apaches learned the use of the local vegetation and the use of mescal from which they derived their name, Mescalero Apaches. Because the Mescalero and Lipan Apaches were troublesome to Coahuila and Chihuahua, another party under Garza Falcon made about the same trip in 1735-36, and with the same unsatisfactory result Berroteran and his men had experienced in 1729.[3]

At Bexar (San Antonio), five hundred Apache Indians attacked the small force of defenders. In an engagement with the Indians, Captain Perez and twenty-five men were defeated after two hours of conflict, suffering a loss of two dead, thirteen wounded and some cattle driven away.

To chastise those Apaches, Governor Bustillo marched up with forces from the province of Coahuila and set out (December 9, 1732) from San Antonio with one hundred fifty-seven Spaniards, sixty mission Indians, one hundred forty pack loads, and nine hundred horses. They fought a large party of Apaches, Lipans, Ysandis and Cheutis at "Little River." After a four-hour battle, the Spaniards captured thirty women and children, seven hundred horses and one hundred mule loads of plunder.[4]

Eleven years later, in 1743, within the vicinity of San

Antonio, the Comanches were first reported to have followed and attacked the Apaches, resulting in an enmity that lasted for years.[5]

One year later, Britain, in fear of possible encroachment by the Spaniards of Florida and the French of Louisiana, established (1733) a settlement at Savannah — the beginning of Georgia.

Soon after, the three missions of San Javier, Candelaria and San Ildefonso, situated on a river called San Javier (Bancroft thought the river to be a branch of the Brazos or Colorado), were guarded by a small number of men (1744-45), varying from twenty-two to fifty soldiers. The resident Indians, not more than three hundred, often ran away[6] to join the ever troublesome and thieving nomadic Indians.

To prevent Apache raids into Mexico (New Spain), the Spaniards again planned to put forts along the Rio Grande, the troops of which might head off the Apaches before they got into Mexico. In late 1747, three separate Spanish parties started to reconnoiter the Big Bend of Texas for that purpose. In converging on the abandoned site of the Apóstol Santiago, Captain Vidaurre was to look over the Rio Grande region below, and Idoyago, the vicinity above. As to Teran, I am not informed other than that he moved down to Apostol Santiago and returned shortly.

Idoyago's party went by San Bartolome (November 3, 1747) and down the Conchos River, passing San Antonio de los Julimes, and arrived in Santa Cruz de los Cholomes on the Conchos. There he was told that the mission Indians at La Junta (Presidio) had abandoned their pueblos in protest against any establishment of a fort or presidio in their midst. When his party came to San Juan Bautista on the Conchos River (November 17, 1747), some twelve miles southwest of La Junta, they found a priest who had been there seventeen years since the Spaniards abandoned the region.

Idoyago visited the ruins of the mission at Cibolos (November 3, 1747), which had been abandoned by the Cibolo Indians because of the Apaches.[7] Idoyago found the Tecolote (Owl) Indians located above La Junta, the Pescados (Fish) at San Antonio de los Puliques, six miles below La Junta on the present Texas side of the Rio Grande; and the Cibolos (Bull or Buffalo) at San Cristóbal, located four or five miles north of La Junta. Mission Guadalupe was situated five miles northwest from San Cristóbal.

Captain Fermin Vidaurre's party went from Durango by Mapimí, reached the Rio Grande below the present Langtry, and followed up its west side, detouring away from the river because of rough country. Vidaurre secured guides, and crossed the Rio Grande at the site of the present Lajitas. They trailed over the rough mountains, reached Alamito Creek about eighteen miles above its mouth, and found many abandoned rancherias of the Apaches, who had traded with the Indians of the deserted missions. Upon traveling down the Alamito to the abandoned mission of Apóstol Santiago, they met Idoyago's party. Teran had been there, but had returned a few days previously.[8]

Seventeen miles down the Rio Grande from La Junta and eleven miles from San Antonio de los Puliques, lay the ruins of the pueblos of the Tapalcomes, with walls yet standing. Some five years after Idoyago made this trip and his recommendations, the Junta missions were reoccupied by the Spaniards.[9]

In the region of San Antonio, following Indian depredations, Don Pedro de Rabago y Teran and Urrutia respectively led expeditions in 1748 and February, 1749, from Monclova and San Antonio to the San Saba area in retaliation. During Urrutia's absence from San Antonio, Indians attacked and stole cattle from Mission Concepción.[10]

In South Texas, following many attacks by the Karankawas in their location on the Guadalupe, the Spaniards in 1749, moved the mission Espíritu Santo and the presidio of La Bahía to a more suitable location, bordering on the San Antonio River.

Up in the Plains country, the Comanches were active. In the early 18th century, in pushing their territory southward, they were reported to have inflicted a severe defeat on the Lipan Apaches on the Rio del Fierro, thought to be the Wichita River.[11] Even the Spaniards of New Mexico were having their difficulties with the Comanches. Following several Comanche raids into New Mexico, (they murdered 150 residents of Pecos alone), the Spaniards in 1750 pursued the raiders down the Arkansas River as far as the region of the Jumano villages. In 1751, three hundred Comanches raided at Taos and then attacked Galisteo, after which they were followed and overtaken on the Arkansas River in a little wood, which was set on fire and resulted in the death of 101 Comanches with the remainder captured.[12]

Because of Apache depredations in South Texas, the missions San Javier, Candelaria and San Ildefonso (formerly San Francisco de la Espada, La Purisima Concepcion and San Juan Capistrano) were transferred from Rio Marcos to San Antonio. The presidio San Agustin de Ahumada was established (1755) on the Trinity in East Texas to levy duty on those French traders engaged in exchanging guns and ammunition with Indians for furs. Nearby this presidio were settled fifty Tlascaltec families.[13]

From the founding of Béxar until 1750, there had been almost continuous warfare between the Spaniards and the Apaches. Numerous expeditions were sent out against the Indians from that place.[14] In view of the increasing encroachment of Comanches into this region, in addition to the already troublesome Apaches, the Spanish made the "Horse and Hatchet" treaty with the Apaches. This treaty had poor results, in that it caused the enmity of the other Indian tribes without bringing any real assistance from the Apaches.

Later (1755), Bernardo de Miranda's party was sent from Adaes, New Spain, into the Llano River country. Samples of ore taken by them near a tributary of the Llano River looked sufficiently rich to cause Don Pedro Terreros to order thirty additional mule loads of it.

After these samples were analyzed, Father Ciraco Terreros, a cousin of Don Pedro Terreros, along with priests, colonists, and a small military detachment under the command of Captain Parilla, left Adaes in April 1757, and went through Coahuila to San Antonio. There, they gathered up fourteen hundred cattle and sheep and moved on to establish the mission Santa Cruz de San Saba on one side and the fort San Luis de las Amarillas several miles from and on the other side of the San Saba River, close to the present Menard.

The Apaches made no effort to settle down, grow crops and become Christianized; but continued their raids into New Spain, bringing back large numbers of horses and mules, and were even somewhat hostile to this settlement. They would have destroyed the Spaniards in this settlement, thought Captain Parilla, except that they were in hopes of using them as allies against the Comanches.[15]

The following year (1758), the Comanches and an assortment of other Indians, some of whom were thought to be friendly with the Spaniards, showed up in front of the mission and drove off sixty-two horses grazing between the presidio and the mission. The soldiers, sent out to retrieve those animals, came back empty-handed, but with alarming reports of much Indian sign. Captain Parilla sent word to the mission occupants and attempted unsuccessfully to get them to seek refuge in the presidio.

On the following morning (March 16, 1758), two thousand Indians armed with firearms, lances and sabers, wearing red and black war paint, wild beasts' skins, headgear of horns, antlers and feathers, approached the mission with loud shouts and frequent discharges of firearms. They made signs of peace by gestures and false professions in broken Spanish. Deceived, and believing that he recognized several friendly Indians, the corporal of the guard reported to Padre Terreros, who was enroute to confer with them. Before the padre got to the gate, however, the Indians had been allowed to throw down the bars and open the gate.

In the resulting slaughter, Padre Terreros was shot dead at the gate; Padre Santistevan was killed and his head severed. The seventeen soldiers were shot or lanced or took refuge in the building. The Indians ransacked the property, and set fire to the palisades and buildings. Hidden, smoke-blackened Spaniards were forced out of those flaming buildings to run the gauntlet for other shelter. Only a few escaped to the woods, eventually to reach the presidio. The following day, Parilla, with his soldiers, marched over from the presidio to find the mission reduced to ashes.[16] Upon reporting to his superiors, Parilla suggested the removal of the presidio or the increase in its force, and an expedition to chastise the savages.

The following year, Parilla, five hundred soldiers, volunteers, and a large number of Apaches, went some one hundred fifty leagues, attacked a ranchería, killed fifty-five Indians and took captives. In the next encounter with six thousand Taovaya Indians, along the Red River a short distance from the site of Nacona, Texas, the mixed force of Spaniards and Apaches was attacked and put to flight, leaving two small brass cannons as trophies for the Indians.[17]

At this time, the four missions in the vicinity of San Antonio had annually raised eight thousand bushels of maize and some cotton. In 1745, they had been the proud possessors of nine thousand head of sheep, horses and goats. But following the destruction of the San Saba mission, the other missions in the vicinity of San Antonio abandoned their ranges and farms, and the people remained near their fortifications in constant fear for their lives.

Out at La Junta in West Texas (1759-60), the Spaniards established a fort or presidio (Belén) on the Rio Grande, close to the Mission Nuestra Señora de Guadalupe. Its exact location is uncertain. Old residents of the Rio Grande had a saying that "the Rio Grande might sleep one night in this place and the next night in a different place." Soon after it was built, some eight hundred Indians, including many Apaches, attacked the presidio. Seven Indians were killed and more than sixty wounded. After the Indians had retreated, the presidio's forces were increased, and campaigns were made against the hostile Indians.[18]

Because of these conditions in 1760, Bishop Tamaron did not visit the Junta de los Rios missions: San Juan Bautista, fifteen miles from the junction; San Francisco at the junction; Guadalupe just across the river from San Francisco; and San Cristóbal some three miles down the river from the junction. San Juan Bautista was credited with 309 Indians, as the Mezquites and Conejos, in two *visitas* (haunts), had been joined to the Cebecera. San Francisco contained 167 Indians and San Cristóbal was credited with 117 Indians, as the Pulique villages, located some thirty miles below, had been abandoned.[19] I cannot reconcile these missions and locations with those made by Idoyago in 1748. Probably the new names and locations were those made in re-establishing the missions around La Junta.

On a State Marker at the site of Old Fort Leaton are the words:

> Proximate Site of Presidio del Norte de la Junta Established by Captain Alonso Rubin de Celis in 1759-1760. . . .

Following the defeat of Parilla's forces on the Red River, the garrison at the presidio Las Amarillas (Menard) was taken over (September 30, 1760) by Captain Rabage y Teran, who attempted to put the presidio in better condition for defense against the Comanches. In addition, he sent a party of forty-one men to find a route to Santa Fe, New Mexico. After twenty-four days, having gone out by the Concho River, the present town of Big Lake and farther west, the party found a river (Pecos), eighteen varas wide, almost two varas deep, flowing from north to south across endless plains. Two salt lakes were found adjacent to this river. Probably one of them was the present salt lake in Crane County, and the other, the Toyah Lake in Reeves County.[20] The Pecos River was then named Puerco, because they had no idea that this river was that on which the Pecos Indians in New Mexico lived. As puerco means dirty or piggish, the name was well applied for the water was dirty and many "javelinas" roamed its banks.

Alone, Padre Calahorra visited and made peace with the Taovaya Indians, who had caused Parilla's defeat, disgrace, and recall. The Apaches commenced raiding and murdering the Northern Indians, planting Spanish articles along the trail of their retreat. The same pratice was carried out against the Spaniards with the identifying objects of the Northern Indians left along the trail. Soon the Spaniards and Northern Indians were at war. Having created hostilities between the Northern Indians and the Spaniards, the crafty Apaches then applied to the Spaniards for protective missions.[21] Although the site of the San Lorenzo Mission was previously settled below the Rio Grande in December, 1754, and a few Apaches settled there, they revolted and burned the buildings in October, 1755.[22]

In January, 1762, the San Lorenzo Mission, located on the east bank of the upper branch of the Nueces River near the present Barksdale in Edwards County, was established at El Cañón, followed in February with the establishing of the Nuestra Señora de la Candelaria Mission at a site some four or five leagues down the same stream.[23]

Although the New Mexico authorities made a peace treaty with a branch of the Comanches in 1762, the Comanches attacked Ojo Caliente in June, 1768. Pursuit was not attempted because of the weakness of the Spaniards' cavalry. In July, the Spaniards chased another band of Comanches to the Arkansas River country without success.[24]

One year and a month after Teran took over the depleted stockade, the Presidio Las Amarillas had been rebuilt with stone and mortar. In pleading for a mission to be placed at Las Amarillas, Teran had simply endorsed the Apache request, resulting in the establishment of San Lorenzo and Candelaria, with some four hundred Apaches. By the end of the summer of 1762, crops of corn had been harvested, and adobes had been made at these two places. To better sustain themselves, those Apaches left the missions during the months of May, June, December and January of each year, at times when the crops were to be planted, or when the produce had become exhausted, in order to hunt buffalo on the plains. Some of the young Apaches then plundered the scattered rancherías of the Comanches. The Comanches would follow the trail of that raiding band until within the regions of the hills where they stopped the pursuit in fear of ambuscade.[25]

In order to convey a message and to locate a route from Santa Fe, Governor Tomas Velas of New Mexico sent Francisco Romero (a Christianized Indian), and Joseph Antonio Miraval, along with seven Indians from the Pecos Mission, to the presidio at San Saba (Las Amarillas). After they traveled down the Pecos for five days, the mission Indians abandoned the party. Two additional days' travel brought the party to Coyote, a village of Lipan Apaches, located at a spring six leagues north of the Pecos River, likely in the vicinity of either the present Dexter, New Mexico, or Comanche, Clark or South Spring, near Roswell. This strong party of three hundred men along with squaws and children was far away from its missions of San Lorenzo and Candelaria.

Romero's small party participated in the battle when twenty-one Comanches and two squaws, armed only with six guns, eight swords, four lances and bows and arrows, attacked these three hundred Lipans. Those few Comanches fought until all but one squaw was killed. She was captured, and her body was roasted and eaten.

After recuperating for three months from the wounds received in that fight, Romero and his companion rode down the Pecos River to a large ranchería of the Faroanes (Pharos), known by the Texans as Mescaleros. This was in the "los medanos" (sand dunes), perhaps in the region of Carlsbad or Loving, New Mexico. There, they found three captive Spanish boys, one from New Mexico and two from Coahuila. Two wounded Mescalero Indians arrived — one severely wounded and the other with his ears cut off, reporting that the Spaniards and Julimes from Paso del Norte had killed their chief and many of their companions. They alone had been mutilated and allowed to live, so that they might tell their people what fate awaited them should they raid the Paso del Norte country.

Then the Mescaleros took the clothes, arms, horses of Romero's party and letters of Governor Velas, declaring they would feast on Romero's party the following morning. The Apache Chief urged the Mescaleros to kill as many Spaniards as possible, and to steal as many of their horses and cattle as they could, *for never again would the Mescaleros make peace with them.* Fortunately, Romero understood Apache. He and his companions escaped that night.

Continuing on down the Pecos for ten days, Romero arrived at the friendly Chief Bigote's Lipan village of Loma Pinta (likely the white rocks or bluff of the Pecos within the vicinity of Iraan, Texas). After Romero left this camp, he was intercepted by a messenger from Bigote at Loma Pinta to tell him that a party of Spaniards from Presidio de La Junta de los Rios had arrived at the village.

That party, likely one of the "flying" columns of cavalry from the presidio on the Junta was enroute to San Saba (Las Amarillas). Romero returned to Bigote's village, and informed Captain Rodriguez of the Junta soldiers, that in his journey he had encountered an open and fertile country, several springs, wild grapes and fruits and abundant salt deposits along the Pecos. Captain Rodriguez, who had escorted Romero to San Saba, afterward verified the meeting of Romero at Bigote's village and Romero's being with him at San Saba. Upon Romero's return to New Mexico, the newly installed Governor Marin del Valle doubted Romero's report that a route from San Saba to New Mexico was available over which one could travel in twelve days.[26]

Captain Rodriguez's information from Romero might have influenced Romero Mirabel and his force from La Junta, in crossing through the present Fort Davis country, Balmorhea and Toyah Lake to the Pecos River, and up that river to Santa Fe in 1763.[27]

During the next thirteen years, the Comanches attacked

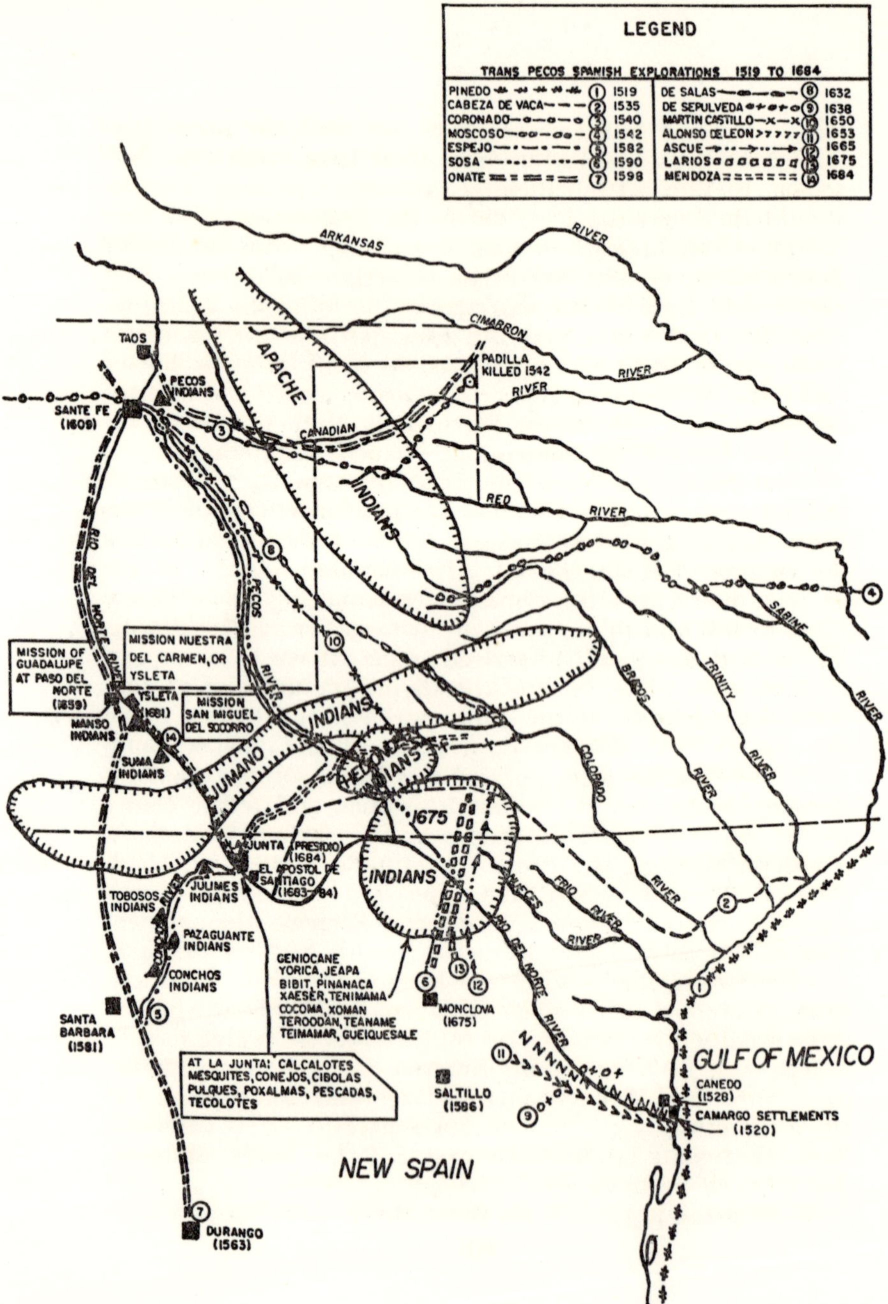

RESEARCH BY C.W. WILLIAMS SR.

MAP BY BILL LAWRENCE

the two missions on the Nueces, harassed the presidio of Las Amarillas, and commenced their long trails into New Spain to kill, loot, and take captives.

Those magnificent horsemen, the Comanches with their Osage Orange bows, dogwood shaft arrows, the stuffed buffalo-hide shields and long, sharp-pointed lances, were more than a match for the Apaches. Subsequent to the destruction of the San Saba Mission, with utter disregard for both the Spanish and the Apaches, the Commanches frequently raided the presidio de San Saba and the settlements around San Antonio and on the Rio Grande.

The Comanches made a serious attack on the presidio de San Saba in 1764. In 1765, a detachment of Spanish soldiers was wiped out by the Comanches as those soldiers were bringing a deserter back to the presidio. Expecting to surprise the Lipan Apaches and the soldiers at the Nueces River missions, three hundred Comanches attacked the defense of San Lorenzo, but retired after a day's siege. From that time until April 26, 1767, more than five attempts were made by the Comanches to surprise the tenants of the presidio of Las Amarillas and of the two missions on the Nueces. On three occasions supply wagon trains were intercepted and destroyed while enroute to those places. In one attack on these trains, over three hundred mules were taken from the Spaniards. At one time three hundred sheep were driven away from the presidio of Las Amarillas.[28] The Comanches were seriously crippling the Spanish outposts and consistently raiding the various Apaches.

Besides having infiltrated within the limits of what is now New Mexico and Arizona, the Apaches were forced into the present West Texas by the Comanches, and were found in large numbers around the vicinity of the presidio of Janos, Mexico. Even around the outskirts of the town of Chihuahua, in 1766, the inhabitants were in constant fear for their lives from the Apaches. La Junta was temporarily abandoned, and its garrison moved thirty miles west to the old Pueblo Julimes, on the Conchos.[29]

Five years after the Spaniards had provided the two missions on the Nueces for the Lipan Apaches, Marquis de Rubi, investigating the conditions on the frontier, reported the main cause of the deplorable situation to be that of the perfidious character of the Lipan Apaches and the imprudent protection which had been extended to them. With their insatiable appetite for robbery and murder, the gravest of evils had been brought down on the province by the fierce attacks of the northern tribes, who in vengeance followed the Apaches to the Spanish settlements. He recommended all-out war on the Apaches, and that those Apaches who submitted be divided into bands and removed into the interior of New Spain. Under such conditions and with no jealousy of French territorial claims since 1762, when France gave Spain that territory west of the Mississippi River, Rubi, for the sake of economy, recommended the abandonment of the northern presidios in Texas, and that the cost of maintaining Espiritu Santo be reduced.[30]

Regardless of Rubi's recommendations, the presidio de San Saba was on its last stand against the advancing hordes of Comanches and Taovayas in their encroachment on both the Spanish and Apaches. A large party of Indians held the Spaniards within the walls of the Presidio de San Saba while the Spaniards' entire herd of cattle was run off. The Indians even butchered, roasted and feasted on several beeves within full view of the garrison.[31]

Two days later another hostile band, mostly Tawakonis with a Tejas Indian as interpreter, rode up in a friendly manner expecting peacefully to take the presidio under the ruse of searching for their enemies, the Apaches. The cautious defenders refused them admittance behind the rock walls, barricaded gates and windows, and distributed presents to the Indians over the low walls of the south corral. The Indians pitched their camps under the walls of the presidio, and spread out their wares for barter, but the Spaniards remained within their defense. The Spaniards obtained the necessary water for man and beast by means of a rock-walled lane extending from the southwest corner of the stockyard to the stream, the safety of such operation being assured by gun-fire from the protective walls of the stockyard. Aware that the Spaniards would not let down their guard and could safely procure water, the Indians moved their camp a short distance away from the presidio. After bringing supplies of buffalo meat and handing them over the three-foot walls of the courtyard of the presidio to the soldiers, the Indians invited the garrison to their camp for a feast. Politely refusing, the Spaniards again gave presents in exchange for the meat. For some time after that ruse failed, there were no Indians in sight.[32]

On December 20th, two soldiers ran into the presidio to inform the garrison of advancing Indians. Soon the walls were rushed by numbers of Comanches and Taovayas. Finding the presidio adequately defended, the Indians raised a flag of truce. For three days a parley went on outside the walls of the presidio, the peace-pipe was smoked, dancing took place nightly and presents were exchanged while the Comanches talked of peace with the Spaniards and war with the Apaches. During such activities, the Indians had allowed a much-needed provision train to enter the presidio. The Indians departed in good spirits on Christmas Eve.

On January 2nd, the presidio withstood another Indian surprise attack. An Indian captured in this encounter told the defenders that the Tawakonis, Tonkawas, Taovayas and Comanches were encouraged by the French to harass the presidio at San Saba. On January 14th, another group of Indians rushed out from the river, took eight horses from near the walls of the presidio and rode off without a soldier daring to follow.[33]

A lieutenant and three soldiers, while hunting turkey near the presidio, were surprised, captured, tortured and killed by the Indians. Confined mostly to the limits of the eight rooms, the patio, the bastion and the stockyard of the presidio, the Spaniards were afflicted with an epidemic which affected the mouth, then the gums, afterward causing a stiffening of the lower limbs. This first struck the women and children, causing death within a few days. With this ailment spreading among the men, Teran sickening with increasing malignant sores, and with the scarcity of supplies, men and equipment, he ordered the abandonment of the presidio Las Amarillas in June. The garrison moved out to arrive at the mission San Lorenzo in the "Valle de José" on the Nueces River on June 22, 1768.[34] Thus ended the untenable position of the Spaniards on the San Saba River, as the last of the soldiers of the presidio de San Saba, in uniforms of blue trousers and red cloaks with silver buttons, departed.

Because the name *San Saba* has been applied to a modern Texas town, there may arise some confusion as to the location of the ruins of the presidio de San Saba. These ruins may be found close to a highway about one mile west of the town of Menard, standing in the midst of a level plain of black, loamy soil. To its south and overlooking the stream bordered on both sides by lovely pecan trees is a picturesque ridge covered with mesquite. To its west, it is decorated with the nice buildings and swimming pool of Menard's recreational facilities. Surrounding the ruins is a modern golf course.

Now, some two hundred years since its abandonment, and symbolic of the frustrated efforts of many noble causes, the abandoned ruins of the mission whose inhabitants were massacred and its timbers burned, have all turned to dust, while the presidio Las Amarillas, although battered and torn by time and the elements, stands defiantly against the world to remind us of the early ravages of the Comanches in Texas at a time some eight years before the American Revolution.

In the rock stockyard of the ruins of the presidio de San Saba is a monument erected by the State of Texas, on which is inscribed:

REAL PRESIDIO DE SAN SABA
ORIGINALLY ESTABLISHED ON THE
SAN GABRIEL RIVER
AS THE PRESIDIO OF SAN FRANCISCO SAVIER

1757-1761

MOVED TO THE PRESENT SITE IN 1757 AS A
PROTECTION TO THE MISSION SAN CRUZ
DE SAN SABA KNOWN AS THE PRESIDIO DE SAN
LUIS DE LAS AMARILLAS IN

1757-1761

AFTER MARCH 1761 THE NAME WAS
REAL PRESIDIO DE SAN SABA
THE STONE BUILDING WAS COMPLETED IN

1761

Early in 1771, the Spaniards of New Mexico made another treaty with the northern Indians, some of whom were Comanches, to join in with them against the Apaches. But on July 4, 1773, five hundred Comanches raided El Valle, fifteen leagues from Santa Fe, and took off the presidial herd of horses.[35]

As the presidio of Cerro Gordo was being occupied and built at this time, it might be well to roll back the time and give some of its background. In an effort to better defend the scattered population on the frontier of New Spain against Apache raids, the Cerro Gordo force and name were moved at times. From the interior in 1680, the force was transferred to form a chain of presidios from Sobrerete, a location ninety miles east of Parral.[36] In 1724, this presidio, San Miguel de Cerro Gordo, was reported to be garrisoned with thirty men and a captain.[37] It continued to exist there until 1748, when it was abandoned.[38] In 1766, as the Apaches from the north began to depredate, the presidio was re-established, presumably at the same location.[39]

Following the Marquis de Rubi's three thousand league trip and investigation of New Spain's frontiers,[40] and his recommendation to reorganize the entire line of presidios,[41] there was a new Reglamento,[42] arranging presidios forty leagues apart and providing that each frontier presidio be occupied by forty-three soldiers, one captain, a lieutenant, *alferez* (chief ensign of the town), chaplain and ten native Indian scouts. Janos, San Juan Bautista, and La Bahia remained at their former sites. San Buenaventura was established at Valle de Ruiz, near Laguna de Guzman; Paso del Norte was moved to Valle de San Elceario; Julimes was moved back to its former site at the Junta de los Rios (Presidio); and Cerro Gordo was located forty leagues below the junction (Junta). Otherwise, the line consisted of Altar, Tubac, Terrenate, Fronteras, Guajoquilla, San Saba, Santa Rosa, Monclova, San Juan Bautista and La Bahia.

San Saba was to be moved to the Rio Grande to form a cordon of posts with Cerro Gordo, Santa Rosa, and Monclova between La Junta (Presidio) and San Juan Bautista.[43]

After making an inspection on the ground, Oconor, military commander of the region, decided that the presidio of San Saba should be placed at San Vicente, near a ford commonly used by the Spanish and the Indians of the Chisos and the "Charamuscos" Mountains. He also selected the site for the presidio of Cerro Gordo (San Carlos) on a small mesa beside a stream, some fifteen miles from its confluence with the Rio Grande.[44] From reports, it would seem that at present the ruins of the old presidio and church are about eight miles down that arroyo from Manuel Benevides, the former town of San Carlos.

In July and August of 1773, Oconór inspected the garrison at the presidio of Cerro Gordo, found it ready, and ordered it to move to its new location.[45] By the fall of 1774, it was reported that the new presidios in Nueva Vizcaya, including Cerro Gordo, were almost completed, but those in Coahuila, including San Vicente, were behind schedule.[46] Following two years of occupation by the garrisons in these remote places of Cerro Gordo and San Vicente on the Rio Grande, Theodore de Croix inspected the northern line of defense. Because of their ineffectiveness in protecting the interior of Coahuila and Nueva Vizcaya as the Indians by-passed them, he recommended their removal to more advantageous positions. Thereafter, Cerro Gordo was moved back to its former location east of Parral. Presumably, San Vicinte was moved out about the same time.[47]

About seventy-five years after this abandonment, M. T. W. Chandler of the U. S. Mexican Boundary Commission reported:

> On a high mesa, some sixty feet above the level of the river bottom, is situated the old Presidio of San Vicente, one of the ancient military posts that marked the Spanish rule in this country, long since abandoned; the adobe walls are crumbling to decay, and scarcely a stick of timber remains in the whole enclosure, except the part devoted to the chapel.[48]

In order for the reader to realize just what the Spaniards were up against on their frontier in New Spain, Bancroft reported that, resulting from Indian raids in Nueva Vizcaya during the years from 1771 to 1776 there were: 1,674 civilians killed, 154 taken captives, 116 haciendas and ranches plundered, and 66,155 cattle stolen. From 1764 to 1784, it was estimated that 16,000,000 pesos worth of property was destroyed by the Indians in Chihuahua.[49]

In New Mexico, between January and September of 1774, the Comanches raided Picuris, Nambe, and made two raids on Albuquerque. One hundred Comanches attacked Pecos, killing a number of people. Upon being followed, they were attacked and routed. Encouraged by this victory, the Spaniards, in September, with one hundred troops set out to chastise the Comanches and engaged an encampment of eighty lodges some fifty leagues east of Santa Fe, where they defeated the Comanches and captured or killed an estimated four hundred Indians in addition to taking a large herd of horses. Regardless of that victory, in 1775 the Indians stole so many horses in New Mexico that the Spaniards were unable to launch a campaign to follow them to their haunts during that year.[50]

1 Castañeda, C. E., as cited, Vol. II, pp. 336-344.

2 Bancroft, H. H., as cited, Vol. I, p. 612.

3 Castañeda, C. E., as cited, Vol. III, pp. 38-42; Bancroft, H. H., as cited, Vol. I, p. 635.

4 Bancroft, H. H., as cited, Vol. I, p. 635.

5 Castañeda, C. E., *History of Texas, 1673-1779 by Fray J. A. Morfi*, Vol. VI, p. 294: The Quivira Society, Albuquerque, 1935.

6 Bancroft, H. H., as cited, Vol. I, p. 641.

7 Castañeda, C. E., as cited, Vol. III, pp. 225-226.

8 *Ibid.* pp. 220-221.

9 *Ibid.*, p. 224; Bancroft, H. H., as cited, Vol. I, p. 593.

10 Reeve, F. D., as cited, Vol. L, No. 2, Oct. 1946.

11 Bolton, H. E., *Athanse de Mezieres and the Louisiana-Texas Frontier, 1768-1780*, Vol. I, p. 25.

12 Thomas A. B., *Forgotten Frontiers*, p. 60: University of Oklahoma Press, Norman, Oklahoma, 1932.

13 Wharton, Clarence, as cited, Vol. I, pp. 53-54; Ramsdell, *San Antonio*, p. 22: University of Texas Press, 1959; Castañeda, C. E., as cited, Vol. III, pp. 38-42; Bancroft, H. H., as cited, Vol. I, p. 635.

14 Wharton, Clarence, as cited, Vol. I, p. 87.

15 Castañeda, C. E., as cited, Vol. I, p. 87.

16 Wharton, Clarence, as cited, Vol. I, pp. 68-72.

17 Bancroft, H. H., as cited, Vol I, pp. 645-649.

18 Castañeda, C. E., as cited, Vol. III, pp. 229-231.

19 Bancroft, H. H., as cited, Vol. 1, p. 601, footnote.

20 Castañeda, C. E., as cited, Vol. IV, pp. 155-156.

21 Bancroft, H. H., as cited, Vol. I, pp. 649-650.

22 Reeve, F. D., as cited, Vol. L, No. 2, Oct. 1946.

23 Castañeda, C. E., *History of Texas — 1673-1679, by Fray J. A. Morfi*, Vol. VI, Art. 2, p. 414: The Quivara Society, Albuquerque, 1935.

24 Thomas, A. B., as cited, p. 61.

25 Castañeda, C. E., as cited, Vol. V, pp. 153-170.

26 *Ibid.*, Vol. IV, pp. 187-188.

27 *Ibid.*, pp. 188-190.

28 *Ibid.*, pp. 182-186.

29 *Ibid.*, pp. 153-186, 236.

30 Bancroft, H. H., as cited, Vol. I, p. 651.

31 Castañeda, C. E., as cited, Vol. IV, p. 195.

32 *Ibid.*, p. 195.

33 *Ibid.*

34 *Ibid.*, p. 197.

35 Thomas, A. B., as cited, p. 61.

36 Hackett, C. W., *Historical Documents Relating to New Mexico, Nueva Vizcaya, and Approaches Thereto, to 7773*, Vol. II, pp. 11, 219-221: Washington, D.C., (Carnagie Institution).

37 Murphy, Henrietta, *Spanish Presidial Administration as Exemplified by the Inspection of Pedro de Riveria, 1724-1728*, pp. 107-129: Ph.D Dissertation at University of Texas, Austin, 1938.

38 *Archivo General de Indias, Audiencia de Guadalajara, 1746-1751*, pp. 62-63: Transcripts, University of Texas Archives, Austin; *Audiencia de Mexico, 1748-1749*, papeleta I, p. 215: Transcripts, U.T. Archives, Austin.

39 *Archivo General de Indias, Audiencia de Guadalajara, 1757-1766*, pp. 79-86: Transcripts, U.T. Archives, Austin.

40 White, T. L., *The Marquis de Rubi's Inspection of the Eastern Presidios on the Northern Frontier of New Spain* — Ph.D. Dissertation, U. of T., 1953: 14, 41, 52.

41 *Archivo General de Indias, Audiencia de Guadalajara, 1768-1772*, pp. 7-62: Transcripts, U.T. Archives, Austin.

42 *Reglamento e instrucción para los presidios que se han de formar en la linea de frontera de la Nueva España, Resuelto por el Rey Nuestro Señor en Cédula de 10 de Septiembre de 1772*, pp. 7-16, 70-78: Mexico, 1790.

[43] Bancroft, H. H., as cited, Vol I, p. 681; Castañeda, C. E., as cited, Vol. IV, 1762-1782, pp. 288, 289-292.

[44] *Archivo General de Indias, Audiencia de Guadalajara, 1773-1774*, pp. 60-73, 83: Transcripts, U.T. Archives, Austin.

[45] *Archivo General de Indias, Audiencia de Guadalajara, 1777*, pp. 45, 46: Transcripts, U.T. Archives, Austin.

[46] *Archivo General de la Nación, Provincias Internas, 1768-1792*, XXIV, p. 239: Transcripts, U.T. Archives, Austin.

[47] *Archivo General de Indias, Audiencia de Guadalajara, 1777-1780*, pp. 42-71: Transcripts, U.T. Archives, Austin; *Report of El Caballero de Croix, Jan. 23, 1780*, pp. 2-29, 60-61: Transcripts, U.T. Archives, Austin.

[48] Emory, W. H., *Report of the United States and Mexican Boundary Survey*, Vol. I, p. 84: 34th Congress, 1st Session, Ex. Doc. No. 135, Washington, 1857.

[49] Bancroft, as cited, Vol. I, p. 681.

[50] Thomas, A. B., as cited, pp. 62-63.

Chapter 6

Synopsis of the American Revolution — (1774-1783)

While events in the southwest were moving along in a pattern governed by the feudal Spanish culture, the colonies on the Atlantic Coast were to begin an experiment in government based upon the principles of British Common Law and the right of the majority of its individuals to determine its law and their enforcement by representation. Ironically, the success of this revolution would eventually cause the end of the feudal systems in both France and Spain, those very governments which were to assist so greatly in the securing of that new pattern of government and the freedom of the colonies.

Those were the days of "Poor Richard's Almanac," frugal living and axioms such as: "Great talkers, little doers"; "Take council in wine, but resolve afterwards in water"; and, "Would you live in ease, do what you ought, and not what you please." The Rockefeller Foundation has reconstructed the towns of Williamsburg, Virginia, and Tarreytown, and Philipse's Castle just north of New York City, with the building, furniture, apparel and utensils in use some two hundred years ago.

Candles, whale oil lamps, pine torches, crude stoves, inefficient fireplaces, powdered wigs, frills and knee pants, bows and buckles, snuff boxes within embroidered cuffs, beaver hides and tobacco for currency, taverns supplying long stem clay pipes and leather mugs — all were a part of our ancestors' everyday life! Unpaid debts were punishable by a long term of confinement. Prisoners suffered in unheated cells in cold weather, unless their friends brought firewood to them. Stocks were used at the gaol to hold prisoners in uncomfortable positions and allow them to be subjected to abuse. The barber cut hair, shaved customers, made wigs, pulled teeth and sold perfume.

The drug store or Apothecary Shop kept portable microscopes, surgical tools such as a crude amputation saw, tools for pulling teeth, barrels filled with dried herbs or plants, bottles of herb seed such as nutmeg, cloves, cinnamon-bark, sassafras, poppy, ginger, etc., along with balance-scales, spouted measuring bottles, and candles.

Few establishments manufactured gunpowder, as most of the supply came from England. For frontier purposes and to save lead and gunpowder, the graceful, light, and accurate Pennsylvania or Kentucky rifle of .40 to .45 caliber with spiraled rifling had replaced the smooth-bore English or French muskets and wheel-locks of .60 to .75 caliber which fired large, round, one-ounce balls. Those Pennsylvania guns became standard equipment for the Pennsylvania militiamen during the American Revolution, constituted Daniel Boone's type of rifle in Kentucky and Missouri, and David Crockett's "Betsy" in Tennessee and Texas. In the hands of the colonists, they played an important part in the victories at Saratoga, at King's Mountain and at Cowpens. These were the rifles that helped to push westward the borders of the United States' frontiers.[1]

Having assisted England in the capture of French Canada and organized their independent militia for their own frontier protection, the colonists began to think of their own freedom from the burdensome taxes and regulations imposed by the British Parliament, such as: the proclamation of October 7, 1763, recognizing the Indian ownership of all land west of the Appalachian Mountains and regulations to prevent Americans on the seacoast from manufacturing goods for settlers who pushed beyond those mountains; the Navigation Act of 1764, ordering customs officers to enforce strictly the laws regulating colonial shipping; the Revenue or Sugar Act of 1764, levying a three-penny tax on each gallon of molasses brought to the colonies from the West Indies Islands or other countries; and the Quartering and Stamp Acts of 1765, requiring colonists to provide quarters, fuel, candles, cider or beer, and transportation for British troops stationed in the colonies, in addition to the requirement to purchase and place stamps on newspapers, playing cards, and various documents. The impetuous and eloquent Patrick Henry, as a member of the Virginia House of Burgesses and in supporting his resolution, a declaration of resistance to this last act, proclaimed: "Caesar had his Brutus, Charles the First his Cromwell, and George the Third (here he was interrupted by cries of TREASON) and George the Third may profit by their example! If this be treason, make the most of it." The thirty colonial newspapers teemed with essays upon colonial rights. With the British tightening their overall regulations and with only Connecticut and Rhode Island in control of their legislative, executive, and judicial branches, the other colonies were chipping away at the British officials' authority through the control of the legislative branch. In October, 1773, the British Parliament passed the Tea Act to enable the English East India Company to pay the Townshend tax and still sell tea cheaper in the colonies than could the Dutch. Regardless of this lower price, the colonists considered that such an act was taxation without representation.

To avoid detection of their secret meetings and sessions, John Adams instigated a courier system to pave the way for authorized assemblies to meet in strange places. In some cases the King's representatives were locked out of duly authorized meetings.

Open hostility existed between the citizens and the British soldiers. Riots occurred. British tea was thrown overboard (December 16, 1773) into the Boston Harbor.

Upon considering Boston's activities as a small revolution, the British Parliament by early 1774 passed the four Intolerable Acts: 1. the Boston Port Bill, ordering the port of Boston to be closed; 2. an act entitling any British soldier or officer charged with murder in the colonies the privilege of being tried in England; 3. an act which changed the Massachusetts Charter altering it to provide for a Crown-appointed council and prohibited town meetings without the governer's permission, except for the purpose of electing officers; 4. and an act requiring the colonists to provide shelter, firewood, drink, bedding, soap, and candles for the British soldiers quartered among them.

The British occupied Boston with a large force, and blockaded its port to paralyze its industry in an effort to force reimbursement for that tea. Adjoining colonies sent subsistence in the form of stock, wheat and other food to the destitute Boston inhabitants. At Williamsburg, George Washington offered to raise one thousand men, support them, and march to the relief of Boston. A few weeks later, he, with Patrick Henry and Edmund Pendleton, rode horseback to the First Continental Congress (October 1, 1774) in Philadelphia.

Patrick Henry delivered the first speech to the Assembly. The young Thomas Jefferson, then only twenty-two years old, being unable to attend this meeting, sent to it his article, *Summary View of Rights of British North America,* for which he was almost convicted of treason. This Congress, in a Declaration of Rights, did not seek representation in

Parliament, but the right of each colonial assembly to draw up its laws on all subjects except foreign trade, being more interested in fair treatment from Great Britain than in independence. Boldest of its actions was the creation of the Continental Association, which bound the colonists not to trade with Great Britain until its taxation policies had changed. In spite of the cautious attitude of this Congress, revolt was in the air.

As England was the principal source of gunpowder, arms and artillery, the colonists were vigorously attacking or ransacking British arsenals for such supplies. The silversmith, Paul Revere, examined the workings of a powder plant and had it reproduced for the benefit of the insurgents.

The Provincial Congress arranged the transfer of ten thousand soldiers to Boston, and passed the Fishery Act, cutting off the colonies' commerce from Britain, Ireland, and the West Indies.

Patrick Henry was the very essence of the sagacious spirit of the revolution. Upon encountering the temporizing, cautious attitude of his colleagues in Virginia's Second Convention (March 23, 1775) and after becoming impatient with the complacency regarding a statement that the King was examining the colonist complaints with favor, Patrick Henry addressed the Chairman and delivered to the Assembly this brilliant and eloquent address:

> Suffer not yourselves to be betrayed by a kiss. Ask yourselves how this gracious reception comports with those warlike preparations which cover our waters and darken our land. Are fleets and armies necessary to works of love and reconciliation? Have we shown ourselves so unwilling to be reconciled, that force must be called in to win us back to our love? Let us not deceive ourselves, sir! These are the implements of war and subjugation; the last arguments to which Kings resort. I ask, gentlemen, what means this martial array, if its purpose be not to force us to submission? Has Great Britain any enemy in this quarter of the world, to call for all this accumulation

of armies and navies? No, sir, she has none. They are meant for us; they can be meant for no other. They are sent over to bind and rivet upon us those chains which the British ministry have been so long forging. And what have we to oppose them? Shall we try argument? Sir, we have been trying argument for the last ten years. . . . We have petitioned; we have prostrated ourselves before the throne, and have implored its interposition to arrest the tyrannical hands of the ministry and Parliament. Our petitions have been slighted; our remonstrances have been disregarded; and we have been spurned with contempt from the foot of the throne. In vain, after these things, may we indulge in the fond hope of reconciliation? There is no longer any room for hope. If we wish to be free; if we wish to preserve inviolate those inestimable privileges for which we have been so long contending; if we mean not basely to abandon the noble struggle in which we have been so long engaged, and which we have pledged ourselves never to abandon until the glorious object of our contest shall be obtained, we must fight! I repeat it, sir, we must fight! An appeal to arms and to the God of hosts is all that is left us.

They tell us, sir, that we are weak — unable to cope with so formidable an enemy. But when shall we be stronger? Will it be next week? Or next year? Will it be when we are totally disarmed, and when a British guard shall be stationed in every house? Shall we gather our strength by irresolution and inaction? Shall we acquire the means of effectual resistance by lying supinely on our backs and hugging the dilusive phantom of hope, until our enemies shall have bound us hand and foot? Sir, we are not weak if we make a proper use of those means which God or nature has placed in our power. Three millions of people, armed in the holy cause of liberty, and in such a country as that which we possess, are invincible by any force which our enemy can send against us. Besides, sir, we shall not fight our battles alone. There is a just God who presides over the destinies of nations, and who will raise up friends to fight our battles for us. The battles, sir, are not to the strong alone; it is to the vigilant, the active, the brave. And again we have no election. If we were base enough to deserve it, it is too late to retire from the contest. There is no retreat but in submission and slavery. Our chains are forged. Their clanking may be heard on the plains of Boston. The war is inevitable! Let it come! . . . It is in vain, sir, to extenuate the matter. Gentlemen may cry peace, peace; but there is no peace! The war is actually begun! The next gale that sweeps from the north will bring to our ears the clash of resounding arms! Our brethern are already in the field! What is it that gentlemen wish? What would they have? Is life so sweet, as to be purchased at the price of chains and slavery? Forbid it, Almighty God! I know not what course others may take, but as for me — (he cried with both arms extended aloft, his brow knit, every feature marked with resolute purpose of soul, and with his voice swelled to its loudest note). . . . GIVE ME LIBERTY OR GIVE ME DEATH!

How true Patrick Henry's predictions were to be! God and the cause of freedom were on their side. On the other hand, the people of England had luke-warm feelings toward the contest. Even the Catholics of France and Spain would eventually join on the side of the revolting Protestants of the colonies to turn the tide and secure the colonies' separation from Britain. The next gale that swept in from the north brought the sound of the clash of resounding arms on the plains of Boston.

British forces from Boston enroute to destroy the patriots' main ammunition supply depot at Concord were attacked (April 19, 1775) by Minutemen at Lexington. Fifteen thousand New England volunteers surrounded the British forces in Boston. The British captured Bunker Hill (June 17, 1775) on the outskirts of Boston, losing one-third of their forces.

After being elected Commander in Chief of the Continental Army by the Second Continental Congress (July 3, 1775), George Washington took charge of the American forces at Cambridge. Although no war had been declared, Boston was under siege and the colonists were making limited preparations to defend themselves. In October, 1775, Congress had voted funds for establishment of a fleet, which preyed on British shipping. On March 3, 1776, a portion of this fleet captured much needed ammunition at Nassau in the Bahama Islands and transported it to New London. In 1775, the patriots sent two expeditions from the region of Boston to Canada, capturing Ticonderoga (May 10, 1775) and Crown Point with needed ammunition and cannon, and occupied Montreal. After attacking and besieging Quebec, they abandoned the long siege and retreated when the British began to land a ten thousand man army in Canada in May, 1776.

Prior to the result of the Canada expedition, the last British governor of Virginia, after collecting an army of British, Tories, and Negro slaves, was defeated at Great Bridge on December 11, 1775, and forced to flee to his ships. Thereafter he raided the coast until he joined the English in New York in 1776. In South Carolina, Josiah Martin's one thousand Loyalists were defeated by the colonists at Moore's Creek Bridge on February 27, 1776.

With their forces surrounded at Boston, their own people not enthusiastic about the war, and recruiting difficult, the British procured twenty-two thousand German-Hessian professional troops.

When Washington's artillery, obtained with the capture of Ticonderoga, was placed on Dorchester Heights, towering over Boston, the British evacuated Boston (March 17, 1776), re-formed their troops with the Hessians in Nova Scotia, and planned to split the colonies by occupying the Hudson River: one force to come down from Canada, and the other to travel up from the mouth of the Hudson. During the summer of 1776, the British thirteen thousand man army advanced from Quebec to Lake Champlain, awaited the establishment of a navy there, and on October 11, 12, and 13, destroyed the patriots' fifteen vessels guarding that approach to the colonies. In the south, the British navy made an unsuccessful attack on Charleston in June, 1776.

In the meantime, the act of perpetual union between the thirteen states was effected May 20, 1776, affording machinery for unified action to provide for a Continental army.

Under such conditions, the Second Continental Congress declared their Independence on July 4, 1776. This declaration, after citing a large number of causes stated:

> These United Colonies are, and of Right ought to be, Free and Independent States; that they are Absolved from all Allegiance to the British Crown, and that all political connection between them and the State of Great Britain, is and ought to be totally dissolved; and that as Free and Independent States, they have full Power to levy War, conclude Peace, contract Alliances, establish Commerce, and to do all other Acts and Things which Independent States may of right do. — And for the support of this Declaration, with a firm reliance on the divine Providence, we mutually pledge to each other our Lives, our Fortunes and our sacred Honor.

During the signing of this Declaration, John Hancock warned the delegates, "We must be unanimous; there must be no pulling different ways; we must all hang together." "Yes," Benjamin Franklin replied, "we must all hang together, or assuredly we shall hang separately." The signing of this Declaration by the delegates of the thirteen colonies did result in the death of some, the loss of all of the fortunes of others, and the harassment of the remainder.

The next day, July 5, 1776, the British landed a large force on Staten Island, established their base there, and thereafter during the months from August through December defeated the patriots and captured New York City, White Plains, Rhode Island, and three thousand colonial troops at Fort Washington.

During the conflict around New York City, one of the heroes of the Revolutionary War, Captain Nathan Hale, volunteered to enter the British lines in disguise to obtain military information. He was captured and hanged the following day. Upon being refused any courtesies and the benefit of clergy before dying, he is quoted as saying: "I only regret that I have but one life to lose for my country."

As the loss of Fort Washington left the route open, the British started an army overland to capture Philadelphia, the seat of the rebellion. Washington's retreating forces in a surprise attack (December 26, 1776) engaged that force at Trenton, capturing one thousand Hessians and halting the British advance.

In the meantime, during August through December, 1776, the small Colonial fleet under John Paul Jones raided British vessels between Nova Scotia and Bermuda, and burned warehouses along the Arcadian coast.

As the British occupied much of the St. Lawrence River, their agents incited the Northern Indians to activity against the colonies. The two settlements near Boonesborough and the fort were unsuccessfully attacked by a large party of Indians on April 15, 1777, followed by a subsequent unsuccessful attack by Indians on July 4, 1777.

One force of British with six thousand regulars and four hundred Indians moved down from Quebec through Ticonderoga (July 6, 1777) to reach the Hudson River at Fort Edward in July, as another force of British and Indians made an unsuccessful attempt to capture Fort Stanwix (August 6, 1777). Two large foraging detachments of the former were wiped out on August 16, 1777, by the Vermont Militia at Bennington and Oriskany. As this occurred, hundreds of Indians overcame several parties of colonists near Fort Henry (September 1, 1777) and unsuccessfully laid siege to the fort (now Wheeling).

Deviating from the original plan, a British army was convoyed from New York City, landed at the mouth of Chesapeake Bay, defeated Washington's army at Brandywine (September 11, 1777), occupied Philadelphia and repulsed Washington's attack at Germantown (October 4, 1777). In failing to capture much of the lower Hudson River and meet the British army from the north, the British lost their advantage when an American army stopped the northern British army's advance south and forced the surrender of its seven thousand men at the battle of Saratoga (October 17, 1777).

Washington's defeated soldiers, following the battles of Brandywine and Germantown, reunited at Valley Forge to train. Desertion and disease soon reduced their number from eleven thousand to five thousand. In spite of the success at Saratoga, the revolution was at its lowest ebb. It took real patriots to stick with the Continental Army when their government currency was worth practically nothing.

Previous to the Americans' success at Saratoga, the French had secretly furnished the colonies with money, arms and ammunition. After the favorable news of that battle, Benjamin Franklin arranged for France's recognition of the colonies' independence (December 16, 1777), an alliance of mutual aid and defense, and France's declaration of war (February 6, 1778) on Great Britain.

As a French fleet was enroute to America, the British evacuated Philadelphia overland, and were attacked by Washington's troops at Monmouth, New Jersey (June 28, 1778). Washington's troops then moved to West Point on the Hudson, which remained their headquarters until the end of the war.

Squadrons of the French and American fleets engaged (July, 1778) a British fleet off the coast of France. Also, upon encountering a portion of the British fleet near Newport, Rhode Island (August, 1778), a French squadron was so badly damaged by a storm that it retired to Boston without an engagement.

In the meantime (June 2, 1778), fifty-two Colonial troops and militia were defeated by four hundred Indians on the upper branch of the Cobelskill in the Schoharie country as Colonel John Butler, with eleven hundred Indians from Niagara, laid waste to Wyoming Valley (July 3-4, 1778).

George Rogers Clark, a pioneer in the Kentucky regions, when denied military aid from Virginia, made this famous statement: "If a country is not worth protecting, it is not worth claiming."

He used his own money to finance, feed and pay soldiers and to carry the fight into enemy territory, which activities left him penniless.

With a small force he floated down the Ohio River, established a base at the site of Louisville, and then captured Kaskakia (July 4, 1778), Vincennes and Kahokia. Five hundred Indians laid siege to Boonesborough (September 9, 1778), without success.

Shortly thereafter (November 10, 1778), two hundred and fifty Continental troops at the fort in Cherry Valley were attacked, the fort and village overrun, sacked, and burned by Tories and Indians.

The British transferred (November, 1778) five thousand of their continental troops to the rich West Indies, increasing naval activities in that region. The French made two unsuccessful naval attacks (December, 1778) on the British at St. Lucia.

Upon capturing Savannah and Augusta (December 29, 1778), the British started the conquest of Georgia from there as the American, George Rogers Clark, went up (February, 1779) to recapture Vincennes, followed by his withdrawal to Ft. Nelson at the Ohio Falls. The French fleet captured Senegambia, but failed to take the Island of Jersey.

On April 18, 1779, five hundred colonists moved up and destroyed three villages of the Onondaga Indians and returned to Fort Schuyler. This action resulted in a raid by the Onondagas on the settlement at Cobelskill, the ambuscade and defeat of the local militia and the plundering and burning of the settlement. During the same day, scalping parties raided Canajoharie, Stone Arabia, and the Schoharie settlements.

Spain joined (June 21, 1779) in the war against England. In an attempt to draw Washington's troops out of the highlands surrounding West Point, the British lost the garrison of seven hundred men at Stony Point on July 16, 1779. The French fleet captured St. Vicente and Granada in the West Indies, resulting in an indecisive naval battle nearby (July, 1779) between the French and English. The American "Penobscott Expedition" from Boston to Castine, Maine, after a long unsuccessful siege was put to flight (August 13, 1779) by a British squadron.

Two of the Colonists' forces, one under John Sullivan, ascending the Susquehanna, and the other under General Clinton from the mouth of the Canajohaire, met at Lake Tioga. The entire force of five thousand men on August 29, 1779, defeated a large force of Tories (Loyalists) and Indians near Conewawah in the battle of Chemung, thereafter destroying the Indian villages, cornfields and orchards from the Susquehanna to the Genesse along with Kanadaseagea, the capital of the Senecas. In the winter of 1779-80, the Senecas took revenge by destroying the Oneidas' castle, church, and villages, and chasing the Oneidas to the protection of the white settlements. Thereafter, joined by Tories, the Senecas destroyed Harpersfield, and raided in Ulster and Orange counties.

In the meantime, England's coast was defended by only thirty-eight British ships and frigates, as sixty Spanish and French ships with frigates lay ready to transport a French army across the channel to land on defenseless England. Panic prevailed as the English called out their militia. Following dissension between the French and Spanish admirals, the invaders' squadrons sailed away.

Spain commenced its unsuccessful siege of Gibraltar, as the Spanish governor of Louisiana captured the British garrisons at Baton Rouge and Mobile in contemplation of capturing West Florida.

Colonial troops along with French squadrons and marines made an unsuccessful attempt (August and September, 1779) to capture Savannah, and departed.

After landing in the harbor of the two forts commanding Whitehaven, England, spiking the forts' guns, and attempting to set fire to British shipping, the small squadron of

John Paul Jones, thereafter encountered a convoy of British merchantmen in the North Sea. As Jones's ship rammed the superiorly armed British "Serapis," the Americans failed to board her on first attempt at a time when Jones's own ship was slowly sinking. Jones was hailed by the commander of "Serapis": "Has your ship struck?" Jones's famous answer was: "I have just begun to fight." Jones's own comrade ship, the "Alliance," in passing by in the dark of night, by error raked poor Jones' "Bon Homme Richard." Quickly concentrating his fire on and destroying the rigging of the "Serapis," Jones caused the "Serapis" to surrender (September 23, 1779), boarding her from his sinking ship.

In the meantime, Colonists of the Pittsburg region during the summer of 1779 made a retaliatory march against the Senecas, destroying the Indians' huts and fruit orchards and defeating the Loyalists at Newton on August 29. Simon Girty, with Indian help, killed all but thirteen of a party of seventy colonists on the Ohio River. British squadrons ran down and confiscated five Dutch vessels on the excuse of searching for contraband. Several conflicts between British and French squadrons during April and May near Martinique ended when a Spanish squadron arrived.

Upon being reinforced with eighty-five hundred soldiers, the British at Savannah destroyed Lincoln's cavalry (April 14, 1780), captured Charleston (May 13, 1780), and thereafter defeated Buford's Virginia regiment.

Six thousand French troops landed at New Port, as the British placed more troops and naval units at New York City.

British and Indians captured Ruddle's and Martin's posts in Licking Valley, while Clark, with a large party of Kentuckians, raided Shawnee, Delaware, and other Ohio Indian villages.

Holland joined in the "Armed Neutrality Act," for protection of commerce of neutral countries, as instigated by Russia, and entered into by Sweden, Denmark, and United Colonies, France, and Spain. Britain declared war on Holland.

Two thousand colonial troops from the Hudson, along

with the recruits from Virginia and North Carolina, upon arriving at Camden were routed (August 16, 1780) by the British and followed into North Carolina. A British force surrendered to Shelby and Williams at King's Mountain (October 7, 1780), and Tarlton's British cavalry was cut to pieces at Cowpens (January 17, 1781) as the Cornwallis British army chased Greene's army of colonists toward the Virginia line.

With the presence of many British sympathizers, there were numerous acts of treason, but the treason of the disappointed officer, Benedict Arnold, has received the most publicity. As a runaway 14-year-old boy, he fought at Lakes George and Champlain in the French and Indian War, then deserted to go home and successfully manage a book and apothecary store. He became a captain in the Connecticut militia at the outbreak of the Revolutionary War; joined the patriot army as a colonel in Cambridge; was with the Green Mountain Boys in the capture of Ticonderoga; led one thousand men into Canada on the unsuccessful venture and attack on Quebec, where his leg was broken in the battle; and as a brigadier general was in the Lake Champlain engagements.

He was extremely disappointed at not becoming one of the five newly appointed major generals in 1777. Subsequently, he took part in the battle of Saratoga; led a relief detachment to the aid of Fort Stanwix; and in the second battle of Saratoga he was severely wounded while leading a courageous charge. Following which, he was promoted to the rank of major general and placed in command of Philadelphia, where he married and lived extravagantly and was court-martialed and cleared of the charges of Tory leanings and using military personnel for personal benefit.

Later, when Arnold was in command at West Point in 1780, his plan for the surrender of the fort to the British was disclosed upon the capture of the British Major John

Andre, a personal friend of and aide to the British General Henry Clinton. During a meeting of the representatives of the conspirators on the Hudson River shore on September 21, 1780, the Americans opened fire on the British sloop, forcing it to retire. Andre traded his uniform for civilian clothes and was thereafter captured a few miles from the British outposts. Upon his person was found a message from Arnold to the British. Arnold, notified of the arrest of Andre, made his escape to the British to become a scorned British brigadier general and receive lands in Canada and 6,315 pounds in money. Andre was tried and hanged.

In the meantime, during Arnold's treasonable acts in the autumn of 1780, Indians and British soldiers met at Unadilla, bypassed Upper Fort (within the limits of the present town of Fulton, N. Y.), raided and applied the torch at Middleburgh, repulsed a detachment from Middle Fort and besieged Middle Fort (near Middleburgh, N. Y.).

After abandoning the siege, this force marched down the valley, destroying and burning all property except that of Tories. At the Lower Fort (Five miles north of Middleburgh), they were repulsed. Following this setback they continued down the river, captured Fort Hunter and burned all of its buildings and those of the adjacent village, killing, and capturing prisoners.

By October, 1780, the British and Indians had pillaged the country surrounding Fort Hunter and were making their retreat. About fifteen hundred patriots, including some Oneida warriors, met and defeated a band of the retreating British and Indians on the south side of the Mohawk at Palatine (October 19, 1780).

By moving up the Mississippi River, the Spaniards captured the British Fort St. Joseph in what is now southwestern Michigan. A British fleet with five thousand troops took possession of the Dutch island of St. Eustatius, its fifty-five soldiers and $20,000 in booty. By means of a Dutch flag flying over that port for the next seven weeks, the British captured fifty additional American ships in its harbor.

In January, 1781, Brant's Indians were so active that supplies could hardly be gotten in to Forts Schuyler, Dayton, and Plain, resulting in the abandonment of Fort Schuyler (May 12, 1781) with its forces retreating to Forts Dayton and Plain.

A French squadron defeated several British vessels around Chesapeake Bay, as the southern British army followed the retreating colonial troops from Camden into North Carolina, and fought an indecisive battle (March 15, 1781) at Guilford Court House (Greensboro)

In the north, five hundred Tories and Indians devastated the village of Johnson Hall (May 21, 1780) as their other forces raided and pillaged the Mohawk at Tripes Hall, and destroyed Caughnawaga and those settlements at the mouth of Cayudutta Creek, thereafter making an unmolested retreat to St. John on the Sorel.

On October 24, 1781, about one thousand British regulars, Indians, and Tories, invading and raiding the settlements, arrived near Johnson Hall. Following news of this situation, four hundred patriots from Fort Rensselaer marched for Fort Hunter on the Mohawk, met the enemy close to Johnson Hall, and forced the invaders to retreat.

In the meantime, the colonial troops marched back into South Carolina. Their commander wrote: "We fight, get beaten and fight again," and were beaten again at Hobricks Hill (April 25, 1781) and repulsed on May 22, 1781, at Ninety-Six. With the way left open, Cornwallis's British army marched northeast, capturing Fredericksburg and Charlottesville, Virginia, and uniting with additional British forces there. The Frenchman, Lafayette, with a detachment of Americans, vainly attempted (July 6, 1781) to stop the British advance at Jamestown Island. The Virginia militia, by continually harassing the British and their foraging parties, forced Cornwallis's army to retire to Yorktown. In the meantime, British and Dutch fleets had a severe naval engagement in the North Sea in August, 1781.

In the far northwest, Clark, with four hundred men expecting to attack Detroit, lost over a hundred Pennsylvania militiamen as Indians and Tories wiped them out while they were enroute to join Clark. The Tories and Indians rushed back to defend Detroit, and Clark's forces moved back to defend the Kentucky settlement.

In the south, colonial forces were partially successful at Eutaw Springs (September 8, 1781), as the British forces gradually withdrew to Charleston.

In the meantime, Washington, with a contingent of his Continental Army from the Hudson River arrived to aid the Virginia militia in their siege of Cornwallis at Yorktown, as squadrons of the French fleet defeated the British fleet (September 5, 1781), in the harbor of Chesapeake Bay. Upon being left without any hope of supplies, and with additional troops on hand to attack him, Cornwallis surrendered his seven thousand man British army.

Spain seized Florida in 1782, (which it held until it was later purchased by the United States in 1819). In 1782, in the region of the Leeward Islands, the British vanquished a French fleet off the islands of Santia, and the French with six thousand troops captured St. Kitts on Christopher Island after a 30-day siege. The war was virtually over in America, with the British abandoning Charleston, Wilmington, and Savannah in December, 1782. French, Spanish, and Dutch naval units battled the British over all the oceans for nearly two years thereafter until a peace treaty was signed in June, 1783.

Benjamin Franklin, John Adams, John Jay, and Henry Laurens represented the United States in Paris in April to sign a separate and preliminary treaty with the British negotiators on November 5, 1782, which was ratified on April 19, 1783. The final peace treaty was signed on September 3, 1783. This gave the United States the British territory from the Atlantic Coast to the Mississippi River on the west, and from the Great Lakes and the 49th parallel on the north, to the 31st parallel on the south. The Americans were also given the right to fish on the Grand Banks off the coast of Newfoundland. Following this, the British soldiers left New York City, the last of them leaving on November 25, 1783.

---

[1] H. E. Resley of Fort Stockton, Texas, as a part time hobby, reproduces the Pennsylvania rifles, and estimates that it would take a smith and his helper two weeks to make that rifle when making their own stocks. Resley is a member of the National Muzzle Loading and National Rifle Associations, having won first place in the State and fifth place in the National muzzle loading shooting contests. Among his ancestors was Joseph Whittlesey, who lost two sons in the American Revolution. His paternal grandfather, George Resley, was with the Snively Expedition, and served as an early surveyor in Texas. Resley's maternal grandfather, Thomas Washington Cox, fought as a private in the Battle of San Jacinto; and was in the Mier Expedition, the fight and surrender.

[2] *Encyclopedia Britanica*—14th Edition: New York and London, 1929; *The World Book Encyclopedia:* Field Enterprises Educational Corporation, Chicago, 1965; Lossing, B. J., *Pictorial Field Book of the Revolution,* Vols. I & II, Harper Brothers, New York, 1859.

Chapter 7

Depletion of Spanish Settlements in Texas —
(1775-1800)

During the period of the American Revolution, the province of Texas was reported as having one villa, two presidios, one outpost, six ranches and seven missions, including the dispersed settlers of Bucareli; all of which contained 780 families — in all, 3,803 persons. The families of soldiers and settlers did not much exceed 2,000, the greater portion being at Béxar with the remainder at La Bahía and Nacogdoches. Morfi wrote that the villa of San Fernando and presidio of San Antonio de Béxar was the most beautiful, suitable and inviting place in all of New Spain in which to establish a settlement.[1]

In the same community with the presidio San Antonio de Béxar was the villa of San Fernando on the site of modern San Antonio. It was the capitol and residence of the Governor and was garrisoned with about sixty soldiers. Something over one hundred houses, some of stone and all of one story, contained its population.[2]

The five missions of Valero, Purísima Concepción, San José de Aguayo, San Juan Capistrano, and San Francisco de la Espada, all within three leagues of each other, were located on the banks of the San Antonio River. Valero, the oldest, with an insignificant parcel of land and neophytes, was situated across the river from Béxar. Down the river two short leagues was the beautiful Purísima Concepción; and below this about one-half league was located San José de Aguayo, the finest mission in New Spain. It had been San José in East Texas, but now, having been moved to San Antonio, Aguayo was added to its name. San Juan Capistrano was one and one-half leagues below Aguayo, and Espada was down the river one league from Aguayo.

Valero, located close to the present site of the Alamo, was reported at its peak to have a population of 275, supported by 1,200 cattle, 300 horses and 1,300 sheep grazing its adjacent lands. Its first hut had been replaced by a stone church shortly after 1744, which had crumbled down and been rebuilt of chiseled stone with two towers, nave, and transept, close to the Alamo. Because of faulty construction, the church collapsed before 1762. By 1778, during the American Revolution, there was not sufficient labor available to rebuild it, as the decreased Indian population was only sufficient to attempt the guarding of their herds.[3]

Purísima Concepción contained a population of 207; with 600 cattle, 300 horses and 2,200 sheep in 1762. Its delayed construction had commenced in 1731 along with that of Espada and San Juan Capistrano. Remaining as the most beautiful and oldest intact mission in Texas, its structure, with its twin towers, majestic dome, and handsomely carved doorway, stands proudly within the now imaginary enclosure of defensive walls and outbuildings.[4]

Aguayo, the alliance between sword and cross, with

its spacious two hundred and sixty square vara plaza enclosed by high, strong walls, and with four gateways opening to each side, fortified and surmounted by bastions over the gates and its walls penetrated with musket loopholes, was a beautiful edifice of masonry consisting of three vaulted aisles and covered by a handsome cupola. The fifth entrance to the grounds was protected by a portcullis and opened into a square in front of the church. The expensively constructed porch was ornamented with fine but reportedly, inappropriate statues and mouldings. An imposing balcony covered the principal portal. The two story commodiously built dwelling for the friars contained accommodation for guests. Muskets, lances and other weapons were kept in a well built armory.[5]

Aguayo had been founded in 1720 with the removal of the East Texas missions. Embittered with its occupation by East Texas Indians, their former enemies, the Apaches had attacked these missions several times in 1745, only to be driven off through prompt succor by the Indians of the San Antonio missions.[6] By 1762, it was reported as having a population of 350 Indians with 1,500 yoke of oxen.[7]

San Juan Capistrano, another of the removed East Texas missions, claimed a population in 1762 of 203 Indians with 1,000 cattle, 500 horses and 3,500 sheep.[8] Not so elaborate as Aguayo, San Juan's simple church formed part of the side of the square surrounded by protective walls. A small tower graced the northwest corner of those walls. Two sides of the walls were bare; the others consisted of dwellings.[9] The stone chapel with a belfry for three bells was commenced in 1756. That building is at present located some seven miles from downtown San Antonio.[10] Within a league of San Juan was Rosario, which had been founded in 1754 and listed some 200 inhabitants and 5,000 cattle.[11]

San Francisco de la Espada had been founded in East Texas among the Tejas Indians, abandoned in 1693, reestablished in 1716 near Mound Prairie, abandoned again 1719-21 and finally transferred to San Antonio in 1731.

By 1762 its population was listed as 207 Indians with 1,200 cattle and 4,000 sheep.[12] Its plan was similar to that of San Juan Capistrano. Located nine miles from downtown San Antonio are the ruins of that old historic edifice.[13]

Now, nearly two hundred years later, the tourist, for a small fee, can view the partially reconstructed remains of the missions San José, Concepción, La Espada, Alamo and Capistrano within the limits of San Antonio, Texas.

The presidio Santa María de Loreta de la Bahía del Espíritu Santo, which had been founded at La Salle's Fort St. Louis on La Vaca River in 1722, had been transferred to the San Antonio River about 1724, and transferred again to the site of modern Goliad in 1749. During the period of the American Revolution, it was garrisoned with about 53 men and contained about 500 Spaniards and Indians within its vicinity.

Across the river from La Bahía stood the mission Espíritu Santo de Zuñiga, which had been transferred along with the presidio's removal. It had a population of around 300, which subsisted on 1,500 cattle and possessed 100 horses.

The two missions San Lorenzo and Candelaria on the upper Nueces River had evidently been swept away by the ravages of the oncoming Comanches and Taovayas.

The mission Guadalupe near Nacogdoches, founded in 1716, had been abandoned temporarily from 1719-21 and was finally abandoned about 1773. To replace it, Bucareli, which had been placed on the Trinity in 1774, was within a few years transferred to Nacogdoches where a few friars and Spaniards lived among the Indians.[14]

Because of Comanche raids and the deplorable condition in New Mexico in 1775, Mendinueta proposed that a presidio be established at Taos for the protection of southeastern New Mexico. Under such conditions, Oconór's detachment, in pushing eastward while following Apaches to the Colorado River in Texas, came to the site of Apache bodies, lodges, large quantities of buffalo meat, etc., where the Comanches had recently slaughtered three hundred Apache families. By January, 1778, the Comanches were reported to have pushed the Apaches into the Organ Mountains and El Cerro Hueco beyond the Pecos River; even as some Comanches were in the Sierra Blanca Mountains some seventy miles southeast of El Paso.[15]

While the British and Indians had kept the thirteen colonies on the Atlantic coast and on their frontiers in trouble for a number of years, by 1784 it was estimated that the Comanches and Apaches had destroyed sixteen million pesos' worth of property in the State of Chihuahua during the preceding twenty years.[16] Chihuahua was being raided from the north by the Seris and Apaches and from the northeast by the Mescalero and Lipan Apaches and Comanches. During those exciting days of Patrick Henry's speech, the Declaration of Independence, and the early encounters between the British and the colonists, the Apaches had been caught between contingents of Spanish forces and the Comanches, and a large number of them were exterminated by either the Spaniards under Oconór or the Comanches.[17]

While the American Revolution was still in progress, plans were made in Monclova, Mexico, and San Antonio de Béxar to organize an expedition of twelve hundred soldiers to make treaties with the Comanches and Apaches, or failing that, to punish them. As to their nearest enemy, the Apache, it was suggested that Spanish soldiers from the area of the present New Mexico should reconnoiter the "Sierra Blanca" and "Sierra Sacramento" regions, while the troops from La Vizcaya (Chihuahua and Sonora) should travel in several large detachments to examine the sierras La Cola, El Aguila, Movano, "El Diablo" and the Guadalupe to the margins of the Rio Puerco (Pecos). Many of the mountain ranges still carry the names which were applied to them by the Spaniards nearly two hundred years ago.

It was thought advisable to move soldiers into the Bolsón de Mapimí and dislodge the hostile Indians from the regions near the presidios San Carlos and San Savas. Those troops were also expected to clean out the Indians to the San Pedro (Devil's) and Nueces Rivers. . . . That was the region of the Lipan and Mescalero Apaches, although Mescaleros also occupied the middle Pecos River area and the Guadalupe Mountains. The junction of the Pecos and the Rio Grande was the refuge most frequented by the Lipans. This officially proposed movement of troops was suggested through dispatches to the King of Spain and conveniently misplaced or forgotten either because of its additional expense or the possibility of Spain's entrance into the British-American War.[18]

Following this proposal, and in order to scout a section of the country in Texas from which the hordes of Comanches were coming down into New Spain, A. Mezierres with a few soldiers from the Béxar garrison, along with his two sons, took a course out of San Antonio (1778) through the rough and trackless regions, where the most southern Comanches had had their corrals and dwellings, finding an incredible number of Castillian cattle and herds of mustangs around the Brazos and Colorado rivers. Evidently those animals which were found were a portion of the sixty-six thousand head of cattle and horses which had disappeared from the ranches of Chihuahua and New Spain during the Apache and Comanche raids up to that time. That was the beginning of those vast herds of mustangs and Spanish cattle which were to inhabit the plains of Texas for many years.

Mezierres reached Bucareli, two days' travel up the Trinity River from the Gulf of Mexico, then moved northwest to reach the village of Tortuga (Tahuacano, Limestone County) were the Tancaguas (Toncawas) lived. Those warriors were suspected by the Spaniards of complicity in the previous raids on and around the presidios of Las Amarillas, Espíritu Santo, and Béxar. West of Tortuga, the Mezierres troops encountered the friendly Tuacanas (Tawakonis), who helped them to cross the swollen Brazos River. The one hundred and fifty warriors of this place complained of the thieving Comanches.

Mezierres proceeded up the Brazos River and through

a portion of the Cross Timbers to meet the Taovayas on the Red River at the location which is now known as "the old fort," situated a short distance north of the present city of Nacona, Texas. The Taovaya Indians reported that a short time before, two English or American traders had come into the Taovaya village from the Arkansas River to establish trade, but the Indians craftily confiscated their goods and allowed the traders to depart.

Mezierres found at these villages the two brass cannons which Parilla had hastily abandoned when he and his soldiers, along with the Apaches, had been defeated there twenty years previously. Ten Spaniards, all natives of New Mexico, had been bought as slaves by these Indians from the Comanches, and were present in the village.

Satisfied that the council's recent recommendations would be put into effect against the Apaches and Comanches, Mezierres sent a messenger to the Comanche tribe with the threat to mend their ways or take the consequences of having a Spanish force campaign against them.[19]

At this place Mezierres was expected to assemble one thousand Indian allies and propose to lead them to join three hundred Spanish troops on the Colorado River in Texas, from where the two allied forces would chase and attack Apaches in the Pecos River and northern Coahuila regions.[20]

Inadvertently attacking and killing a party of ten Comanches enroute to meet with the Spaniards, Mezierres and his small force wisely retired over the many miles south to Bucareli near the Gulf of Mexico. Not far behind him was a large, angry band of Comanches, who raided and captured a herd of 240 horses being escorted from Béxar to Bucareli, in substitution for their intended revenge on the party of Mezierres.

Inspired by recent reports of Mezierres' trip to northeast Texas, and not intimidated by the Comanches' recent foray, Gil y Barbo, with a number of settlers, moved into East Texas in 1779 to establish what is now known as Nacogdoches, around the old abandoned site of the mission of Guadalupe.[21] As the Comanche and Apache raids were seriously damaging the Texas settlements, Mezierres went out again in 1779 to visit the same Indians for the same purpose. While stopping at the small settlement of Nuestra Señora de los Dolores (St. Augustine), he was informed that the small settlement of Bucareli had been attacked by the Comanches and the few remaining settlers had moved from their location on the lower Trinity River to a site near the present Nacogdoches, not far from the mission of Nuestra Señora de los Dolores.

At this stage, when Spain had joined France in the American Revolutionary War against Britain, Mezierres reported that the Spaniards on the Mississippi River were using six-ton barges with two swivel guns in the prow and manned by sixteen rowers and eight alternate rowers to convey parties of seventy-five men in patrolling the river from New Orleans.

For some unknown reason, the Mescalero Apaches and other Apaches of the plains attacked the Lipan Apaches in their resorts in Coahuila; after which, the Lipans moved back into the area between Laredo, San Antonio and Goliad to make raids on those Spanish settlements. When peace was made between the Apaches and the Tonkawa Chief, El Mocho, whose trade with French merchants supplied them with arms and ammunition, the combination of Lipans and Apaches ravaged the regions of Texas and Coahuila. Juan Ugalde, Governor of Coahuila, took the field against the Apaches and inflicted minor defeats on them in northwestern Coahuila and on the lower Pecos River.[22]

Although Colonel Juan de Ugalde's campaigns out of Monclova, New Spain, from May, 1779, to February, 1783, against Mescalero Indians in the Bolsón region of New Spain and below the Pecos and Devil's rivers in Texas were not very impressive in stopping the Indian uprisings, they served to give the Spaniards some knowledge of the routes, streams, and Indian camping grounds.

Beginning May 3, 1779, Ugalde with two hundred men

with the usual impedimenta searched for over thirty days, covering a portion of the Carmen Mountains nearest to Monclova, resulting in the killing and the capturing of a few Indians and the recovery of some horses. Again beginning on November 11, 1781, Ugalde's forces scouted the regions of the Rio Grande, Pecos and Colorado for two and one-half months, only managing to attack several small rancherías and one large camp with the outcome that the Indians made a safe retreat into the hills. In an attempt to drive the Apaches from the hills of Boca de Tres Picos, after the town of Parras, Alamo, Hacienda de Amelo and towns of Nuevo Reino (de Leon) and other towns in Coahuila had been raided, eighty persons killed and slaves and horses stolen, Ugalde's forces made a three and one-half month campaign, beginning on March 9, 1782, and terminating in a four-day battle, the capture of 36 braves, and 517 Apache women.

In September, 1782, and for six months thereafter, Ugalde with 250 men, Indian guides, 250 loads of supplies, 48 mule-drivers, and 2,000 horses traveled as far out as eighty leagues in the Bolsón from Monclova, resulting in the killing and capturing of a few Indians. Even while he was out, Apaches raided the towns of Saltillo, Patos, Parras, and others. By October, Ugalde's forces were combing the Betanillas Canyon and its tributaries; then they crossed to Cuatro Ciénagas on the east of the Bolsón de Mapimí without meeting an Indian. In November, after refitting at Monclova, procuring some cavalry and two thousand horses, Ugalde crossed from Hacienda de Ciénagas on the east of the Bolsón, going west across the Bolsón to Presidio Guajoquilla, where he obtained supplies and fresh horses, then searched through to La Cruz in the center of the Bolsón de Mapimí, moved over to what he called Paso del Chisos or Charamusco on the Rio Grande. This is not the Chisos as we know it, but a location, I believe, on the Rio Grande east of the Carmen Mountains. Up to this time Ugalde was reported to have traveled 540 leagues and to have found only 29 abandoned Mescalero camps.

The next fourteen days were occupied in going to the Guadalupe River in Texas to arrive there on January 29, 1783. After scouting, then sending some men and over eight hundred worn-out horses back to Monclova, the force started north toward the Devil's and Pecos rivers, then veered west and south to arrive at the region of Aguage, from whence he had departed on March 3. Soon thereafter his force encountered and attacked a large, inhabited Indian ranchería, located on a high, rough, rock-covered hill, spent six hundred rounds of ammunition, resulting in some casualties on both sides and the Indians' retreat. The loot was forty-one tents and eighty-one beasts. The next day, March 4, Ugalde's forces started home by way of Apaches de Santo Domingo, Bahía, Tositas, Escondido, and the Rio de Sabina to Monclova.[23]

Informed of El Mocho's activities in obtaining arms and ammunition from the French, the Spaniards in Texas murdered him while he was on a visit to La Bahía, resulting in the abatement of hostilities for only a short period. But the following year, the Apaches again started raiding, killing forty-six persons and stealing over six hundred horses and mules during June, 1784.[24]

The Texas settlements had incurred serious losses from the Indians by 1785. The Bahía (Goliad) region claimed the loss of fifteen thousand cattle during the preceeding eight years and now had only three thousand cattle. Because of its depleted manpower, it was experiencing limited agricultural production and was forced to buy its grain yearly. Its population had decreased by several hundred. The presidio Bahía included some five hundred inhabitants by counting the garrison and possibly those of the small adjacent communities of Chayopin, Pataquilla, Cabras, San Francisco, Mora and Las Mulas, all of whose occupants varied from a few persons to twenty-six.[25]

Around San Antonio the herds and population of the missions had also been greatly depleted by the Indian raids. At Concepción only 71 people remained, compared with its previous number of 207 some 13 years earlier. The fabulous Aguayo contained less than one-third of its previous population and Capistrano had been reduced to one-fifth of its population, in spite of the addition of the refugee citizens from the abandoned Rosario in 1781. The herd of five thousand head of stock was gone from Rosario. Espada had likewise been reduced to one-fourth of its population and its stock was negligible. Valero, which stood next to the presidio of Béxar, was in a similar condition with most of its livestock now in the hands of the Apaches or Comanches.

Some Spaniards had retreated to Mexico. Many of the domesticated Indians, tiring of the drudgery of everyday work, deserted to the short mesquite and cholla thickets to join those roving bands who lived off the buffalo, berries, sotol and the stock stolen from the Spaniards.

Twenty-three years earlier, the Mescalero chief on the Pecos River had been heard to make his threat "never again to make peace with the Spaniards." Those Apaches raided far into Mexico, wiping out Sabana Grande and Grunidora in July, 1786, near Mexico City. In retaliation, two hundred Spanish soldiers under command of Lieutenant José Menchaca repulsed an attack of over three hundred Comanches, following which they destroyed a Mescalero ranchería in Coahuila.[26]

Unable to stop either the Apache or Comanche raids, the Spaniards had previously abandoned the presidio of San Vicente and Cerro Gordo on the Indians' Trail in the Big Bend of the Rio Grande as a superfluous expense and fostered a policy of appeasement. Peace under any conditions was the order! Any kind of treaty with the Indians was better than no treaty. Instructions were given to donate ornaments, trade freely, and encourage the use of alcohol among the Indians. In some cases entire villages of Indians were given year-round subsistence and furnished ornaments at the Government's expense. This plan, added to the cost of maintaining troops in Nueva Vizcaya, was a strain on the King's depleted treasury.

But Juan de Ugalde, a veteran soldier of the campaign

in Peru and at this time seventy years old and second in command of Nueva Vizcaya, was not content with such appeasement, especially following the Mescalero raid near Mexico City. After arranging for one out of every three military units in the province to accompany him and obtaining subscriptions of money and provisions, he left Santa Rosa, New Spain, to meet the other contingents at the Hacienda de Sardinas in the eastern edge of Bolsón de Mapimí. Their departure (January 26, 1787) from this place was delayed while awaiting the arrival of a portion of the Alamo Company, which was then engaged on a punitive expedition out of Parras.

With 289 soldiers, 76 muleteers, 20 corporals, 3,000 horses and pack mules, Ugalde struggled northeast through deep snow for five days to arrive finally at Hacienda de Cuatro Ciénagas (Four Marshes), the last frontier on the northeast. The cavalcade tediously worked its way by easy stages up to the Sierra de San Antonio (Acatite la Grande), the heart of the desolate country, where they made their headquarters while their scouts searched the region.

The crafty Ugalde had his scouts dressed in tanned deerskin jackets and trousers with brown cloaks or blankets and Mescalero moccasins. Each was supplied with a pistol, knife, lance and an escopeta, the barrel of which was of tinted blue steel to prevent the sun's reflection. His troops traveled on jerky and coffee and put the beans on to boil only when they expected to camp for several days. Experienced in campaigning, he established his service of supply to the rear with pack trains and guards.

Northeast from the Sierra de San Antonio, Ugalde, with a patrol, discovered the trail of Indians near Tinajas del Viento, leading towards the Big Bend of the Rio Grande. After gathering his entire force and following this trail for several days, he camped (March 24, 1787) next in the shade of the deserted presidio of San Vicente near the Rio Grande. For four days his horses and men rested while his Lipan scouts searched the regions before news was brought in that the trail led into the Chisos Mountains (in the Big Bend Park of Texas). The next morning, worn-out horses were put out to graze under guard, while Ugalde's forces crossed the Rio Grande with their faces to the northwest where the dark shadows of the Sierra de los Chisos loomed upon the horizon. By noon the next day, the Mescalero ranchería had been located two leagues beyond the first water hole they had reconnoitered.

They planned a night or early morning attack, when four squads of unmounted men were to climb the slopes of the mountains to surround the ranchería, while the mounted men were to conduct the main attack. After laboring all night to attain their proposed positions and at the appointed time, daylight (March 31, 1787), the slender, seventy-year-old Ugalde led the horseback charge across the stream or arroyo into a shower of arrows from the alert Mescaleros. As the men on foot had not reached the conflict at the appointed time, Ugalde's horsemen were forced to dismount and take shelter among the rocks for three-quarters of an hour until their reinforcements arrived. Even then it was a serious encounter and in spite of the Spaniards' precautions, the Mescaleros managed to make a rearguard defense for their retreating squaws and children, abandoning their horses, mules, tents and food and scattering among the rocks. In doing that, some twelve Indian men and women were captured, and a Spaniard recovered, who had been in captivity for a long period, having been captured along with two older companions by the Indians while enroute between Parras and Alamo. Four Indians lay dead on the field.

While the Spaniards were examining their loot and chaining the prisoners, a lone Mescalero warrior exposed himself from behind a boulder and made signs of surrender. His squaw and two sons were among the prisoners and he would rather join them as a prisoner in chains than be separated from them. It was Chief Zapato Tuerto (Crooked Shoe), who afterward was very useful to Ugalde. Influenced by both the loyalty of this Indian Chief to his family and by his voluntary surrender, Ugalde humored the Indian and in return received valuable information from him on his subsequent expeditions.

At the time of his capture, Crooked Shoe informed Ugalde that the retaliatory expedition of the Spaniards was expected and that most of the Mescaleros had just made peace with the commander of troops at Presidio del Norte and had moved their camps close to its protective walls to avoid punishment for their recent acts in New Spain. At the Presidio del Norte, the Mescaleros were rewarded with gifts of guns, ammunition and horses for having sought peace even though openly showing their plunder and Spanish captives.

As Ugalde was occupied with his preparations for attacking the Mescaleros in the Chisos Mountains his guards and supply train, while traveling between Sierra de San Antonio and San Vicente, followed an Indian trail and suddenly came upon a ranchería whose occupants escaped. Along with camp plunder, mules and horses found in the camp, was an instrument in writing of safe conduct for these Indians and signed by the commandant of the Presidio del Norte. This certified that the bearers had sought peace in the presidio in the previous February. From the brands on the mules and horses and the type of booty in the abandoned ranchería, the Spaniards concluded that this little band with the safe conduct paper had just returned from raiding several places in Coahuila.

After the encounter with the Mescaleros in the Chisos Mountains, Ugalde's troops casually took their course back, arriving at their camp near San Vicente on the third day. Crooked Shoe, no doubt, was thoroughly interrogated and gave them other information relative to the Mescaleros and their native ranges. The commandant from Presidio del Norte, with a small detachment, dropped down to spend some time with Ugalde to impress the force with the peacefulness of the Mescaleros and his intentions to comply with the provinces' recent orders of peace at any price. In turn he listened to a lecture from Ugalde and then made his way back to Presidio del Norte.

On April 12, Ugalde's expedition moved out to destroy the enemy everywhere, excepting those who were camped under the walls of the Presidio del Norte. Five days' travel up the Rio Grande brought them to a point where they looked down upon the regions of the Presidio del Norte and could see the dust rising from Indian parties making their way into the presidio. In another direction they saw the black smoke issuing up in the sky. The signals signified that the escapees had notified the other Indians of Ugalde's approach. Only one visible tribe paid no heed to the warnings.

Ugalde had the location scouted and thereafter made an early dawn attack, resulting in a serious encounter and the near defeat of the Spaniards. The Mescaleros successfully defended themselves and made an orderly retreat, leaving eighty-three horses and mules which had been stolen from Coahuila and Nueva Viscaya. While the Spaniards were occupied in gathering the stock and loot, the Mescaleros sent a detachment over and attacked the guard of Ugalde's pack train, causing several additional Spanish casualties there.

Ugalde's forces moved up to San Felipe, located about thirty miles up the Alamito from the presidio (La Junta) and searched the regions without additional engagements.

Subsequently, in order to thoroughly search out and chastise the originators of some of those serious raids far down into New Spain, Ugalde marched his troops 150 miles northeast through the mountains and over the deserts to the regions of the Guadalupe Mountains and the Pecos River. They crossed the swollen Pecos River by swimming their horses and mules, making a vain pursuit of the Nit-agende (Seed Sowers) Indians and capturing a few squaws and horses. Informed by one of the captured squaws of a large encampment of Cendés and Mescaleros at "Aguaje del Tobaco," a water hole far to the northwest, Ugalde's troops moved out nearly to Paso del Norte and found that the ranchería had recently been exterminated by the Comanches. Enroute, however, his forces had a small engagement in the Guadalupe Mountains where they rescued a Spaniard who had been in captivity for fourteen years.

We leave Ugalde here to go on his way down the Pecos (Puerco) River where he met with the "Lipiyan" (Llanero) Apaches on the lower Pecos River to seek an alliance with them against the Mescalero Apaches and Comanches.[27] This is just one sample of the punitive expeditions sent out from New Spain in retaliation for many of the Indian raids, which had already occurred and would continue through the next century, regardless of treaties.

With the usual thefts and depredations going on between various tribes and all of them double-crossing the Spaniards, a combined group of Comanches, Taovayas, Wichitas, and Tawakonis was defeated by the Apaches on the Pedernales River.[28] Soon thereafter, in 1789, Colonel Juan Ugalde with his troops pursued the Mescaleros and Lipan-Apaches to the site of former presidio de San Saba (Menard). Following which, on December 21, at San Antonio, an Indian scout and a Chief Sofias of the Comanches with a small escort of Spanish soldiers, just in from Ugalde's forces at Las Amarillas, brought a request from the colonel. The colonel wanted a reinforcement of eighty-five soldiers or men and two thousand cartridges to be sent to his aid at the abandoned presidio, a short distance from where Ugalde's forces with two hundred Comanches would attempt to defeat a group of Lipans and Mescaleros with whom Ugalde had had a brief encounter on the Pedernales River.

Eleven soldiers and fifty-two volunteers from San Antonio joined Ugalde's forces, which along with Comanches, Tawakonis, Taovayas, and Wichitas surprised and attacked a big camp of the Lipans and Mescaleros on Solidad Creek on January 9, 1790. The engagement lasted several hours, resulting in the defeat of the Apaches, a number of casualties, and the capture of a large number of women and children, horses and mules. In celebration of this victory over their common enemy, the Comanches went into San Antonio, where they stayed for several days.[29]

Resulting from their experiences with the Indians, the

Spaniards under Viceroy Revillagigedo, in 1791, issued a new set of instructions as to their relations with the Indians of the Interior Provinces. Any tribe desiring peace must give up its nomadic life, settle within four leagues of a presidio, take part in all Spanish campaigns against enemies, and not leave the ranchería without permission from the nearest presidio's commander. In turn, the Spaniards would provide rations to the Indians for a reasonable period, allowing for the Indians' establishment of a camp and the raising of crops.[30]

Under such circumstances, it was but a few years until the Comanches were pillaging and stealing from the Spanish settlements. Early in 1795, one party of Comanches raided and drove off a herd of cattle from the San Juan Bautista mission, located across the Rio Grande; and another group attacked a Spanish wagon train enroute from La Bahía to Nacogdoches, while still another Comanche party raided in the vicinity of Laredo. The following year, the friendly visits by Comanches to San Antonio were accompanied by their theft of considerable property. By 1797, the Comanches were actively stealing cattle and raiding in the region of the mission of San Bernardo, near San Juan Bautista, causing considerable concern to Governor Cordero of Coahuila.[31]

In Texas, the Comanches were reported to have stolen horses from Philip Nolan in December, 1798, and later to have stolen cattle from the presidio of Rio Grande, some mules from Don Antonio Baca in Texas, and animals from others in the early part of 1799. It is of interest to note that Philip Nolan of Ireland, then Kentucky, and subsequently of Nacogdoches and New Orleans, since 1790 had spent much time in trading horses, lived two years among the Indians, and with a passport from the Governor of Louisiana, frequently visited San Antonio.[32]

---

[1] Morfi, Juan Agustín, *Memoirs, Libro IV, History of Texas, 1673-1779:* The Quivira Society, Albuquerque, 1935.

[2] Bancroft, H. H., as cited, Vol. 1, p. 665.

[3] Ramsdell, Charles, as cited, pp. 17, 18; Bancroft, H. H., as cited, Vol. I, p. 665.

[4] Bancroft, H. H., as cited, Vol. I, p. 665; Ramsdell, Charles, as cited, p. 121.

[5] Bancroft, H. H., as cited, Vol. 1, pp. 657, 658.

[6] Ramsdell, Charles, as cited, p. 24.

[7] Bancroft, H. H., as cited, Vol. I, p. 665.

[8] *Ibid.*

[9] Ramsdell, Charles, as cited, p. 41.

[10] *Ibid.*, p. 143.

[11] Bancroft, H. H., as cited, Vol. I, p. 665.

[12] *Ibid.*

[13] Ramsdell, Charles, as cited, pp. 41, 119.

[14] Bancroft, H. H., as cited, Vol. I, p. 665, footnote.

[15] Thomas, A. B., as cited, pp. 63, 64.

[16] Castañeda, C. E., as cited, Vol I, pp. 594-600.

[17] Reeve, Frank D., *Southwestern Historical Quarterly*, Vol. L, October, 1946, No. 2, pp. 189-219; Bancroft, H. H., as cited, Vol. I, p. 681.

[18] Morfi, Juan Agustín, *Excerpts from the Memoirs for the History of the Province of Texas*, p. 429: Translated by F. C. Chabot and revised by C. E. Castañeda, San Antonio, Private Publication, The Naylor Co., San Antonio, Texas, 1932.

[19] Bolton, H. E., *Athanase de Mezierres and the Louisiana-Texas Frontier*, Vol. II, pp. 186-216; Castañeda, Carlos E., *History of Texas, 1673-1779*, p. 429: The Arthur Clark Co., Cleveland, 1914.

[20] Bolton, H. E., *Athanase de Mezierres and the Louisiana-Texas Frontier*, Vol. II, pp. 147-170.

[21] *The Texas Almanac, 1941-42*, p. 44: Dallas News, Dallas, Texas.

[22] Bolton, H. E., *Athanase de Mezierres and the Louisiana-Texas Frontier*, Vol. II, p. 150; Bancroft, H. H., as cited, Vol. I, pp. 594-600.

[23] "Campaigns of Colonel Don Juan de Ugalde" in *Historia 349*, Vol. XXIX, *Archivo General of Mexico*, pp. 197-234 in the Bexar Archives, University of Texas, Austin, as taken from a translation by José Luis Coro — October 14, 1966.

[24] Castañeda, C. E., as cited, Vol. V, p. 8; Domingo Cabello to Viceroy

Maliasde Gálvez, Sept. 30, 1784. A. G. I., Provincias, Vol. LXIV, pp. 123-134, 135-140.

25 Bancroft, H. H., as cited, Vol I, p. 659.

26 Nelson, Al B., "Campaigning in the Big Bend of the Rio Grande in 1787, "*Southwest Historical Quarterly XXXIX, January, 1936 (201 F)*, p. 203.

27 *Southwest Historical Quarterly* XXXIX, pp. 203-227, Juan Ugalde.

28 Bolton, H. E., *Texas In The Middle Eighteenth Century*, p. 127: New York, Russell & Russell Inc., 1962.

29 Castañeda, C. E., as cited, Vol. V, pp. 16, 17.

30 *Ibid.*, p. 21.

31 *Ibid.*, pp. 117-120.

32 Letter of Pedro Nava to the Viceroy (July 23, 1799), *Internal Provinces*, Vol XII, p. 64: General Archives, University of Texas as translated by José Coro.

Chapter 8

Comanche War Trails to Mexico

The Spanish feudal system was in effect in New Spain (Mexico), where the influential Dons had established their domains over fertile lands and vast grazing areas. Domesticated Indians had become their vaqueros and farm hands. To prevent any possible insubordination in their establishments and to forestall revolutions among the seventeen different Indian tribes, none but the few soldiers and Dons were allowed the possession of firearms. Those haciendas, often remote and far from any military aid, were built in style and with protective walls around them in which their occupants could seek shelter from the weather or small banditry. Those generous and courteous Dons sat in ease and pomp as their immense herds of stock ranged for miles around the haciendas until the Comanches and Apaches found the defenseless Mexicans an easy prey for their war parties.

The Apaches, located in what is now western Texas and New Mexico, had only a comparatively short distance to go on those frequent raids into New Spain. They had previously established trails into Mexico which the Comanches used thereafter.

Years earlier in 1785, the Spaniards, in order to protect their New Mexico frontier and to encourage the Comanche tribes of "Yupes" and "Yamparicas," who lived on the border of New Mexico, and the "Cuchanec" or "Cuchanticas," who lived in northern Texas, made an agreement with those tribes that all of the Indians' captives were to be brought in for redemption; that no other foreigners were to be allowed within the Comanche camps; that the Spaniards would furnish dealers to supply goods in exchange for furs in addition to an annual gift by Spain to the leaders of the Comanches; that the Lipan Apaches were a common enemy; and that the Comanches would ask permission to move to the borders of Coahuila only when they were on a mission against the Apaches.[1]

The most northern Comanches, Caschotethkes (Buffalo Eaters), Quahadas (Antelopes), and Yapparethkas (Yap Eaters named for the root eaten by the Shoshones) inhabited the Red and Arkansas rivers and Great Plains region. The Kiowas and Kiowa Apaches bordered them on the west. The Noconys (moving in a circle or wanderers) and the Tanimas (Liver Eaters) and the Tanawas lived to the south of the northern Comanches. The most southern Comanches, Penatekas (Honey or Sugar Eaters), also known as the Wasps, were located southwest of the Cross Timbers along the headwaters of the Colorado and Brazos rivers.[2]

In the 1790's some branches of these southern Comanches were accused of raiding across the lower Rio Grande. As these raids continued farther into New Spain (afterward Mexico), the Kiowa warriors had become a party to them by the winter of 1834-35, when "a war party set out against the Tonhen-t'a ka-i (Mexicans of the waterless country, or Chihuahua)."[3]

I have been unable to establish the date of the commencement of the Comanche War Trails through this vicinity to Chihuahua. I assume that those trails and raids originated in the early 1800's. The Comanches from the Red, Arkansas, and Brazos rivers developed the habit of going down in the fall, raiding and gathering their booty during the winter and bringing back their stolen herds, booty and captives in the spring. Their wealth was counted in their ownership of horses and squaws. They were the early "trail drivers" of the region with their captives, stolen herds of cattle, horses and mules.

Their rancherías in the regions of the Arkansas and Red rivers were fairly orderly with their tepees of poles and cured hides of the buffalo, deer, antelope or bear. Squaws, in long tunics with high necks and long sleeves, which were decorated with embroidered flowers, colored by the shades of the porcupine quills, wore their hair clipped short and painted theirs faces with red ochre only when traveling, to protect their skin from the weather. The squaws made cream-colored chamois shirts with beautiful designs for their warriors from the hides of the agile mountain sheep.

The warrior's wearing apparel consisted of fringed buckskin trousers similar to the abbreviated cowboy chaps of today. A front and rear flap was attached to the belt for the convenience of nature's calls. Their feet were covered with buckskin moccasins. In general, they were a short, stocky breed of men with straight, coarse hair hanging down in long tresses. Their headdress of feathers denoted their rank by its length and color. Excepting an ornamental necklace and bracelet, they were bare from the waist to their headdress.

These magnificent horsemen, equipped with their shields, bows, arrows, lances, tomahawks, knives, and excellent horses were more than a match for the Apaches. The shields, two inches thick with an inside padding of buffalo hair between two thick buffalo skins, were hardly penetrable by the bullets of those days. Their Osage Orange bows were strengthened with deer sinews to forcefully project their flint or metal pointed, dogwood stem arrows. The trajectory of the arrow was regulated by three feathers at a forty-five degree angle with the shaft. Long ash-wood lances, either pointed with metal or with a burned and tempered point, gave them a good weapon at fairly close quarters.

Attached to and hanging over the warriors' backs were quivers, made of various animals' skins and filled with arrows. Tomahawks and knives were conveniently placed in their belts. Some warriors placed buffalo horns and other ornaments on their shields. Mule tails were placed on the shields of those who had participated in the treks and raids into New Spain or Mexico, denoting the number of such raids that warrior had made.[4]

Their horses were ridden and guided by means of an improvised saddle composed of a blanket "cinched" to the horse's body with a horsehair rope or a leather strap and a bridle of a leather thong attached to the horse's lower jaw. Sometimes in order to provide mobility on that crude saddle, a crude stirrup was attached to the cinch. A horsehair rope or leather strap was woven into the horse's mane in the form of a loop to support a warrior's arm when shooting arrows from behind the body of a horse in motion.

In writing of the Comanche horsemanship, George Catlin had the following comment:

> The exercise of these people, in a country where horses are so abundant, and the country so fine for riding, is chiefly done on horseback; and it stands to reason that such people, who have been practicing from their childhood, should become exceedingly expert in this wholesome and beautiful exercise. Amongst their feats of riding, there is one that has astonished me more than anything of the kind I have ever seen, or expect to see, in my life — a stratagem of war, learned and practised by every young man in the tribe; by which he is able to drop his body upon the side of the horse at the instant he is passing, effectually screened from his enemies' weapons (Fig. 167) as he lies in a horizontal position behind

the body of his horse's back; by which he has the power of throwing himself up again, and changing to the other side of the horse if necessary.[5]

This feat was accomplished by leaning the body to one side of the horse, placing the elbow and arm in a loop of hair rope which was around the horse's neck and braided to the mane on the withers, and leaving the far lower leg and heel on the other side of the horse to steady and restore the Comanche to his upright position on the horse's back.[6]

Relative to the horsemanship of the Comanche women, R. B. Marcy wrote:

> Many of the women are equally expert as equestrians, with men. They ride upon the same saddle and in the same manner, with a leg upon each side of the horse. As an example of their skill in horsemanship, two young women of one of the bands of the Northern Comanches, while we were encamped near them, upon seeing some antelopes at a distance from their camp, mounted horses, and with lassos in their hands set off at full speed in pursuit of the fleetist inhabitant of the plains. After pursuing them for some distance, and taking all the advantage which their circuitous course permitted, they finally came near them, and, throwing the lasso with unerring precision, secured each an animal and brought it back in triumph to camp.[7]

In recent years, the late Ray Baumgardner of Fort Stockton, who spent many years in piloting airplanes and killing eagles and coyotes for the ranchers of this region, stated that he had checked the speed of the antelope from an airplane, as being sixty miles per hour and that of the deer as fifty-five miles per hour.

Several years before the American Revolution, the Comanches made their long rides from the Arkansas River into New Mexico and Texas. About 1800, they commenced their raids into the interior of New Spain. In preparing for this

155

venture, the warriors discarded their long chamois shirts, put their buffalo robes in order and painted their faces and chests with red ochre. Each man supplied himself with a war pony bridled with only a rawhide thong attached to its lower jaw and equipped with a blanket or a rawhide-covered wooden saddle. With extra packhorses to carry additional war equipment and a herd of spare ponies, the party started on that long trek. Only the young, stout warriors, in search of fame, captives and booty, could stand the strain of the arduous journey.

Before leaving the regions of those two rivers, they equipped themselves with an extra supply of deer sinews, flint or metal arrow points and food in the form of rolled-up, thin tortillas of maize, cattail rush, and jerky from the plains buffalo. With the warriors equipped in this manner, as the late O. W. Williams wrote:

> The Comanche War Trail became a moving picture show, where parties of these barbaric warriors, in troops of a half dozen to a hundred or more Comanches, Kiowas, Plains Apaches, Utahs from the Rocky Mountains, outlaws from other tribes, and even renegades from Mexico, all were hurrying forward to the Carnival over the Rio Grande . . . to scourge the fertile valley of the Conchos River, up to the very walls of Chihuahua or . . . to carry fire and lance into the confines of Durango . . . or to the mines and to the farming valleys, but most of them sought the haciendas where they might find horses and cattle, the great source of savage wealth.[8]
>
> These raids were made with such regularity on this route in the September or 'Mexican Moon,' that the Mexicans in August of each year stationed sentinels on a high mountain overlooking the trail where it crossed the river. Two sentinels stood this guard and at the expiration of two weeks were relieved by another pair — when they caught sight or found the trail of the Comanches crossing into Mexico — they set fire to their signal pile on some mountain point.

This was seen from some other signal station and the signal was then made at that point. So the word was flashed from hill top to hill top until it reached the Presidio — that the Comanches had come on their usual raid — then the word was sent to all out-lying villages, and men, women, and children came into the towns everywhere for protection, bringing their goats and burros to escape the hands of the Indians.[9]

The Mexican Moon in the fall of the year was the time when there was a great deal of moonlight by which to travel. During the full of the moon the signs and trails could better be seen by night. During the nights, sentinel duty and patrol of their "remuda" (horse-herd) was required.

In making this long trek from the Red and Arkansas rivers, the Comanches skirted the east side of the waterless great Llano Estacado, crossing the headwaters of the Brazos to the Colorado where their favorite camping grounds were at the present site of Big Spring, Texas. They had passed through a country of rolling hills and red lands tenanted only by the buffalo, jack rabbit, and antelope. It was a land sentinelled by the buzzard and hawk, where the sumac, Greggs ash, juniper, piñón and scrub oak occassionally adorned the hillsides, and where the water courses supported the Mexican buckeye, desert willow, and western walnut. They came from a region of scattered trees; and gradually, as the annual local rainfall decreased southwestward on the plains, they came to a land of stunted plant growth.

In riding on toward the North Concho, they passed through a country of scattered shrubs of mesquite, hop tree, polled hackberry, Mexican buckeye, the white prickly poppy, nightshades and the wild rose. Continuing on to the Mustang Ponds, up Centralia Draw, Wild China Ponds to Castle Gap, they had gone through mesquite trees, the scattered Spanish daggers and prickly pear. They now observed to the north and a little to the west, the great Sand Dunes from which they could obtain additional food from the acorns of the shinnery. Just as the quicksand and abrupt, steap bank of the crooked, snake-like Pecos resisted any crossing, that long heavy one hundred-mile stretch of sand dunes, parallel to the Pecos, created a barrier to man or beast, on the west side of the Llano Estacado.

Upon crossing through the rough pass in Castle Gap they viewed the desolate, tree-barren regions of the Pecos River. At Horsehead Crossing, they camped, quenched their thirst, watered their animals, and prepared a supply of jerky from the horse herd for food to supply them on those long, hard and parching rides across the salt grass bumps to the few and hidden springs in the mesas of the Edwards Plateau and mountainous, basalt regions of the Rio Grande. While traversing the mesa country west of the Pecos, they saw principally the creosote bush and cacti, but also the Spanish oak, cedar, mesquite, hackberry and live oak trees along with the gramma, needle, buffalo, running and curly mesquite grasses. Prominent among the plants were the Indian paintbrush, the blue and red verbenas, bush honeysuckle, red bud, Mexican buckeye and persimmon, mountain laurel, juniper, piñon, wild cherry, and buttercups. They found those buckskin leggings useful in protecting them from thorns and the prickly spikes of the catclaw, mesquite, prickly pear, cholla, allthorn, lechuguilla, and the tasajillo.

If they had proceeded by Pecos Spring, Independence and Myers Springs, they would have encountered the plum. By going through the regions of the Big Bend, they might have climbed the heights of the Chisos Mountains among the maple, western yellow pine, quaking asp and black thorn to visit the only native Douglas spruce and Arizona ash in Texas. Should they have ventured into the Davis Mountains, they would have seen the mountain live oak and western yellow pine.

The salt grass and "Chamizal" of the Pecos Valley were seeding and full of nourishment. At the watering places were found the metates and pestles for grinding the seeds and grasses for food. Permanent springs and streams of

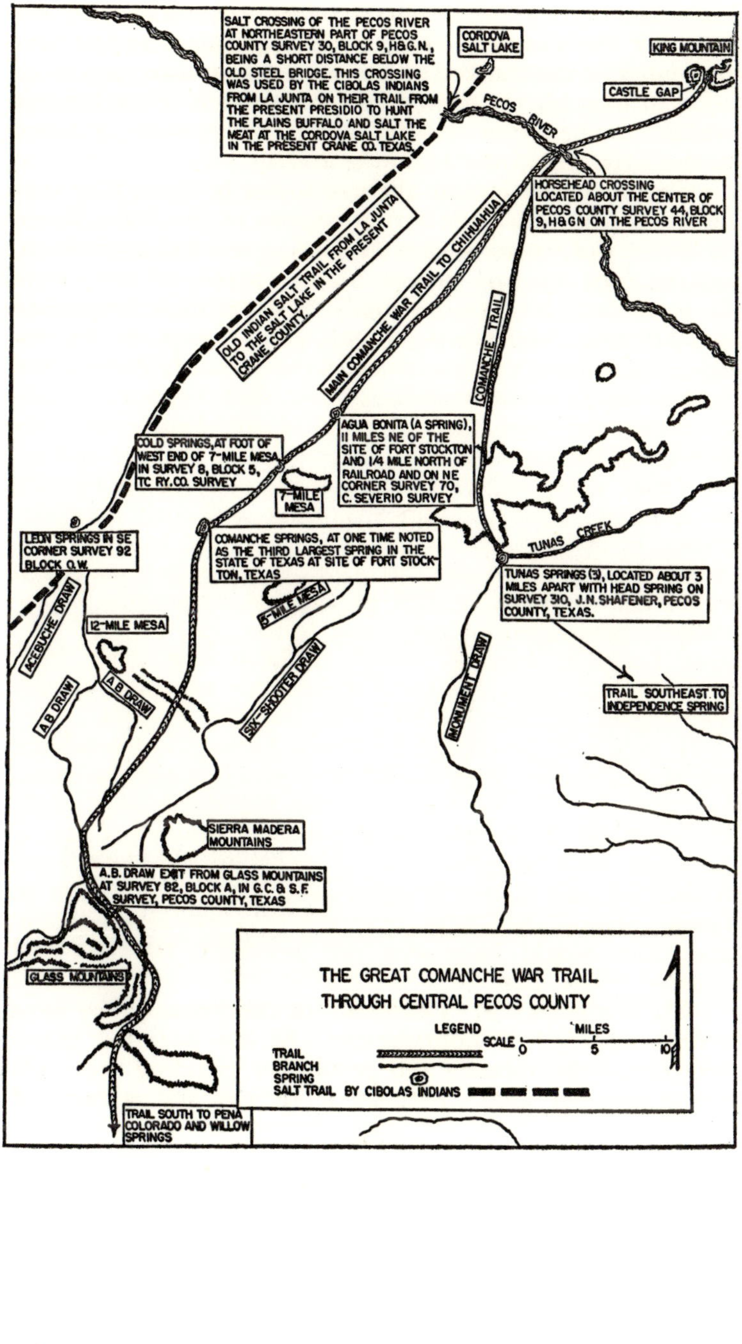
SALT CROSSING OF THE PECOS RIVER AT NORTHEASTERN PART OF PECOS COUNTY SURVEY 30, BLOCK 9, H&G.N., BEING A SHORT DISTANCE BELOW THE OLD STEEL BRIDGE. THIS CROSSING WAS USED BY THE CIBOLAS INDIANS FROM LA JUNTA ON THEIR TRAIL FROM THE PRESENT PRESIDIO TO HUNT THE PLAINS BUFFALO AND SALT THE MEAT AT THE CORDOVA SALT LAKE IN THE PRESENT CRANE CO. TEXAS.
CORDOVA SALT LAKE
KING MOUNTAIN
CASTLE GAP
PECOS RIVER
HORSEHEAD CROSSING LOCATED ABOUT THE CENTER OF PECOS COUNTY SURVEY 44, BLOCK 9, H&GN ON THE PECOS RIVER
OLD INDIAN SALT TRAIL FROM LA JUNTA TO THE SALT LAKE IN THE PRESENT CRANE COUNTY.
MAIN COMANCHE WAR TRAIL TO CHIHUAHUA
COMANCHE TRAIL
AGUA BONITA (A SPRING), 11 MILES NE OF THE SITE OF FORT STOCKTON AND 1/4 MILE NORTH OF RAILROAD AND ON NE CORNER SURVEY 70, C. SEVERIO SURVEY
COLD SPRINGS, AT FOOT OF WEST END OF 7-MILE MESA IN SURVEY 8, BLOCK 5, TC RY. CO. SURVEY
7-MILE MESA
LEON SPRINGS IN SE CORNER SURVEY 92 BLOCK O.W.
COMANCHE SPRINGS, AT ONE TIME NOTED AS THE THIRD LARGEST SPRING IN THE STATE OF TEXAS AT SITE OF FORT STOCKTON, TEXAS
TUNAS CREEK
TUNAS SPRINGS (3), LOCATED ABOUT 3 MILES APART WITH HEAD SPRING ON SURVEY 310, J.N. SHAFENER, PECOS COUNTY, TEXAS.
5-MILE MESA
12-MILE MESA
ACEBUCHE DRAW
A.B. DRAW
A.B. DRAW
SIX-SHOOTER DRAW
MONUMENT DRAW
TRAIL SOUTHEAST TO INDEPENDENCE SPRING
SIERRA MADERA MOUNTAINS
A.B. DRAW EXIT FROM GLASS MOUNTAINS AT SURVEY 82, BLOCK A, IN G.C. & S.F. SURVEY, PECOS COUNTY, TEXAS
GLASS MOUNTAINS
TRAIL SOUTH TO PENA COLORADO AND WILLOW SPRINGS
THE GREAT COMANCHE WAR TRAIL THROUGH CENTRAL PECOS COUNTY
LEGEND
TRAIL
BRANCH
SPRING
SALT TRAIL BY CIBOLAS INDIANS
SCALE
MILES
0
5
10

the valleys were supplemented by small springs in the mesas resulting from the fall showers. The potholes in the mesa escarpments were again full of water from the September rains. Although the days might be warm or even hot, the nights would be cool and refreshing. This was the practical time of the year for the young Indian braves to travel to New Spain or Mexico in quest of glory, horses, stock, mule tails and captives!

For a little over seventy-five years, the Comanches, unmolested by enemy patrols, passed through the regions between San Antonio and Paso del Norte to raid and plunder in Chihuahua and Coahuila. They often took the shortest route down and the route back which would best accommodate the plunder. Water was no problem until they passed westward from the present Big Spring and the Concho River country in Texas.

Their route from the great plains to Coahuila took them by the Conchos, and Devil's (San Pedro) rivers and across the Rio Grande. Another route went from the site of the present Big Spring by way of Grierson Spring, Live Oak Creek, Independence Spring and Meyers Spring.

The trails to Chihuahua and northern Coahuila came by the present Big Spring, Centralia Draw, Castle Gap, and Horsehead Crossing to Agua Bonita Springs, located some fifteen miles northeast of the present Fort Stockton. Thence, several trails led to New Spain. One route took the Comanches by Horsehead Crossing to Tunas Springs, Independence or Meyers, to the Rio Grande by way of Lozier Canyon. Another, from Meyers Springs, went close to Langtry to cross the Rio Grande. Several good crossings which were later named by the white man, were located along the rough borders of the Rio Grande in this vicinity.

A picture drawn by Emory's crew, the "Lipan Crossing" as described by them, appears much like that scenery at the mouth of the Lozier Canyon, according to the late Joe Graham of Marfa, Texas. Emory's crew estimated that this crossing was ninety miles above the mouth of the Pecos.

The McKenzie Crossing, named for General McKenzie, is some ten miles above the mouth of the Devil's River.

The second route out of Agua Bonita or Antelope Springs went west of the Seven Mile Mesa and passed by way of Comanche Springs (Fort Stockton), turned south, roughly paralleling the present Marathon Road until it reached the crest of the east extension from the Nine Mile Mesa. There, taking a straight course for the mouth of the A. B. Draw in the northern foothills of the Glass Mountains, it followed up this draw for a short distance, then passed southeast over the small hills, and the site of the old Joe Moss homestead to either Peña Colorado or Willow Springs.

According to Travis Roberts of Marathon, Texas, the Comanche War Trail split in southern Pecos County. One trail went into Brewster County and passed a couple of miles east of the present Highway 385, continued south and a little west to cross the present Southern Pacific Railroad some eleven or twelve miles east of Marathon, and passed by Horse Mountain, where it separated. The western branch went along Hackberry Creek to the west of the Tinaja Mountains, curving south and southeast to follow the Maravillas Draw on the east side of the Santiago Mountains to pass due south through the Persimmon Gap to Bone Spring. Two miles south of Bone Spring, the trail crossed Nine-Point Draw, continued south and a little east about ten miles to form two branches. The west branch went southwest on the north side of Grapevine Hills, passed Croton Springs, crossed Cottonwood to the north of Burro Mesa and continued on to Santa Elena Junction and the present Ranger station, where it branched again. The western branch went west and a little south, crossed Terlingua Creek about seven miles above its confluence with the Rio Grande, and continued westward to the Lajitas Ford on the Rio Grande. From the present Ranger station at Santa Elena Junction, the other branch went south and a little west down Willow Creek to the Rio Grande two miles west of the present Castolon.

The east branch, commencing at just east of Horse

Mountain, went due south, crossed Kincaid Draw and negotiated through the small hills to join the previous trail at a point about five and one-half miles north of Persimmon Gap. The main trail continued on to and through Bone Spring and beyond for some thirteen miles where it departed from the previous trail to continue south, crossing Avery Canyon and going east of Nuget Mountain and west of Chilicotal Mountain to Glenn Spring. From there it skirted the western edge of Talley Mountain to go due south to the Rio Grande at a point some eight miles from the present Reed Camp. The trail that led to the San Vicente ford, left the prior trail at a point just east of Nuget Mountain and one mile northwest of Dugout Wells and made almost a straight line by Chilicotal Spring to a point on the Rio Grande, a mile west of the old Presidio San Vicente.

The other main Comanche trail as reported by Roberts, branched off the main trail just north of Brewster County to pass by the present Marathon, Texas, and then passed the site of old Camp Peña Colorada, from where one branch went down Peña Colorada Draw, passed east of the Cochran Mountains, and down Maravillas Draw to join the former trails about three or four miles north of Persimmon Gap. The other trail went south from Peña Colorada Spring by way of Woods Hollow Creek to join the above trail at Maravillas Gap.

Another Indian trail, as reported by Travis Roberts, went from Peña Colorada Spring to Presidio, going southwest by Monument Draw from Peña Colorada Spring, passing through Del Norte Gap of the Cochran Mountains (five miles south of the present Roberts' ranch) then turning west, southwest and skirting around the south end of the foothills of Elephant Mountain to come to Terlingua Creek, just north of Turney Peak. It then went up Terlingua Creek and Paradise Draw, passed through Jordan Gap and on to the present location of Perdiz siding on the present Panhandle and Santa Fe railroad. From this point, it joined the Alamito Creek trail to Presidio (La Junta).

As reported to him by the Mexicans, the late O. W.

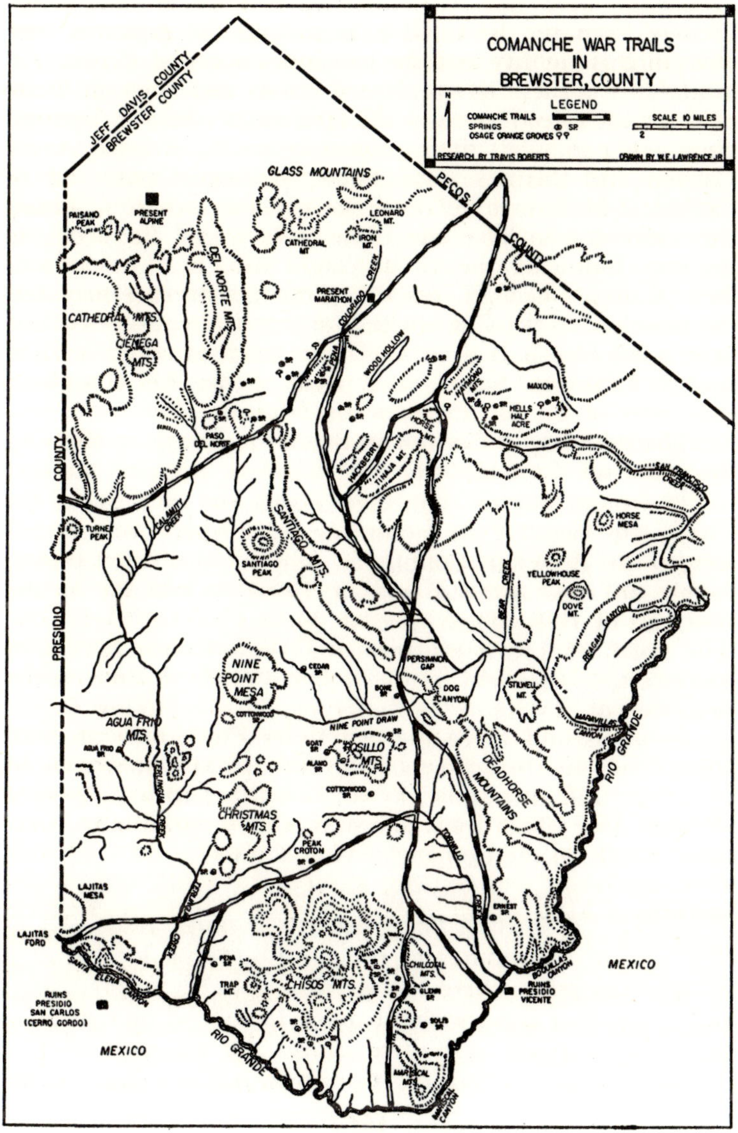

COMANCHE WAR TRAILS
IN
BREWSTER, COUNTY
LEGEND
COMANCHE TRAILS
SPRINGS
OSAGE ORANGE GROVES
SCALE 10 MILES
RESEARCH BY TRAVIS ROBERTS
DRAWN BY W.E. LAWRENCE JR.
JEFF DAVIS COUNTY
BREWSTER COUNTY
PECOS COUNTY
PRESIDIO COUNTY
GLASS MOUNTAINS
PRESENT ALPINE
PAISANO PEAK
DEL NORTE MTS.
CATHEDRAL MT.
LEONARD MT.
IRON MT.
PRESENT MARATHON
COLORADO CREEK
CATHEDRAL MTS.
CIENEGA MTS.
WOOD HOLLOW
MAXON
HELLS HALF ACRE
PASO DEL NORTE
HACKBERRY
TINAJA MT.
HORSE MT.
SAN FRANCISCO CREEK
HORSE MESA
TURNEY PEAK
CALAMITY CREEK
SANTIAGO MTS.
SANTIAGO PEAK
YELLOWHOUSE PEAK
BEAR CREEK
DOVE MT.
REAGAN CANYON
NINE POINT MESA
CEDAR SR.
PERSIMMON GAP
BONE SR.
DOG CANYON
STILWELL MT.
COTTONWOOD SR.
NINE POINT DRAW
MARAVILLAS CANYON
AGUA FRIO MTS.
AGUA FRIO SR.
GOAT SR.
ALAMO SR.
ROSILLO MTS.
DEADHORSE MOUNTAINS
RIO GRANDE
TERLINGUA CREEK
CHRISTMAS MTS.
PEAK CROTON
TORNILLO CREEK
LAJITAS MESA
ERNEST SR.
LAJITAS FORD
SANTA ELENA CANYON
PENA SR.
TRAP MT.
CHISOS MTS.
CHILICOTAL MTS.
GLENN SR.
BOQUILLAS CANYON
MEXICO
RUINS PRESIDIO VICENTE
RUINS PRESIDIO SAN CARLOS (CERRO GORDO)
SOLIS SR.
MARISCAL MTS.
MARISCAL CANYON

Williams stated that the Comanches brought the Osage Orange from the Red River region and transplanted the trees in this vicinity in order to have the limbs of that tree available for their bows. The warriors had such little regard for the effectiveness of the Spanish or Mexican fighting ability that they left their guns at home. The Government Gardens (to this day surrounded by Osage Orange trees), located some five miles northeast of Fort Stockton, Texas, were reported to have had those trees placed there by the soldiers, following the Civil War. Also, in the southern part of Pecos County, on the present Allison ranch and located close to the Comanche War Trail is a survey corner, known as The Bois d' Arc (Osage Orange) corner. Close by is a thicket of Osage Orange trees. Travis Roberts places this location on the east side of Highway 385, some two and three-fourths miles northeast of the Moore ranch and the Brewster County line.

The other Bois d' Arc groves adjacent or near to the Comanche War Trails, according to Travis Roberts, are located in Brewster County as follows: on Peña Blanca Creek, on the northeast end of Horse Mountain; at the west end of Hell's Half Acre; at Maxon Spring, about one mile north of Tres Hermanos; on Alsate Creek, five miles southwest of Marathon; at the Roberts' ranch, thirteen miles southwest of Marathon; on the Upper Woods Hollow Creek, about seven and three-quarters miles due south of Marathon; and in the valley of the Tinaja Mountains about seventeen and three-quarters miles south and a little west of Marathon, which leads to a draw that empties into Hackberry Creek on the Comanche War Trail.

Most of these groves are on the Comanche War Trail or nearby, the farthest being about ten miles away. All of them are in the mountains or foothills, being located at a suitable campsite, where the warriors could leisurely season and make their bows without much likelihood of a surprise attack. It appears that these groves are all located in a region extending along the Comanche trails from a point twenty miles northeast of Marathon to eighteen miles south of Marathon.

Many unfortunate captives came to know these campsites. Among the Mexican captives taken by the Comanches and Kiowas, the men were killed and the boys and the attractive young women and girls were taken to the distant homes of the warriors to become slaves at first and later good Indians. The young captives were tied upon horses or mules, not always very gentle, to follow dusty herds of long-horned cattle, or mules and horses, the hoofs of which churned little geysers of dust. They traversed the Indians' trails over rocks, mountains thick with the Spanish daggers, and terraces covered with the numerous spear-like points of the lechuguilla.

After toiling over and through the Carmen Mountains to come to and cross the Rio Grande in the present region of the Big Bend Park of Texas, nature wore a dreary look across the scrawny vegetation, where God had put thorns all over the stunted trees. Blood trickled down the young captives' limbs from frequent punctures by the Spanish daggers, prickly pears, catclaws, tasajillos, mesquites and various thistles. There was no dampness to provoke "daily ague," but heat waves danced before their eyes as the certainties of life lost all meaning. Many of the young girls and women had been taken from the comfort of frills, perfume, and pink; and after weeks of toil, and pain from the unaccustomed position of being tied on animals, they were then subjected to, among other indignities, sweat and unpleasant odors, where the sky furnished the only vaulted-arch corridor and the parched land was so hot that rain might evaporate before hitting the ground. They were in the Devil's Hell of Texas, where (as described in a familar verse) sometimes it is reported too dry for Hell, and where some water, with dregs of a cathartic nature, smells like bad eggs; where the rattlesnake bites; the scorpion stings; the sand-burrs prevail; the toads have horns; the centipedes' feet are poisoned; and the tusked wild boar (javelina) roams through the black chaparral. The ants are so thick that one who sits down needs half soles on his seat. Even the rabbits have an addition to their ears. It is a hell of a place for the Devil's Hell.

The captives, after being continually guarded and doing slave duty at night camps, traveled the fifty to sixty miles to the region of the Tenaja Mountains, where small springs of good water and small shade trees were occasionally available nearby or on the trail for camping. Having subsisted on jerky, occasional fresh meat as procured by the Indians, the tuna from the prickly pear, and what food the Comanches had stolen from the Mexicans, they were then to wade out in the small springs and streams to gather the cattail roots to supply the warriors with one of their common foods. Those captives who were stubborn, failed to make good slaves, or were too fatigued and worn out to continue were killed. By the time the captives had reached the Pecos River at Horsehead Crossing, some of the adaptable captive boys were allowed to ride and guard the extra herd of horses. Very few of such captives ever managed to escape as they were prized as slaves, whose release from such captivity could only be purchased by lengthy negotiations and large sums of money. This was a practice that could have resulted from the Spanish Treaty of 1785, which provided that all of the Indians' captives were to be brought in for redemption.

---

[1] Letter of Pedro de Nava to the Viceroy (July 23, 1799), *Internal Provinces*, Vol. XII, p. 64: General Archives, University of Texas, as translated by José Coro.

[2] Wallace & Hoebel, *The Comanches, Lords of the South Plains:* 1952; W. W. Newcomb, *The Indians of Texas*, p. 157: University of Texas Press, 1961; W. L. Clark, *Indian Sign Language*, p. 118: L. R. Hamersly & Co., 1885, Philadelphia.

[3] Powell, J. W., *Annual Report of the Bureau of American Ethnology 1895-96, Part 1*, p. 269: Government Printing Office, Washington, 1898.

[4] Barreiro, Pina, *Three New Mexico Chronicles*, pp. 100, 129: Quivira Society Publication, Albuquerque, 1942.

[5] Catlin, George, *The North American Indians*, Vol. II, p. 73: Leary, Stuart and Co., Philadelphia, 1913.

[6] *Ibid.*, p. 74.

[7] Marcy, Randolf B., *Exploration of the Red River of Louisiana*, pp. 95-97: A. O. P. Nicholson, Public Printer, Washington, 1854.

[8] Williams, O. W., *Baja el Sol*, a privately printed brochure, written before 1914 and printed after 1919.

[9] Letter from O. W. Williams, Alpine, Texas, March 16, 1902, to My Dear Children.

Chapter 9

United States Expands Westward in Its Louisiana Purchase and Fights Britain as the Spaniards Attempt to Hold New Spain (1800-1821)

The United States was growing, with the carving of Vermont out of New York in 1791, the creation of Kentucky out of Virginia in 1792 and the formation of Tennessee out of North Carolina in 1796. The Anglo-Americans with their fur and coonskin caps, and Kentucky rifles, were exploring and settling to the west.

Besides the possibility of finding gold, silver and other metals, the "grab box" of the West was wide open to the venturesome spirits from the East — even those wild mustangs and Spanish cattle found by Mezierres on the Brazos and Colorado rivers were a harvest to be plucked by the pioneers. The regions of Texas were penetrated early by the citizens of the United States. Learning of Philip Nolan's expedition in 1801, which was engaged in capturing mustangs on the Brazos River near the site of Waco, the Spaniards from San Antonio and Nacogdoches surprised and killed Nolan and a few of his companions. The survivors of Nolan's unfortunate party were sent to prisons in New Spain.

In 1803, upon the United States' purchase of the immense unknown territory of Louisiana from France, Spain guarded more zealously than ever the questionable limits of that boundary. She considered the United States to be more aggressive and more to be feared for its transgression of territory from the east of the Sabine River than Louisiana's former owner, France. The doubtful status of the actual boundary between the Sabine River and east to Arroyo Hondo resulted in a neutral zone filled with desperate characters and freebooters, accountable to no law.[1]

Ohio had been admitted as a state in the United States in the same year that Louisiana had been purchased. Lewis and Clark with their party, under arrangements perfected by Thomas Jefferson and financed by the United States, started their ascent of the Missouri River. By April, 1805, they had reached the three forks of that river in Montana, and were safely piloted across the Rocky Mountains, along the Snake River and on to the Columbia River by November of 1805.

Zebulon Pike, with twenty-three men, in an official capacity of looking over the newly acquired Louisiana for the United States, made his way from St. Louis to the Great Bend on the Arkansas and explored to its headwaters to make camp in the high mountains of the Rockies in January, 1807. Upon being found by a Spanish scouting party, he willingly came into Santa Fe where he was officially under arrest.

In Santa Fe he met a carpenter named Pursley, from

Kentucky, who informed him that in the previous year, his party, while hunting on the plains, was followed and driven by the Sioux Indians into the high grounds in the rear of Pike's Peak and near the headwaters of the Platte River. There he found gold, and being uncertain as to whether that gold was within the newly acquired Louisiana or in Spanish territory, he delayed several months before coming in alone to Santa Fe. After he had informed the Spaniards of his gold, they attempted to get him to show them its location, which he shrewdly declined to do. Confined and put to work by the Spaniards, he was never able to return to his companions for fear of disclosing the location of his gold.[2]

Pike's party, officially under arrest, was ordered from Santa Fe to report to General Saucedo in Chihuahua, to which place they journeyed, passing through Paso del Norte (Juárez) to arrive in Chihuahua City on April 2, 1807. There Pike diplomatically arranged for the release of several trappers in prison in Santa Fe and for his own trip back through San Antonio and Texas. After a century and a half, Pike is better known now as the name of a snow-covered peak which majestically overlooks the city of Colorado Springs in the State of Colorado.

More closely associated with our country of the Pecos River and Rio Grande was the trip of Francisco Amangual, with one company of the New Kingdom of Leon, two companies of the Kingdom of Santander, and one of Bahia, all on horseback and equipped with carts for their luggage. Starting from the mission of San Antonio and slowly making their way across mesquite and chaparral-covered rolling hills, passing the Leon Creek and Pedernales River, they met two Comanches of Cordero's rancherías and viewed the abandoned ruins of the mission and the desolate rock walls and fortress of the deserted presidio of San Saba, near the present Menard.

They joined Cordero and his Comanches in killing buffalo for their mutual benefit, as those Indians were in need of meat, because their young warriors were most likely in New Spain on a raid. Amangual gives the impression that he met mostly old men.

Leaving Cordero's Comanches, Amangual's party proceeded to the Colorado River. After encountering a delay because of bad weather and the necessity of recovering their "remuda," they traveled up the Colorado River for several days and met and camped with the friendly "Yamparica" (Yamparika Comanches) on the headwaters of the Colorado River until their scouts had found sufficient water for their next camping site.

At this new campsite, they met Chief Isambanbi of the Yamparika Comanches, who took them on the following day to his ranchería where the old Indian men put on a special display for the benefit of the Spaniards. The Comanches were dressed in unusual clothes, such as very long red coats adorned with blue collars and cuffs with trimmings of white buttons and yellow, imitation gold galloons. One was dressed in ancient Spanish style with a short red coat, blue trousers, white stockings, English spurs, a three-cornered hat worn cocked, and a cane with a silver handle shaped like a hyssop. The others, with their nicely braided hair trailing the ground and their bodies and faces covered with chalk and red ochre, were wearing red neckties, sashes made of otter skin adorned with beads and shells. Excepting the English spurs and otter skin sashes, those were the relics and souvenirs taken from the massacred Spanish soldiers at the missions of San Saba, San Antonio, Espíritu Santo and San Lorenzo and the presidios of San Saba, La Bahia and others in Texas and New Spain.

After hunting with these Indians for several days, Amangual's party moved on, passing through a country inhabited by other rancherías of Chief Isambanbi, and on to the country of Chief Queque. By May 27th, their guides informed them that they were on the Red River. Following up this river and across and up the Canadian River, they passed over the hills and the Upper Pecos River to arrive at Santa Fe.

Completing a short rest at Santa Fe, they came down the Rio Grande to "The Royal Presidio of San Elizerio."[3] With the aid of two Apache guides from "San Elizerio," they followed down the Rio Grande for a distance of eleven leagues and arrived at "San Antonio Crossing," pushed east through the "Sierra Blanca," the "Guadalupe Mountains" and arrived at the Pecos River. Enroute they rescued a lone, forlorn, tiny, slowly moving little Mexican lad who had been recently captured by the Apaches in a raid upon the New Mexican settlements, and had managed to make his escape out on that desert hundreds of miles from his home.

At the Pecos River, evidently the recognized boundary between the Comanches and the Apaches at that time, the two Apache guides were unwilling to continue and departed to return to "San Elizerio." Amangual's party traveled with their carts down the winding, desolate Pecos River, with the occasional abandonment of a worn-out horse, to arrive at about the location of Live Oak Creek.[4] There, they encountered two Comanches who guided them east to the Middle Concho where their friendly Comanche chief, Cordero, was then camped, some one hundred miles from where they had previously met him.

In making its way from "San Elizerio" to the Middle Concho, Amangual's party contained probably the first white men to cross those regions in carts, excepting Sosa's group, which came up the Pecos River in 1598. Chief Cordero courteously exchanged some fresh horses for Amangual's worn-out horses so that Amangual's party might reach San Antonio. Upon arriving in San Antonio, the report was written that Amangual's party had averaged a speed of fifteen miles per day even though there had been no roads for their carts.[5]

In spite of her many exploring parties and vast domains, the Spanish empire was beginning to fall apart. With insufficient Spanish protection from the numerous Indian raids, with persecution of individuals and with racial difficulties in maintaining law and order among the peoples of seventeen different languages, internal trouble was brewing in New Spain. Just two years after Amangual's party had explored the plains country and the Pecos River, Miguel Hidalgo headed an unsuccessful Mexican revolution in New Spain.[6]

The Spaniards' troubles included, also, the aggression of the Anglo-Americans from the East. The earlier Anglo-American traders, settlers and trappers came into extreme west Texas from the northeast by way of the Santa Fe Trail and south along the Rio Grande and the Jornada del Muerto to Paso del Norte and its regions.

The names of Mexico and New Spain, the reports of Pursley's gold and Chihuahua's silver mines, the rumored sources of Montezuma's riches and Coronado's Seven Cities of Gold, always possessed an invincible allure for the people of the western frontier of the United States. Though jealously guarded from foreign intrusion by Spanish despotic power, with a sentence of imprisonment in Chihuahua for life, or labor in the mines as the inexorable penalty for every attempt to penetrate, prospect or trap in the forbidden country; nevertheless, this fascinating region lured the bright imaginations of the venturesome spirits of the great West to move into this hazardous, forbidden area. The failure, misfortune, chains and labor of some were not sufficient to intimidate the others. The journal of Pike set flame to those pioneer spirits and induced new adventurers and frontiersmen to risk the fate of their predecessors.

Foremost among those daring spirits were the trappers who moved out from the rolling hills and plains of the Missouri Territory. Among those to earn the name of "Mountain Men," were Jim Bridger, James Pursley, Kit Carson, Ezekiel Williams, Charles Beaubien and Ceran St. Vrain. Independently or in the employment of the great fur companies, they blazed the trails to the running waters and streams of the Rocky Mountains in search of the fine soft furs of the beaver, which supplied the demand for fancy hats in New York, London and Paris.

Although many of the trappers had suffered the confiscation of their furs and equipment and years of confinement in the dungeons of New Spain, the first commercial caravan of goods to reach Santa Fe from the United States was received with enthusiasm, as the citizens of Santa Fe were eager to secure the scarce products of calico and other merchandise previously transported from Mexico City by way of Chihuahua and Paso del Norte.

The new trail of commerce was opened by Captain Becknell, because the Indians on the plains informed him that Santa Fe would be a good market for his goods. The following year, in 1812, he, along with an escort of thirty men and with $5,000 worth of goods transported by pack animals, traveled up the Arkansas River to the "Caches" where he boldly directed his party away from the Arkansas and towards Santa Fe. They were soon upon the desert; and having started with a small supply of water, within two days they were suffering the tortures of thirst. First their dogs were killed, then the ears of the mules were cut off for the warm blood, and finally a lone buffalo bull was killed for the soured contents of its bladder. Some of the stronger members of the party followed the back tracks of the buffalo to the Cimarron River where they filled canteens and returned to their comrades. Relieved of thirst and unfamiliar with the route to Santa Fe by way of the Cimarron they returned to the Arkansas River to follow up its course and then cross to Taos and travel down the established trail to Santa Fe.[7]

In the meantime, the United States had progressed rapidly since the Revolution. The cotton plant had been introduced to Georgia, and the cotton gin had been invented to give an impetus to that industry. Benjamin Franklin had died. The city of Washington had been chosen to replace New York City as the nation's capital. Washington served a second term, and died December 14, 1799. John Adams served as the second President and Thomas Jefferson as the third President, during whose term of office Louisiana had been purchased from the

French. Under that purchase, the United States claimed that territory which was thought by some to include Texas to the Rio Grande.

The steam engine had become a reality and locomotion was in its infancy. Livingston and Fulton built the "Clermont" in 1807 and established a regular packet service between New York City and Albany. The steamboat "New Orleans" was launched at Pittsburgh in October, 1811, to carry freight and passengers on the Ohio River.

Industry was beginning to boom. Coal, produced in Pennsylvania, Virginia, Ohio and Rhode Island, with iron ore from the mines in the mountains of Virginia, Rhode Island and Maryland was being used to make iron by furnaces in Lancaster, Coatsville, and Juanita Valley, Pennsylvania, and in plants in New Jersey and Maryland.

New Jersey produced lead, copper, silver, iron nails, leather goods, cotton and wheat. New York with its navigation on the Hudson River and its ocean outlet for commerce, raised grains and produced gypsum, limestone, marble, porcelain, clay, and salt; while New York City's great factories of linen and woolen cloth, with its 300,000 tons of shipping facilities enabled the state to produce and market an annual $20,000,000 worth of goods. Close behind Virginia's coal production was her cultivation of tobacco and manufacture of cigars, cigarettes, chewing and smoking tobacco, and snuff. Maine was important because of its production of wheat, Indian corn, rye, barley, the roughage of native grass, the growing of the finest potatoes, the production of fruit and berries from its orchards, and timber from its immense forests for boatmaking, fuel and export.

Massachusetts' great fishing industry along the Atlantic coast, its fine harbors for the import of cheap cotton goods from India, and its vast cotton factories kept its population employed.

The state of Rhode Island, in addition to its coal and iron industry, produced copper ore. Besides its iron factories, Connecticut produced porcelain clay, black lead and cobalt. Its fruit orchards, "Goshen" butter and cheese, together with its foreign shipping capacity of 60,859 tons, provided ample commerce for its citizens. Wheat, tobacco, hickory, fruits, sweet potatoes, some cotton, exports of flour, pig iron, lumber and grain provided the commerce of Maryland.

Delaware was prosperous with its mills for flour, cottons, wool, paper and gunpowder. Dupont de Nemours and Company had been operating as a factory in making gunpowder since 1802. The regions of Kentucky furnished one of the elements of gunpowder from a deposit which contained about 50% nitre. Steamboats on the Ohio River were conveying large quantities of nitre to the growing gunpowder factories.

Pennsylvania had built its turnpike from Philadelphia to its manufacturing city of Lancaster. Roads and stagecoach routes had been established in every direction. Blacksmithing was big business with six or seven smiths in every establishment where metal tires were shrunk on to carriage wheels, horses were shod, trace chains were forged, varmint traps were made, and carriages and harnesses were manufactured and repaired.

Some citizens of the United States had long borne a grudge against Great Britain because of her refusal to give up western ports following the Treaty of 1783, resulting in a long and costly Indian war and the massacre of many Americans by the Indians. Others were incited over Britain's actions in prohibiting neutral trade with France and her allies in the early stages of Napoleon's European conflict. And now in a single year, Britain, the master of the seas, had injured American commerce, captured and impressed thousands of free Americans into the British navy by the seizure of several hundred ships, cargoes and men. Even so, a large number of Americans were opposed to the ensuing war. On June 18, 1812, the United States declared war on Great Britain. But prior to any actual engagements between the United States and Britain, was that expedition into Texas by ex-lieutenant Augustus McGee of the United States Army. Induced by discontented refugee citizens of New Spain or those who had fled to New Orleans after the unsuccessful revolution of Hidalgo, McGee resigned his commission in New Orleans and joined their cause. The venture of taking Texas for the United States was not a new idea, as the outcast ex-vice president of the United States, Aaron Burr, together with General Wilkinson, had been exposed in their complicity relative to the contemplated capture of Texas from Spain. Burr was tried for treason in Richmond, Kentucky, and acquitted.

With a "Green Flag," McGee, along with a band of freebooters and pirates, joined by Bernardo Gutiérrez and his Mexican forces, the "Republican Army of the North," attacked and captured La Bahía, the veteran presidio for Spanish protection of its mission Espíritu Santo and its tenants. During the fierce siege and slaughter of the Spaniards under command of Salcedo, McGee was mysteriously killed.

Gutiérrez took command and moved up to capture San Antonio and proclaim Texas free from Spain. After becoming unpopular with his followers, Gutiérrez was removed and Toledo was selected to replace him. Spanish troops advanced from New Spain and met the Toledo forces in the battle of Medina, causing the Toledo forces to retreat out of the province and ending a short term of so-called freedom for Texas.[8]

Relative to the war between United States and Britain, an overconfident band of Americans attacked the fortified Queenstown in Canada, and upon being repulsed, surrendered. Another small expedition of Americans from the vicinity of Albany and Plattsburg moved into Canada, defeated a small party of British and Indians, and returned.

The United States' naval units, in separate engagements, captured the British frigate "Querriere," the sloops "Frolic," "Java," and the "Peacock."

Soon, seventeen thousand Americans who were conveyed across Lake Ontario, captured York, and then occupied Fort George. Shortly thereafter, the British from

Detroit captured five hundred Americans at Frenchtown, then departed, leaving the prisoners under Indian guard. Following the massacre of most of those prisoners, the few escapees carried the news to the Kentuckians, joined the Harrison's Kentuckians in marching to the rapids of the Miami, assisted in the building of a fort there, and then successfully withstood the attack of a large force of British and Indians. Fort Meigs, defended by a few Americans, also repulsed an attack by British and Indians. Soon after, the few American defenders and refugees at Fort Mimms on the Alabama River were wiped out by a large band of Creek Indians.

Meanwhile, with most of the American troops located in the Great Lakes and St. Lawrence River regions, the British forces landed at Chesapeake Bay. Encountering only feeble resistance, they marched to Washington, burned many buildings, and retreated to sail away in their ships.

In the meantime, three thousand Americans took possession of Fort Erie, defeating the British on the plains of Chippawa, and followed the retreating British to the heights of Burlington. There, the British received reinforcements, engaged the Americans and forced the American retreat to Fort Erie. As the Americans then were reinforced, the British again retreated.

As the above events were taking place, the British navy took the Spanish port of Pensacola, and attempted to capture Fort Bowyer at the entrance of Mobile Bay. Even as the last encounter was in progress, General Andrew Jackson marched south with his army, capturing Pensacola and forcing the British to evacuate Florida.

As the relief force coming to the aid of Americans at Fort Erie had left Plattsburg almost defenseless, the British moved their navy in to destroy the American flotilla on Lake Champlain and marched troops to Saranac River, hoping to capture Plattsburg. Simultaneously, the British troops were defeated at the river, and the British naval units were forced by the American squadron to retreat from the harbor of Plattsburg.

The conflict had not been popular among many Americans. Ten million dollars and an army of thirty-five thousand men had been voted by Congress to sustain the war. Only eight million of the ten million had been subscribed. Many Americans called it "Mr. Madison's War." The Connecticut governor refused to obey President Madison's call for troops, and the Connecticut Assembly declared the state to be free, sovereign and independent. Daniel Webster denounced the draft of men as unconstitutional. The Massachusetts Legislature appropriated one million dollars to support a ten thousand man state army.

Discord between the parties of John C. Calhoun and Henry Clay (The War Hawks) and the representatives of the New England states interested in the commerce of the seas put the nation's policies in chaos. Delaware, Massachusetts, Connecticut and other New England states sent delegates who convened at Hartford to devise means of defense against foreign powers and to safeguard States' Rights against federal encrouchment. Some of the states now realized that more must be done if liberty were to be retained, resulting in negotiations by the United States for a peace treaty with Britain.

In the meantime, the British squadrons defeated a small group of American gunboats in Lake Borgne, the nearest avenue of approach to New Orleans. Jackson's army, in New Orleans, after organizing the militia, erected fortifications and declared martial law. Under the cover of navy power, the British convoyed twenty-four hundred troops up the Mississippi and debarked them nine miles below New Orleans. That very night the Americans attacked the British landing force, and were defeated.

In the middle of these arrangements for conflict and unknown to the parties involved, the United States and Britain signed the Peace Treaty at Ghent — but because of slow communications, the war went on.

Reinforced by twelve thousand men, the British advanced towards New Orleans as six thousand Americans retreated to their fortifications surmounted by large cotton bales located four miles below New Orleans between the Mississippi River on one side and a large cypress swamp on the other. After bombarding the American defenses for eight days, the British columns advanced under a heavy fog. At three hundred yards from the defense works, the British were severely damaged by the American artillery, but managed to overrun the first line of American defense where the American artillery concentrated on them. By night time, with two thousand British dead, dying and wounded on the battle field, the invading forces were in confusion and retreat. By the 18th of January, the British had evacuated the Mississippi.

Long before this war ended, the venturesome American pioneers were again heading commercial caravans towards Santa Fe. McKnight, Beard, Chambers and about a dozen partners successfully made the trip across from St. Louis to Santa Fe. At Santa Fe their goods in the value of thirty thousand dollars were confiscated and they were sent to Chihuahua where they remained in prison for nearly ten years.[9]

Auguste P. Chouteau, with a large party of hunters and trappers were located on the beautiful island in the Arkansas River which now bears Chouteau's name, when some three hundred Pawnee Indians attacked them. The Indians, inexperienced against fortified trappers, were repulsed with the loss of thirty killed or wounded.[10]

Such were a few of the many incidents on the Santa Fe Trail at that time. Down on the Gulf of Mexico coast, the buccaneer, Jean Lafitte, a leading citizen of New Orleans under suspicion by the United States of piracy, and finding himself plagued by that government's officials, moved his base of operations from the Louisiana coast to Galveston Island off the shores of Texas, to deal in slave traffic and piracy on the high seas.[11] There he joined forces with Luis Aury, who like Gutierrez, had been involved with the unsuccessful Hidalgo revolution and had since been operating out of that harbor of pirates. After Aury failed to return from one of those privateering expeditions on the coast of New Spain, Lafitte succeeded him in command.[12]

The Florida Treaty between the United States and Spain acquired Florida for the United States. In negotiations leading up to the final settlement of this treaty, Spain offered to give up that portion of Texas lying between the Red and Arkansas rivers, but because of the slavery question in Missouri's admission to the Union and an oncoming presidential election, Congress compromised by passing up the opportunity to take in that portion of Texas.[13]

Following the purchase of Louisiana, the boundary line between New Spain and the United States had been indefinite. In 1819, the line was agreed upon as commencing at the Gulf entrance to the Sabine River, thence up that river to its junction with the Red River of Natchitoches at 100 degrees west longitude, thence due north to the Arkansas River and up it to 42 degrees north latitude and to follow that parallel west to the Pacific Coast.[14]

The United States sent Major Jacob Fowler along with his wagon train from Fort Smith to explore the Arkansas River in September, 1821. Long had come down the Arkansas and Canadian rivers in 1820. Previously, pack animals afforded the only mode of travel across the plains, but Fowler and his men and wagons ascended the Arkansas River from Fort Smith to the location of the present Pueblo, Colorado.[15]

While Major Fowler was exploring Louisiana, Spain was in difficulty. Seriously crippled by the destruction of the Armada in 1588, troubled with incessant European wars during the intervening years and followed by an inspired movement for liberty on its mainland, Spain had by now lost its position as a great nation. In January, 1820, before Fowler had completed his reconnaissance on the Arkansas River, the Spanish military forces mutinied and placed King Ferdinand VII in prison, resulting in political confusion. During this period Mexico gained its independence and was no longer termed New Spain.

Many years after the unsuccessful revolutionary efforts in New Spain by the Indians and mestizos in 1809, the subsequent race war led by Hidalgo and Captain Allende, their defeat and the execution of Allende in 1815, the following guerilla warfare, and the expeditions into Texas by refugee Spaniards from New Orleans, opponents of liberalism entertained the plan of absolute separation from Spain.

Selected by a group of influential men to take the leading role in that task, Agustín de Iturbide, an ex-officer in the Spanish army, easily influenced the unsuspecting Viceroy to authorize him to take the field against the rebels. Fortified with government troops and finances, he bypassed the Viceroy's authority and with intrigue, signed the Plan de Iguala Agreement with the rebel leader, Guerrero, on February 24, 1821.

That agreement laid the basis for a limited independent monarchy, for continuation of the Roman Catholic Church as the established church of the new government and for equal rights for Spaniards and for various classes of native-born inhabitants. Iturbide then approached the Viceroy, Apodaca, for the cooperation he desired, and was refused. It was too late for Apodaca to stem the flow of support for the agreement.

Here we shall interrupt the account of the intrigue and political manipulations in Mexico or New Spain, to relate briefly Dr. James Long's experience in Texas during this period. As a citizen of the United States, and after distinguishing himself in the battle of New Orleans, he was named the "Young Lion" by General Jackson. Dedicated to the attempted capture of Texas, he had recruited men in Natchez, marched west and occupied a rudely constructed stockade at Bolivar Point on Galveston Bay in 1820.[16]

In the following year, Long left his wife, daughter and twenty-five men at the stockade on Bolivar Point and with seventy-five men started for his intended conquest of Texas. He felt some assurance that his family was well protected by that small force, for just across the bay could be seen the activity of Lafitte's pirates on Galveston Island.[17]

Long's party marched up to La Bahia and without any opposition, compelled it to surrender, only to be forced to surrender himself within a few days to Colonel Perez and his forces. As prisoners, Long and his followers were sent to San Antonio de Béxar and treated with leniency, perhaps because of the existing revolution in Mexico, and because Long's cause could not properly be identified; also because the "Act of Independence of the Mexican Empire" had not been signed until the last of September of that year. Long and his men were transferred to Mexico City where they were released. Upon attempting to enter the barracks of Los Gallos and being refused, Long struck the sentinel, who, in turn, shot and killed him.[18]

Mrs. Long's long wait for her husband's return and her experiences should be included in "Believe It or Not." In that location on Galveston Bay where it seldom freezes, Mrs. Long reported that a terrible snow came, which weighted down the top of her tent. Frozen fish were picked up for food, and the salt water of the bay was converted into a sheet of ice so thick that Mrs. Long stated: "A bear calmly pursued its way across the bay, unmolested save by the barking of Mrs. Long's dog, Galveston."[19]

In the midst of the turmoil and intrigue in New Spain, young Stephen F. Austin, at his dying father's request, had taken over the Moses Austin grant of colonization from the Spanish government. Unlike the expeditions of Nolan, Dr. James Long's and the piratical operations of Lafitte, McGee and Gutierrez, Moses Austin had proceeded through proper channels obtaining the permission of the authorities of New Spain in getting his territory for colonization. In August, after Stephen Austin had come to agreement with Governor Martinez at San Antonio relative to the establishment of the colony, he had chosen that region between the Colorado and Brazos Rivers below San Antonio Road as the site for his colony where he was to be permitted to settle three hundred families. Each single man and each head of a family was to receive 640 acres with 320 acres allowed for a wife, 160 acres for each child and

80 acres for each slave. For such acreage, Austin was to receive 12½ cents per acre.

With its resident Viceroy's authority nullified and his life in jeopardy, Spain sent Juan O'Donoju from Spain as the new Viceroy; and he arrived at Vera Cruz in July, where he was captured and held in confinement until he signed the treaty of Cordoba, recognizing the independence of New Spain. On September 27, 1821 a provisional junta signed the "Act of Independence of the Mexican Empire." At that time Texas, along with a large portion of western North America, came under the control of the Mexican Republic. The occupation of many of its presidios ceased while the new government was attempting to organize and arrange its finances.[20]

---

1 *The Texas Almanac*, 1941-42, p. 46.

2 Inman, Henry, *The Old Santa Fe Trail*, pp. 29, 30: Colonel Henry Inman, Topeka, Kansas, February 13, 1897.

3 *Ibid.*, pp. 30-37.

4 Live Oak Creek enters the Pecos River in Crockett County, a few miles below Sheffield, Texas.

5 Don Amangual, Francisco, "Diary of the Incidents and Operations which took place in the Expedition made from the Province of Texas to the Province of New Mexico in Compliance with Superior Orders": University of Texas Archives, Barker Library.

6 Vincent, Benjamin, *Haydn's Dictionary of Dates:* 15th Edition: E. Moxon, Son & Co., London: 1, Amen Corner Paternoster Row — 1876.

7 Inman, Henry, as cited, pp. 38-40.

8 Chabot, F. C., *With the Makers of Texas*, pp. 75-77: Chabot, F. C., San Antonio, Texas, 1937; Wharton, Clarence, as cited, Vol. I, pp. 120-121.

9 Inman, Henry, as cited, pp. 40-41.

10 *Ibid.*

11 Wharton, Clarence, as cited, Vol. 1, p. 121.

12 *Texas Almanac, 1941-2*, p. 46.

13 Benton, Thomas H., *Thirty Years in the U.S. Senate*, Vol. I, pp.

15, 17: Appleton & Company, 346 and 348 Broadway, London: 16 Little Britain, 1854.

[14] Inman, Henry, as cited, p. 46, footnote.

[15] Coves, Elliott, *Journal of Jacob Fowler*, p. 20: Francis P. Harper, 1898, New York.

[16] Brown, John Henry, *Indian Wars and Pioneers of Texas*, p. 92: L. E. Daniel, Austin, Texas.

[17] *Ibid.*, p. 123.

[18] Bancroft, H. H., as cited, Vol. II, p. 51.

[19] Brown, John H., as cited, pp. 10, 189; Wharton, as cited, Vol. I, p. 24.

[20] *The Texas Almanac, 1941-42*, pp. 46-47.

Index

A. B. Draw: 161
Acatite la Grande: 143
Acoma (pueblo): 49, 58, 63, 79
Acorns: 17, 24, 158
Act of Independence of the Mexican Empire: 183, 184
Adaes (Indians): 84
Adams, John: 116, 130, 174
Aes (Indians): 84
Agarita: 16, 21, 27
Agua Bonita Springs: 160, 161
Aguage: 141
Aguaje del Tobaco: 146
Aguayo, Marquis de San Miguel de: 85, 86
Aguayo Mission. *See* San José y San Miguel de Aguayo
Alameda (pueblo): 60-61
Alamillo (pueblo): 59, 60, 77
Alamito Creek: 20, 50-51, 68, 86, 87, 94, 162
Alamo, The. *See* San Antonio de Valero

Alamo (Mexico): 140
Alarcón, Martín de: 84
Albany, New York: 54
Albemarle, North Carolina: 57
Albemarle Point (South Carolina): 57
Albuquerque, New Mexico: 50, 109
Alder: 27
Allende, Ignacio María de: 182
"Alliance" (ship): 126
Allison ranch: 164
Alsate Creek: 164
Altar (presidio): 108
Alto, Texas: 75
Alvarez de Pineda, Alonso: 39
Amangual, Francisco: 170-172
American Revolution: 113-131
Amistad Dam: 2
Anacahuita: 17
André, John: 127-128
Animals: prehistoric, 1-2; in West Texas, 6; Indians use of, 18-19
Antelope: 2, 6, 155

Antelope Springs: 161
Antelopes (Comanche band): 152
Ants: as source of honey, 17, 23
Apaches (Indians): and mescal, 14; burial of, 29; smoke signals of, 29; in revolt against Spanish, 58, 72-73; origin of name of, 64; attack Domínguez de Mendoza, 70, 71; locations of, 72, 81, 92, 94, 103, 136, 152; missions for, 72, 99-100; Roque de Madrid's campaign against, 73; as horse thieves, 74; missions destroyed by, 81, 99; Flores' battle with, 86; missions abandoned because of, 86, 93; Spanish alliance with, 91, 95, 96, 97, 136; Bustillo's defeat of, 92; attack San Antonio, 92; presidios built as protection against, 93, 107; and San Saba settlements, 96; attack Belén, 97; Rubí recommends war on, 104; Ugalde's campaigns against, 139-147 *passim;* captives of, 147, 172; guide Amangual, 172. See also Faraones; Hapaches; Lipans; Lipiyans; Llaneros; Mescaleros; Vaqueros; Warm Springs Apaches
—as enemies of other tribes: of Jediondas, 70; of Comanches, 81, 91, 93, 95, 96, 100, 103, 135, 136, 147, 152; of Jumanos, 86; of Cíbolas, 93; of Northern Indians, 99, 107
— raids of: in Mexico, 57, 67, 73-74, 93, 96, 136, 139, 140; in New Mexico, 53, 77, 79; in Texas, 86, 95, 139, 141
Apalachen province: 40
Apodaca, Juan Ruíz de: 182
Appalachian Mountains: 115
Aranamos (Indians): 87
Arizona: Marcos de Niza in, 46-47; Espejo in, 50
"Ark" (ship): 55
Arkansas River: Spanish fight Comanches on, 95; Spanish chase Comanches to, 99; Zebulon Pike on, 169; Becknell on, 174; Fowler's explorations of, 181
Armed Neutrality Act: 126

Arnold, Benedict: 127-128
Arroyo Hondo: 169
Ascue (Spaniard): 57
Ash: 154, 158
Augusta, Georgia: 124
Aury, Luis: 180-181
Austin, Moses: 183
Austin, Stephen F.: 183-184
Avery Canyon: 162
Azaleas: 24
Aztecs (Indians): 35-39

Baca, Antonio: 148
Bakersfield, Texas (San Ygnacio): 70
Balcones Research Center (Austin, Texas): 2
Balmorhea, Texas: 101
Balmorhea Springs: 50, 51
Barksdale, Texas: 99
Barrel cactus. See Cactus
Basket Makers (Indians): 9-10, 42, 44
Basket making: 26-27, 28
Baton Rouge, Louisiana: 125
Baumgardner, Ray: 155
Bay City, Texas: 55
Beans: 43, 44
Beard, James: 180
Bear grass: 26
Beaubien, Charles: 173
Becknell, William: 174
Belén (presidio): 97
Beltran, Father: 73
Bennington, Vermont: 122
Beranger, M.: 85
Bermuda: 122
Bernalillo, New Mexico: 47
Berroteran, Captain José: 91-92
Betanillas Canyon: 140
Béxar. See San Antonio, Texas
Bibit (Indians): 58
Big Bend (Texas): O. W. Williams on, 5; cinnabar found in, 27; cliff paintings of, 28; O. W. Williams surveys in, 31; Cabeza de Vaca in, 43; Indian cultivation of corn in, 44; Spanish reconnoitering of, 93; Ugalde's expedition to, 143-145
Big Lake, Texas: 98

188

Bigote (Lipan chief): 101
Big Spring, Texas: 160
Biloxi, Mississippi: 81-82
Birds: 2, 6
Birth control pill: 25
Bison. *See* Buffalo
Black brush: 4
Black Gap: 27
Blackhawk (Oregon firm): 7-8
Black locust: 9
Blazing star: 22, 23
Bluewood: 16
Boca de Tres Picos: 140
Bois d'Arc. *See* Osage Orange
Bois d'Arc Corner: 164
Bolivar Point: 182
Bolsón de Mapimí: Spanish propose expedition to, 136; Ugalde in, 139, 140, 143
Bone Spring: 161, 162
"Bon Homme Richard" (ship): 126
Boone, Daniel: 114
Boonesborough, Kentucky: 122, 124
Boston, Massachusetts: 116-117, 119, 120
Brandywine Creek: 122
Brant, Joseph (Mohawk chief): 129
Brazos River: 48, 62
Bridger, Jim: 173
Brown, M.D. (Chico): 19
Brownwood, Texas: 56, 86
Bruchlos, Baron: 15
Bryant, Vaughn M., Jr.: 2
Bucareli: dispersed settlers of, 132; locations of, 135, 139; Mezierres at, 137, 138
Buckelew, F. M.: 11
Buena Vista, Texas: 51
Buffalo: prehistoric, 2; locations of, 18, 50; Indian use of, 18-19; fuel made from chips of, 26; Spanish attempt to capture, 53
Buffalo Eaters (Comanche band): 152
Buford, Abraham: 126
Bunker Hill (Massachusetts): 119
Burlington, New Jersey: 178
Burr, Aaron: 177
Burro Mesa: 161
Bustillo y Ceballos, Juan Antonio: 92

Butler, John: 123
Buttercups: 24
Butterfly bush: 17, 19
Buzzard: 6

Cabeza de Vaca, Alvaro Núñez: 9, 30, 41-45, 46, 48, 49, 50, 63
Cabot, John: 54
Cabras (Texas): 141
Cacaxtles (Indians): 57
Caches, The: 174
Cactus: 4, 16, 17, 23, 44; barrel cactus, 26, 28; petaya, 16, 17, 21; prickly pear, 21, 27, 41; tasajillo, 5; tunas, 7, 9, 16, 42, 166. *See also* Peyote
Cahokia, Illinois: 124
Calabashes: 43
Calahorra y Sáenz, Joseph de: 99
Calhoun, John C.: 179
Calleros, Dr. Cleofas: 55
Calvert, Leonard: 55
Camalote: 69
Camargo, Diego de: 39
Camargo, Mexico: 39
Cambridge, Massachusetts: 120
Camden, South Carolina: 127, 129
Camel (prehistoric): 1, 2
Camp Peña Colorada: 162
Canada: 120-131 *passim*, 171
Canadian River: 171
Canagra: 19
Canajoharie, New York: 124, 125
Canary Islands: 92
Candelaria: *See* Nuestra Señora de la Candelaria
Canedo, Sancho de: 39
Cannibalism: among Aztecs, 37; among Ascue's Indian allies, 57; among Lipans, 100; and Mescaleros, 101
Carlsbad, New Mexico: 100
Carmen Mountains (Mexico): 140
Carransa, Guero: 14
Carrizo: 8
Carson, Kit: 173
Casas Grandes (Mexico): 63
Caschotethkes (Comanche Band): 152
Castaño de Sosa, Gaspar: 30, 51-52, 172

189

Castillo, Alonso del: 43
Castillo, Diego: 55-56
Castine, Maine: 125
Castle Gap: 70, 88, 158, 160
Castolon, Texas: 161
Catclaw: 4
Cattail (tule): 10, 19, 20, 69, 70, 156, 166
Cattle: wild herds in Texas, 137
Caughnawaga (Canada): 129
Cave paintings: 27-28
Cayudutta Creek: 129
Cedar Spring: 42
Cendés (Indians): 146
Centralia Draw: 88, 160
Century plant: 21, 23. *See also* Lechuguilla
Cereus gregii: 17
Cerrillo Mountains: 65
Cerrillos, New Mexico: 65. *See also* Los Cerrillos
Cerro Gordo (presidio): 107-109, 142
Cervid (prehistoric): 2
Chama River: 51
Chambers, Samuel: 180
Chamiza: 20
Chamois: 30
Chandler, M. T. W.: 109
Chaparro prieto: as oak, 29; as Mimosa, 34
Charamuscos Mountains: 108, 140
Charleston, South Carolina: 57, 121, 126, 130
Charlottesville, Virginia: 129
Chayopin (Texas): 141
Chemung, New York: 125
Cherries: 16, 24
Cherry Valley, New York: 124
Chesapeake Bay: 122, 129, 130, 178
Chester, Pennsylvania: 55
Cheutis (Indians): 92
Chibitty, Rev. Steve: 13
Chihuahua, city of: 103, 170
Chihuahua, state of (Nueva Vizcaya): soldiers in, 49, 142; Indian raids in, 73-74, 92, 136, 152-165 *passim*; presidios of, 108-109; Bancroft's report on, 109; Kiowa name for, 152; silver mines of, 173
Chilicotal Mountains: 162
Chilicotal Spring: 162

Chilipitín: 19, 23
Chinara (Indians): 72
China tree: 26
Chippawa, plains of: 178
Chisos Mountains: 5, 108, 143-145, 158
Chittam bush: 8
Chouteau, Auguste P.: 180
Chowan River: 57
Cíbola, Seven Cities of: 46-47, 53
Cíbolas (Indians): 20, 93, 94
Cicuya (Cicuye): 47, 50. *See also* Pecos (pueblo and Indians)
Ciénaga Creek: 87
Cieneguilla (New Mexico): 77
Cimarron River: 174
Cinnabar: 27
Ciudad de Victoria (Durango): 62
Clark, George Rogers: 124, 126, 130
Clark Spring (New Mexico): 100
Clark, W. P.: 29
Clay, Henry: 179
"Clermont" (steamboat): 175
Clinton, Henry: 128
Clinton, James: 125
Coahuila: 92, 108-109, 138, 139, 140
Coal: 175
Coatesville, Pennsylvania: 175
Cobleskill (New York): 123, 124
Cochiti (pueblo and Indians): 58, 61, 65, 77, 79
Cochran Mountains: 162
Cocoma (Indians): 58
Colorado River (Texas): called Nueces River, 55; pearls in, 56; Guadalajara's expedition to, 56, 71; described, 64; Domínguez de Mendoza visits, 68, 71, 74; Amangual's expedition to, 171
Colorado, state of: 47, 181
Columbia River: 169
Comanches (Indians): burial of, 29-30; attack Pecos Pueblo, 53; Shoshonean relationship of, 64; as horse thieves, 74, 138, 148; attack Taos, 81; locations of, 81, 94, 136, 152-153; Apache conflicts with, 91, 92-93, 94-95, 96, 100, 103, 135-136, 147; Apache-Spanish alliance against, 91, 96; and Lipans, 94-95, 100; encroach upon Bexar,

190

95; raid New Mexico, 95, 99, 109-110, 135; Spanish defeat of, 109-110; and San Saba, 96-97, 101, 103, 104-105; Spanish treaties with, 99, 107, 136, 152; attack missions, 103, 136; war trails of, 103, 151-166 *passim*; shields of, 103, 153-154; weapons of, 103, 153-154, 164; horsemanship of, 103, 154-155; raid into Mexico, 136, 152-166 *passim;* Tawakonis complain of, 137; and Mezierres, 138; captives of, 138, 152, 165-166; attack Menchaca, 142; attack Aguaje de Tobaco, 146; and Ugalde, 147; visit San Antonio, 147-148; and Philip Nolan, 148; raid Spanish settlements, 148; bands of, 152; paint uses of, 153; dwellings of, 153; dress of, 153, 156, 171; horse gear of, 156; food of, 156, 158, 166; Amangual's visit with, 170-172
Comanche Peak: 27
Comanche Spring (in Big Bend): 28
Comanche Spring (New Mexico): 100
Comanche Springs (Fort Stockton): Indian trail from Cordova Lake to, 20; named San Juan del Río, 69; springs of, 88; on Comanche War Trail, 161; Osage Orange trees near, 164
Compostela (Mexico): 61
Concho River (Texas): 55, 71. *See also* Middle Concho River
Conchos (Indians): 10, 49, 56, 63, 72
Conchos River (Mexico): 48, 56, 63
Concord, Massachusetts: 119
Conejos (Indians): 98
Conewawah: 125
Connecticut: 55, 115, 175-176, 179
Continental Congress: first, 116-117; second, 120, 121
Continental Divide: 79
Copper oxide: 27
Cordero (Comanche chief): 170-172
Cordero, Joe: 24
Cordero, Manuel Antonio: 148
Córdoba, treaty of: 184

Cordova Lake: 20
Corn: 20, 41, 43, 44
Cornwallis, Charles: 127, 129-130
Coronado, Francisco Vázquez de: 30, 47, 48, 61
Coronado Museum (New Mexico): 47
Corpus Christi de la Isleta. *See* Isleta del Sur
Cortez, Hernando: 36-39, 48
Cotton: Aztecs' use of, 35; introduced in Georgia, 174
Cotton gin: 174
Cottonwood Creek: 161
Cowpens, South Carolina: 114, 127
Cox, Thomas Washington: 131
Coyote (Lipan village): 100
Coyotes: 6
Crane County: 20, 70, 98
Creosote: 25, 30
Crockett, David: 114
Croix, Theodore de: 109
Croton Springs: 161
Crown Point, New York: 120
Crusate, Domingo de: 73, 77
Cuatro Ciénegas: 140
Cuba: 36, 37
Cuchanec, Cuchanticas (Comanche band): 152
Cuiteas (Indians): 56, 64
Culberson County: salt lakes of, 20
Culiacán: 41, 45, 46, 61
Cuyamungue (pueblo): 77

Daughters of Founders and Patriots of America: 64
Davis Mountains: trees of, 158
Declaration of Independence (American): 121
Deer: 2, 6, 44, 155
Delaware (Indians): 126
Delaware, state of: 55, 176
Del Norte Gap: 162
Denmark: 126
de Soto. *See* Soto, Hernando de
Detroit, Michigan: 130
Devil's River: 41-42, 51-52, 63, 137
Devil's root. *See* Peyote
Dewberries: 16
Dexter, New Mexico: 100

191

Diamond Y Draw: 20, 51
Díaz, Melchior: 46-47
Dientes Negros (Indians): 73
Dinosaur: 1
Dittert, Dr. Alfred E., Jr.: 7
Dogs: 52
Dogwood: 8, 10, 23, 27, 103, 154
Domínguez de Mendoza, Juan: with Guadalajara, 56; scouts pueblos, 60-61; West Texas expedition of, 68-73; on Colorado River, 74
Douglas spruce: 158
"Dove" (ship): 55
Drake, Sir Francis: 54, 57
Dryden, Texas: 92
Dugout Wells: 162
Du Pont de Nemours and Company: 176
Durango, city of: 48, 62, 63
Durango, state of: 156
Dutch: New York settlements of, 54; aid Spanish monarchy, 67; in American Revolution, 126, 128-129, 130
Dyes: 27

Eagle: 6
Eagle Nest Canyon: 28
Eagle Pass, Texas: 41
Eastern Gamma grass: 20
Edwards County: 41
El Aguila: 136
El Apóstol Santiago (Julimes rancherías): Domínguez de Mendoza at, 68, 71
El Apóstol Santiago (mission): established, 72; Vidaurre and Rábago at, 93-94
El Cañón Missions: established, 99-100
El Cerro Hueco: 136
El Diablo: 136
El Mocho (Tonkawa chief): 139, 141
El Morro (New Mexico): 79
El Paso del Norte: Espejo at, 50, 63; Oñate at, 51; mission established at, 56-57; Jumanos plea to Spanish at, 68; Indians killed at, 73; New Mexico reoccupied by residents of, 81; Indian raids at, 86; Mescaleros defeated by Spanish from, 100-101; garrison moved from, 108. See also Juarez, Mexico
El Paso valley: 72
El Valle (New Mexico): 107
Elephant Mountain: 162
Elephant (prehistoric): 2
Emory, William H.: 160
English: early colonies of, 54, 55, 57, 93; aid Spanish monarchy, 67; and American Revolution, 113-131; Parliamentary acts of, 115-116; and War of 1812, 176-180
Escanjaques (Indians): 64
Espada Mission. See San Francisco de la Espada
Espejo, Antonio de: 10, 30, 49-50
Espíritu Santo. See Nuestra Señora del Espíritu Santo de Zúñiga; Santa María de Loreto de la Bahía del Espíritu Santo
Espíritu Santo, Bay of (Saint Bernard): 85
Estevanico: 43, 46, 50
Eutaw Springs (South Carolina): 130
Evergreen sumac: 8

Faraones (Indians): 72, 77, 100
Ferdinand VII: 181
Fire-making: 28-29
Flores, Nicolás: 86
Florida: Spanish exploration of, 39-40; de Soto in, 48; Saint Augustine established in, 49; Spanish plan invasion of, 125; U.S. acquires, 130, 181; British forced out of, 178
Flute: Indian use of, 57
Fort Bowyer: 178
Fort Davis: 101
Fort Dayton: 129
Fort Edward: 122
Fort Erie: 178
Fort George: 177
Fort Henry: 122
Fort Hunter: 128, 129
Fort Leaton: 72, 98
Fort Meigs: 178
Fort Mimms: 178
Fort Nassau: 54
Fort Nelson: 124

192

Fort New Gottenberg: 55
Fort Plain: 129
Fort Rensselaer: 129
Fort Saint Joseph: 128
Fort Saint Louis: 74-75, 86, 88, 135
Fort Saint Louis de Carlorette: 84
Fort Schuyler. *See* Fort Stanwix
Fort Stanwix (Fort Schuyler): 122, 124, 127, 129
Fort Stockton. *See* Comanche Springs
Fort Washington: 121-122
Fowler, Jacob: 181
Franklin, Benjamin: 113, 121, 123, 130, 174
Fray Cristóbal Mountains: 66
Fray Cristóbal (New Mexico): 58, 59, 65-66, 77
Fredericksburg, Virginia: 129
French: in Florida, 49; at Parris Island, 57; in Texas, 67, 70, 74-75, 81-82, 85, 95, 105; explore Mississippi River, 70; reinforce Louisiana, 84; give land to Spain, 104 and American Revolution, 123-130 *passim*; sell Louisiana to U.S., 169, 174-175
Frenchtown, Michigan: 178
"Frolic" (sloop): 177
Fromme, Ed: 24
Fronteras (presidio): 108
Fulton, New York: 128
Fulton, Robert: 175

Galisteo (pueblo): 53, 58, 65, 79, 95
Gallegos, Hermando: 49
Galveston Bay: French at, 85; Dr. Long at, 182; Mrs. Long at, 183
Galveston Island: Lafitte on, 182
Garay, Francisco: 39
García, Juan Antonio: 82
Garza Falcón, Miguel de la: 92
Gatún: 5
Genesee River: 125
Geniocane (Indians): 58
Georgia: 93, 124
Gerald, Rex E.: 72
Germans: in American Revolution, 120, 122
Germantown, Pennsylvania: 123
Ghent, Treaty of: 179
Gibraltar: 125

Girty, Simon: 126
Glass Mountains: 32, 161
Glenn Spring: 162
Goatbush: 23, 25
Gold: in Apalachen province, 40; near Pike's Peak, 170
Goliad, Texas. *See* Santa María de Loreto de la Bahía del Espíritu Santo
Gooseberry: 16
Gosnold, Bartholomew: 54
Gourds: 28, 44
Government Gardens (Texas): 164
Graham, Joe: 160
Granada (West Indies): 125
Grand Canyon: 47
Granjeno: 17, 25
Grants, New Mexico: 53
Grapes: 16-17, 21
Grapevine Hills: 161
Grasses: 20-21
Great Bridge, Virginia: 120
Green Mountain Boys: 127
Greene, Nathanael: 127
Greensboro, North Carolina: 129
Gregorio, Padre: 82
Grierson Spring: 70-71, 88, 160
Grijalva, Juan: 37
Grunidora, Mexico: 142
Guadalajara, Diego de: 56, 71
Guadalupe Cathedral (Juarez, Mexico): 57
Guadalupe Mission. *See* Nuestra Señora de Guadalupe
Guadalupe Mountains: Cabeza de Vaca's route through, 41; Spanish propose expedition to, 136; Mescaleros near, 137; Ugalde's expedition to, 146-147; Amangual in, 172
Guadalupe Peak: 77, 89
Guadalupe River: 94, 141
Guadiana (Durango): 62
Guajillo: 42, 45
Guajoquilla (presidio): 108, 140
Guatemala: 84
Guayule: 30
Gueiquesale (Indians): 58
Guerrero, Vicente: 182
Guilford Court House (Greensboro, North Carolina): 129
Gulf of California (South Sea): 53

193

Gulf of Mexico: 39
Gunpowder: 114, 117, 176
Gutiérrez, José Bernardo: 177, 180
Gypsum: 27

Hacienda de Amelo: 140
Hacienda de Ciénegas: 140
Hacienda de Cuatro Ciénegas: 143
Hacienda de Sardinas: 143
Hackberry Creek: 161, 164
Hale, Nathan: 122
Hancock, John: 121
Haozous, Sam: 12-13
Hapaches (Indians): 68
Harpersfield: 125
Harrison, William Henry: 178
Hartford, Connecticut: 55, 179
Hawikuh (pueblo): 47
Hedeoma reverchoni: 17
Hell's Half Acre: 164
Hematite: 43
Henry, Patrick: 115, 116-119
Hidalgo, Francisco: 82
Hidalgo, Miguel: 173, 177, 180, 182
Hignett, Mrs. S. F.: 64
Hill, Robert: 41
Hillin, T. W.: 11-12
Hinde, Frank: 12, 22, 23
Hobkirk's Hill: 129
Hoffman, Dr. George: 7
Honey. *See* Ants
Honey Eaters (Comanche band): 152
Honeysuckle: 27
Hopi (pueblos): 58. *See also* Moqui
Horehound: 23
Horse and Hatchet treaty: 95
Horse beans: 20
Horse Mountain: 161-162, 164
Horsehead Crossing: 158, 160
Horses: prehistoric, 1, 2; wild herds of, 137
Hot Springs, Texas: 28
Howard's Well: 42
Hudson River: 120, 121, 123, 126, 128
Hueco Mountains: 77, 89. *See also* El Cerro Hueco
Hueco Tanks: 28
Huitzilipochtli: 36
Hyacinth: 16

Iberville, d', Pierre le Moyne: 81
Idoyago: 93-94, 98
Iguala, Plan of: 182
Independence Spring: 158, 160
Indian breadroot: 17, 20
Indians: food of, 9-21 *passim*, 43; clothing of, 10, 19; dwellings of, 10, 29, 42, 70; cures of, 17-30 *passim*; fishing methods of, 18; tanning methods of, 18-19; alcoholic beverages of, 21; containers of, 26-27, 28; fire-making methods of, 26, 28-29; dyes and paints of, 27; cave paintings of, 27-28; and smoke signals, 29; burial of, 29-30, 44; metallurgy of, 35; and use of travois, 52; first efforts in Texas to Christianize, 55, 64; captives of, 100, 109, 138, 144, 145, 147, 152, 165-166, 172; shields of, 103, 153-154; in American Revolution, 122-130 *passim*. *See also under tribal names*
— weapons of: bows and arrows, 2-4, 6-9, 18, 19, 52-53, 103; atlatl, 7; boomerang, 9; lance, 9, 103; club, 42; flint knives, 42
Indian tea plant: 27
Inkberry: 27
Inscription Rock: 53
Intolerable Acts: 116
Iraan, Texas: 101
Iron: 175
Iron Mountain: 43
Isambanbi (Comanche chief): 171
Isleta (New Mexico): 59, 60, 61, 62, 65, 79
Isleta del Sur (Texas): 60, 62. *See also* Ysleta, Texas
Iturbide, Agustín de: 182

Jackson, Andrew: 178, 179, 182
Jamestown, Virginia: 54
Jamestown Island, Virginia: 129
Janos (Indians): 72, 73
Janos Mission. *See* La Soledad de los Janos
Janos (presidio): 103, 108
Japonin (Saponin): 26
"Java" (sloop): 177
Javelina. *See* Peccary

Jay, John: 130
Jeapa (Indians): 58
Jediondos (Indians): 70-71, 88
Jefferson, Thomas: 116, 169, 174
Jemez (pueblo): 53, 58, 79
Jerky: 18
Jersey, Island of: 124
Jesuits: 70
Jocome (Indians): 72
Johnson Hall (New York): 129
Jones, Dr. Charles: 15-16
Jones, John Paul: 122, 126
Jones, William Moses: 75
Jongopavi (pueblo): 79
Jordan Gap: 162
Jornado del Muerto: 60, 77
Juanita Valley (Pennsylvania): 175
Juarez, Mexico: founding of, 56; cathedral of, 57. See also El Paso del Norte
Julimeños (Indians): 87
Julimes (Indians): 68, 72, 86, 100-101, 103, 108
Jumanos (Indians): 50, 55, 56, 63, 68, 72, 86, 92. See also Xumanos
Juniper: 17, 27
Jupiter's staff: 23

Kanadaseagea (Seneca capital): 125
Kansa (Indians): 64
Kaolin: 27
Karankawas (Indians): 87, 94
Kaskakia (Illinois): 124
Kentucky: nitre production in, 176
Kentucky rifles: 114
Keresan (Indians): 65. See also Queres
Kiamichi (geological formation): 27
Kincaid Draw: 162
Kingdom of Santander: 170
King Mountain (Texas): 70, 88
King's Mountain (South Carolina): 114, 127
Kiowas (Indians): 152, 165
Kiowa Apaches (Indians): 152
Kokernot Springs (San Lorenzo): 20, 43, 51, 68
Kuaua (pueblo): 47

La Bahía Presidio. See Santa María de Loreto de la Bahía del Espíritu Santo
Lacky, Jim: 22
La Cola: 136
La Cruz (Mexico): 140
La Junta de los Ríos (Presidio): Salt Trail from, 20; Cabeza de Vaca in vicinity of, 41, 44, 50; Fray López party at, 49; named by Espejo, 50; Domínguez de Mendoza in vicinity of, 68, 73; missions in vicinity of, 72, 82, 86, 90, 94, 98; presidios of, 93, 97, 98, 103, 108, 145-146; Idoyago visits Indians near, 94; Mirabel's expedition from, 101; Rodríguez' expedition from, 101; Comanche War Trail near, 162
La Salienta: 59-60
La Salle, Sieur de: 70, 74-75, 88
La Soledad de los Janos (Mexico): 60, 73
Lafayette, Marquis de: 129
Lafitte, Jean: 180-181, 182
Laguna de Guzmán: 108
Lajitas Ford: 161
Lajitas, Texas: 44, 94
Lake Borgne: 179
Lake Champlain: 120-121, 127, 178
Lake Tezcuco: 35, 36
Lake Tioga: 125
Lancaster, Pennsylvania: 175, 176
Langtry, Texas: 91, 94, 160
Laredo, Texas: 148
Larios, Father: 54
Larkspur: 25
Las Amarillas. See San Saba Presidio
Las Barrancas (pueblo): 77
Las Mulas (Texas): 141
Las Peñuelas (New Mexico): 77
Laudoniere, Rene de: 49
Laurens, Henry: 130
Lava beds (New Mexico): 79
Lechuguilla: 10, 16, 21, 25, 26
Leeward Islands: 130
Lemon verbena: 25
León, Alonso de: 74-75
Leoncita Springs: 20, 43, 51, 68, 87
Leon Creek: 170
Leon Farms: 24

195

Leon Springs: 20, 51, 69, 87
Lewis and Clark Expedition: 169
Lexington, Massachusetts: 119
Licking Valley, Kentucky: 126
Lime: 27
Limonite: 27, 43
Limpia Creek: 50
Lincoln, Benjamin: 126
Lipan Crossing: 160
Lipans (Indians): food of, 11-12, 17; locations of, 58, 100, 101, 137, 139; origin of name, 65; and the French, 82; Spanish relations with, 87, 152; missions established for, 91, 104; defeated by Bustillo, 92; raids of, 92, 136, 139; as enemies of other Indians, 94-95, 100, 104, 139, 152; defeated by Ugalde, 147
Lipiyan (Indians): 147
Little Harbor (Rye, New Hampshire): 54
Little River: 92
Little Rock (New Mexico): 79
Live Oak Creek: 42, 160, 172
Liver Eaters (Comanche band): 152
Livingston, Robert R.: 175
Llaneros (Indians): 147
Llano River: 95
Loma Pinta (Lipan village): 101
Long, Dr. James: 182-183
Long, Mrs. Jane: 183
Long, Stephen H.: 181
López, Father Nicolás: 68, 72-73
López, Fray Francisco: 49, 50
Loreto (La Junta mission): 82, 90
Loreto (presidio). *See* Santa María de Loreto de la Bahía del Espíritu Santo
Los Cerrillos (New Mexico): 58, 65
Los Gallos (Mexico): 183
Los Médanos (New Mexico): 100
Lotus: 16
Louisiana Purchase: 169, 174-175, 181
Louisville, Kentucky: 124
Loving, New Mexico: 100
Lower Fort (New York): 128
Lozier Canyon: 160
Luján, Natividad: 14
Luna, Tristán de: 49

McBryde, W. D.: 21
McGee, Augustus: 176-177
McKenzie (Mackinzie) Crossing: 161
McKenzie (Mackinzie), General R. S.: 161
McKnight, Robert: 180
Madison, James: 179
Maine: 125, 175
Maize: 20, 156
Mamillaria grahami: 17
Mammoth: 2
Mangus Colorado: 12
Manhattan. *See* New York City
Mansos (Indians): 50, 56-57, 58, 60, 63, 68, 72
Manuel Benevides. *See* San Carlos
Marathon, Texas: 30, 162, 164
Maravillas Draw: 161, 162
Maravillas Gap: 162
"Marechal d'Esdres" (ship): 85
Martin (American soldier): 126
Martín, Hernando: 55-56
Martin, Josiah: 120
Martínez, Antonio María: 183
Martinique: 126
Maryland: 175, 176
Mascale: 10
Massachusetts: 55, 175, 179
Massanet, Father Damian: 75, 82
Matagorda Bay: 74, 85, 86, 87, 88
Maxon Spring: 164
"Mayflower" (ship): 54
Medina, Battle of: 177
Meeks, Jack: 12
Menard, Texas: 96, 106
Menchaca, José: 142
Mendinueta: 135
Mendoza. *See* Domínguez de Mendoza, Juan; Zaldívar Mendoza, Vicente de Menéndez de Avilés, Pedro: 49
Mercury. *See* Quicksilver
Mesa de Angular: 44
Mesa del Cangelón: 65
Mescal, Mescal button. *See* Peyote
Mescaleros (Indians): food of, 17; alcoholic drinks of, 21; origin of name, 26, 92; locations of, 26, 137, 142; Vargas' party among, 77; Mexican raids of, 92, 136, 139, 142; defeated by Spanish and

196

Julimes, 100-101; threaten Romero's party, 101; Ugalde's expeditions against, 139-147 *passim;* captives of, 144, 145
Mescal pit. *See* Sotol pit
Mesquite: 7, 9, 19, 20, 21, 23, 26
Mexía (New Mexico): 77, 79
Mexican buckeye: 18
Mexican Moon: 156-157
Mexican persimmon: 17, 23
Mexican tea plant: 19
Mexicans, remedies of: 23, 24
Mexico. *See* New Spain
Mexico City: 30, 35-38, 48
Meyers Spring: 28, 158, 160
Meyersville, Texas: 87
Mezierres, A.: 137-139, 168
Mezquites (Indians): 98
Miami River: 178
Michigan: 128, 130
Middle Concho River: 71, 88, 172
Middle Fort (New York): 128
Middleburgh, New York: 128
Midland Woman: 1-2
Mier Expedition: 131
Milkweed: 22, 24
Mimosa laxiflora: 34
Mirabel, Romero: 101
Miranda, Bernardo de: 95
Miraval, Joseph Antonio: 100
Mississippi River: 139, 180
Mississippi, state of: 81-82
Missouri River: 169
Missouri, state of: 181
Mistletoe: 24
Mobile, Alabama: 125
Mohawk (Indians): 129
Mohawk River: 128
Monclova, Mexico: 51, 91, 108, 140
Monmouth, New Jersey: 123
Montana: 169
Montezuma: 37-38, 48
Montgomery, J. M.: 32
Montreal: 120
Monument Draw: 162
Monument Springs: 51
Mooney, John: 13
Moore ranch: 164
Moore's Creek Bridge (South Carolina): 120
Moqui (Hopi Indians): 79

Mora (Texas): 141
Morfi, Juan Agustín: 132
Moscoso de Alvarado, Luis de: 30, 48, 62
Mosquitos: 25
Moss, Joe: 161
Mountain laurel: 21, 24
Mountain mahogany: 27
Mountain Men: 173
Mountain pink: 23
Movano, Sierra: 136
Moving in a circle (Comanche band): 152
Mulberry: 9, 16
Mushroom, sacred. *See* Peyote
Mustard plant: 26

Nacogdoches, Texas. *See* Nuestra Señora de Guadalupe de los Nacogdoches
Nail, Sam: 44
Nambe (pueblo): 58, 65, 79, 109
Narváez, Pánfilo de: 38, 39-41, 49
Nassau: 120
Natchez, Mississippi: 182
Natchitoches Island: 82, 84
Natchitoches (Louisiana): 84, 85, 87
Natoges (Indians): 72
Navigation Act: 115
Nayarit, Jalisco: 13
Nazones (Indians): 84
Neches River: 75, 84
Nets 7, 9, 18
New Braunfels, Texas: 41
New Hampshire: 54
New Jersey: 175
New London, Connecticut: 120
New Mexico: Spanish exploration of, 47; Oñate's contract to settle, 51; Spanish recapture of, 75, 77, 79, 81; Indian treaties with, 99, 107; Comanche raids in, 109-110, 135
"New Netherlands" (ship): 54
New Orleans, Battle of: 179-180, 182
"New Orleans" (steamboat): 175
New Spain (Mexico): 152, 173, 180, 181-182, 184
New York City: 54, 121-122, 126, 131, 174, 175

New York, state of: 54, 121, 125, 128, 168, 175
Newfoundland: 131
Newport, Rhode Island: 123, 126
Newton: 126
Nightshade: 25
Nine Mile Mesa: 161
Nine-Point Draw: 161
Ninety-Six, South Carolina: 129
Nit-agende (Indians): 146
Nitre: 176
Niza, Marcos de: 46-47
Noachis (Indians): 84
Nocona, Texas: 97
Noconys (Comanche band): 152
Nolan, Philip: 148, 169
North Carolina: 57, 127, 129, 168
North Sea: 130
Nova Scotia: 120, 122
Nueces River: 99, 101, 103, 104, 136-137. *See also* Colorado River
Nuestra Señora Begoña del Cuchillo Parado: 82, 90
Nuestra Señora de Aranzazu: 82, 90
Nuestra Señora de Guadalupe (La Junta mission): 82, 90, 94, 97, 98
Nuestra Señora de Guadalupe de los Nacogdoches: 84, 132, 135, 138-139, 148
Nuestra Señora de Guadalupe del Paso: 56-57, 60, 61, 73
Nuestra Señora de la Candelaria: 93, 95, 99, 100, 135
Nuestra Señora de la Purísima Concepción: 94, 95, 133, 141
Nuestra Señora de los Dolores: 84, 139
Nuestra Señora de los Dolores de los Tejas (presidios): 84
Nuestra Señora del Espíritu Santo de Zúñiga: 86, 87, 94, 135
Nuestra Señora Pilar del Paso del Río del Norte (presidio): 72
Nuestro Padre San Francisco de los Sumas: 60
Nueva Vizcaya. *See* Chihuahua; Sonora
Nuevo Almadén: 51
Nuevo León: 51, 74, 140, 170
Nuget Mountain: 162

Oak: 24, 29. *See also* Acorns
Oates' Hills: 27, 43
Ochre: 27, 153
Oconór, Hugo: 108, 135, 136
O'Donojú, Juan: 184
Ohio: 126, 169, 175
Ohio River: 124, 126, 175, 176
Ojo Caliente (New Mexico): 99
Ojo Pescada (New Mexico): 79
Oklahoma: Spanish exploration of, 47
Old Butcher Knife: 23-24
Old Salt Trail: 20
Oleander: 25
Oñate, Juan de: 30, 51, 52, 53-54, 75
Oneidas (Indians): 125, 128
Onion, wild: 16
Onondaga (Indians): 124
Organ Mountains: 136
Oriskany, New York: 122
Ortega, Father Juan de: 13, 54-55
Osage Orange: 8, 153, 164-165
Otermín, Antonio de: 59-61
Otumba (Mexico): 39

Painted Cave: 28
Painted Springs: 28
Paisano Pass: 68, 87
Palatine, New York: 128
Pale dock: 26
Panhandle and Santa Fe Railroad: 162
Panhandle (Texas): 47, 85
Panther: 6
Pánuco: 39
Paradise Draw: 162
Parilla, Diego Ortiz: 96-99, 138
Paris, France: treaty signed at, 130
Parral, Mexico: 48, 63, 77
Parras, Mexico: 140
Parris Island: 57
Paso del Chisos: 140
Pataquilla (Texas): 141
Patillo, S. D.: 44
Patos, Mexico: 140
Pawnees (Indians): 180
Pazaquantes (Indians): 10, 49
"Peacock" (ship): 177
Pearls: 56

198

Peccary (javalina): 2, 99
Pecos (pueblo and Indians): 30, 47, 50, 52, 53, 58, 77, 81, 95, 109. *See also* Cicuya
Pecos Mission: 100
Pecos River: Salt Crossing of, 20; Indian paintings near, 28; Pontoon Crossing of, 41; and Cabeza de Vaca, 42-43; and Espejo, 50; as Río de las Vacas, 50; and Sosa, 51-52; Spanish priests on, 54; Guadalajara on, 56; as Salado River, 69-70; salt deposits near, 69-70, 101; Vargas on 79; as Río Puerco, 98-99; Ugalde on, 146, 147; description of, 98, 158; Spanish plan expedition to, 136; Mescaleros and Lipans located near, 137; Mezierres' proposed expedition to 138; Apache raids on, 139; Amangual on, 171, 172; as Comanche-Apache boundary, 172
Pecos Spring: 158
Pedernales River: 147, 170
Peña Blanca Creek: 164
Peña Colorada Draw: 162
Peña Colorada Spring: 161, 162
Penatekas (Comanche band): 152
Pendleton, Edmund: 116
Pennsylvania: 55, 116, 130, 175, 176
Pennsylvania rifles: 114, 131
Penobscott Expedition: 125
Peñol de Acoma. *See* Acoma
Pensacola, Florida: 178
Perdiz siding: 162
Pérez, Captain: 92
Pérez, Colonel Ignacio: 183
Persimmon Gap: 161, 162
Pescados (Indians): 94
Petaya. *See* Cactus
Peyote (devil's root, mescal, mescal button, sacred mushroom): 11-16, 21, 23, 26, 41-42, 68, 92
Pharos. *See* Faraones
Philadelphia, Pennsylvania: 116-117, 122-123, 127
Philipse's Castle (New York): 114
Picuris, Picuria (pueblo): 47, 59, 62, 66, 79, 109
Pike, Zebulon: 169-170, 173
Pike's Peak: 170

Pinanaca (Indians): 58
Pine: 17, 21
Pinole: 14
Piñón: 17, 28, 42
Piro (Indians): 72
Pittsburgh, Pennsylvania: 126, 175
Platte River: 170
Plattsburg, New York: 178
Pleistocene Age: 2
Plums: 17
Plymouth, Massachusetts: 54
Pojoaque (pueblo): 58, 65, 79
Pokeberry: 16, 25
Pontoon Crossing: 41
"Poor Richard's Almanac": 113
Port Lavaca, Texas: 41, 88
Potato: 25
Pottery: 28
Presidio de Conchos (Mexico): 91
Presidio del Norte. *See* La Junta de los Ríos
Prickly pear. *See* Cactus
Printz, John: 55
Providence, Rhode Island: 55
Puaray (pueblo): 60-61
Pueblo, Colorado: 181
Pueblo de los Mansos: 60
Pueblo rebellion: 58-61
Puerco River. *See* Pecos River
Puliques (Indians): 72, 98
Pulque: 21
Pulques (Indians): 72
Pursley, James: 169-170, 173
"Put Your Little Foot": 20
Pyramids (Aztec): 36

Quahadas (Comanche band): 152
Quartering Act: 115
Quebec: 120, 122, 127
Queen's delight: 23, 26
Queenstown, Canada: 177
Queque (Comanche chief): 171
Queres (Indians): 52, 58, 65, 73, 77
"Querriere" (ship): 177
Quetzacoatl: 48
Quicksilver (mercury): 77, 79
Quivira: 47

Rábago y Terán, Felipe: 98, 99, 106
Rábago y Terán, Pedro de: 75, 93,

Rabbit: 2, 9, 42
Rabbit Catchers (Indians): 10, 42, 44
Raleigh, Sir Walter: 54
Ramón, Domingo: 82, 84, 87
Raspberries: 16
Rats' nests: as fuel, 26
Rattlesnake: 6, 21-23
Real de San Lorenzo: 60, 61, 68
Real de San Pedro de Alcántara: 60
Real del Santísimo Sacramento: 60
Real Presidio de San Saba: 107
Red bud: 10, 23
Red River: 97, 171
Reed Camp: 162
Reeves County: 98
Republican Army of the North: 177
Resley, George: 131
Resley, H. E.: 32, 33, 131
Revenue Act: 115
Revere, Paul: 117
Revillagigedo, Conde de: 148
Rhode Island: 55, 115, 121, 126, 175
Rhubarb: 24
Ribaut, Jean: 49
Río de Fierro: 95
Río de las Palmas: 39, 40
Río de las Vacas. *See* Pecos River
Río Grande: Indian paintings near, 28; Spanish exploration of, 39-50 *passim*; Oñate on, 51; Berroteran on, 91-92; Spanish forts on, 93
Río Grande Presidio: 148
Río Puerco. *See* Pecos River
Rivera, Pedro de: 87
Roanoke Island: 57
Robeline, Louisiana: 84
Roberts, Travis: 8, 161, 162, 164
Rockefeller Foundation: 114
Rocky Mountains: 169
Rodents (prehistoric): 2
Rodríguez, Fray Agustín: 49, 50
Rodríguez, Manuel: 101
Romero, Francisco: 100-101
Rooney & Butz store: 24
Rooney Farm: 24
Roque de Madrid, Captain: 73
Rosario (Texas): 134, 142
Roswell, New Mexico: 100

Royal Presidio of San Elizerio: 172
Rubí, Marquis de: 104, 108
Rubin de Celis, Alonso: 98
Ruddle (American soldier): 126
Russia: 126
Rye, New Hampshire: 54

Sabana Grande (Mexico): 142
Sacramento Mountains: 16, 136
Sacred mushroom. *See* Peyote
Sage: 19
Saint Augustine, Florida: 49
Saint Bernard. *See* Espíritu Santo, Bay of
Saint Denis, Louis: 82, 84, 85
Saint Eustatius Island: 128-129
Saint John (on Sorel River): 129
Saint Kitts Island (Saint Christopher): 130
Saint Lawrence River: 122
Saint Lucia Island: 124
Saint Vincent Island: 125
Saint Vrain, Ceran: 173
Salado River. *See* Pecos River
Salas, Juan de: 54-55
Salcedo, Manuel de: 177
Salinero (Indians): 72
Salt: 20, 101
Salt Crossing: 20
Salt lakes: 20, 69-70, 77, 98
Saltillo, Mexico: 140
San Agustín de Ahumada: 95
San Angelo, Texas: 55, 64
San Antonio Crossing: 172
San Antonio de los Julimes: 93
San Antonio de los Puliques: 72, 94
San Antonio de Valero (The Alamo): 84, 133, 142
San Antonio (La Junta mission): 82, 90
San Antonio River: 94, 133
San Antonio, Texas: French at, 82; called San Pedro Springs, 82, 85, 87, 88; missions of, 84, 86, 95, 97, 133-135, 141-142; Aguayo at, 85, 86; Rivera at, 87; and Indian raids, 92, 95, 103, 141-142; as San Fernando de Bexar, 92, 95, 132-133; Bexar presidio of, 132-133;

Philip Nolan at, 148
San Augustine, Texas: 139
San Bartolomé: 48, 49, 63, 93
San Bernardo: 148
San Buenaventura (presidio): 108
San Carlos Indians: 27
San Carlos (Manuel Benevides), Mexico: 108
San Carlos (presidio): 136
San Cristóbal (mission): 72, 82, 90, 94, 98
San Cristóbal (pueblo): 79
San Diego (mission): 77
San Diego River (Texas): 71
San Elizario (San Elceario): 86, 108
San Elizerio: 172
San Felipe (New Mexico): 58, 59, 60, 61, 65, 77
San Felipe (Texas): 146
San Fernando de Bexar. *See* San Antonio, Texas
San Francisco (Bahía community): 141
San Francisco de Asis de La Junta: 82, 90
San Francisco de la Espada: 95, 133-135, 142
San Francisco de los Julimes: 72
San Francisco de los Neches: 82, 84
San Francisco de los Sumas. *See* Nuestro Padre San Francisco de los Sumas
San Francisco de los Tejas: 75, 84
San Francisco (La Junta mission): 98
San Francisco Savier: 107
San Francisco Vizarrón de los Pausanes: 87
San Francisco Xavier (Leon Springs): 69
San Geronimo (Mexico): 51
San Honofre (Spring): 71
San Ildefonso (mission): 93, 95
San Ildefonso (pueblo): 58, 79
San Isidro Labrador: 71
San Jacinto, Battle of: 131
San Javier (mission): 93, 95. *See also* San Xavier
San Javier River: 87, 93
San José (La Junta mission): 82, 90
San José (Nazone mission): 84

San José y San Miguel de Aguayo: 85, 133-134, 142
San Juan Bautista: 82, 90, 91, 93, 98, 108, 148
San Juan Capistrano: 95, 133, 134
San Juan del Río (Comanche Springs): 69
San Juan (pueblo): 58, 79
San Lázaro (pueblo): 79
San Lorenzo. *See* Real de San Lorenzo
San Lorenzo (Coahuila mission): 99
San Lorenzo de la Santa Cruz: 99, 100, 103, 106, 135
San Lorenzo (Kokernot Springs): 68
San Luis de las Amarillas. *See* San Saba Presidio
San Marcos (pueblo): 59, 65, 66, 79
San Marcos River (Texas): 71, 82, 95
San Miguel de Cerro Gordo (presidio): 107-109
San Miguel de Cuéllar: 84
San Miguel de Linares: 84
San Miguel de los Adaes: 84
San Miguel del Socorro: 60
San Miguel (Santa Fe mission): 59
San Pedro Alcántara (mission): 72
San Pedro de Alcántara. *See* Real de San Pedro de Alcántara
San Pedro de Alcántara (Leoncita Springs): 68
San Pedro (Colorado River site): 71
San Pedro River (Devil's River): 137
San Pedro Springs (Bexar County). *See* San Antonio, Texas
San Pedro Springs (Pecos County): 69, 88
San Saba Mission (Santa Cruz de San Saba): established, 96; massacre at, 96-97, 171; and State Marker, 107; Amangual at, 170
San Saba Presidio (San Luis de las Amarillas): established, 96; Parilla recommends removal of, 97; and Rábago y Terán, 98, 99; and route to Santa Fe, 100; Comanches attacks on, 103; Indian harassment of, 104-105; epidemic at, 105-106;

201

abandoned, 106; State Marker at, 106-107; relocation of, 108; Ugalde at, 147; Amangual at, 170
San Saba River: 94, 96, 106
San Saba, Texas: 106
San Sabas (presidio): 136
San Vicente ford: 162
San Vicente (presidio): 108, 109, 142, 143, 162
San Xavier de Naxera: 86
San Ygnacio. *See* Bakersfield
Sánchez, Francisco: 49
Sandía Mountain: 47
Sandía (pueblo): 59, 60, 61, 62, 66
Sand dunes (New Mexico): 100
Sandstone: 27
Santa Ana del Torreón (Mexico): 81
Santa Ana (New Mexico): 58, 65, 79
Santa Bárbara (Mexico): 48, 49, 63
Santa Clara (New Mexico): 58, 79
Santa Cruz de los Cholomes: 93
Santa Cruz de San Saba. *See* San Saba Mission
Santa Elena Junction: 161
Santa Fe, New Mexico: museum of, 7; Spanish settlement at, 54; siege of, 59; as capital of New Mexico, 64; Spanish recapture of, and route to San Saba, 98, 100; Zebulon Pike at, 169; Amangual at, 171-172; Becknell at, 174
Santa Fe Trail: 173, 174, 180
Santa María, Juan de: 49
Santa María de las Carretas: 81
Santa María de Loreto de la Bahía del Espíritu Santo (presidio): established, 86; moved to Guadalupe River, 87; Ramón killed at, 87; moved to San Antonio River, 94; Rubí's recommendations regarding, 104; in chain of forts, 108; during American Revolution, 132, 135; locations of, 135; Indian raids in vicinity of, 141; population of, 141; and Amangual's expedition, 170; captured by McGee's expedition, 177; captured by Dr. Long, 183

Santa María la Redonda: 72
Santa Rosa (presidio): 108
Santa Rosa Springs (Texas): 51
Santia Islands: 130
Santiago de la Ciénega del Coyame: 82, 90
Santiago Mapimí: 91
Santiago Mountains: 161
Santiago Peak: 44
Santiestevan, Padre: 96
Santísimo Nombre de María: 75
Santísimo Sacramento. *See* Real de Santísimo Sacramento
Santo (Spaniard): 84
Santo Domingo (pueblo): 58, 59, 65, 77
Saranac River: 178
Saratoga, New York: 114, 123, 127
Saucedo, General: 170
Savannah, Georgia: 93, 124, 125, 126, 130
Schoharie, New York: 123, 124
Screw bean: 17, 20
Seed Sowers (Indians): 146
Senecas (Indians): 125, 126
Senecu del Sur (Chihuahua): 62
Senecu (New Mexico): 59, 60
Senegambia: 124
Senna: 23
"Serapis" (ship): 126
Seris (Indians): 136
Serna, Captain: 81
Seven Cities of Cíbola: 46-47, 53
Seven Mile Mesa: 27, 43
Sevilleta (pueblo): 59, 60
Shawnee (Indians): 126
Sheffield, Texas: 52, 63
Shelby, Isaac: 127
Sherrill, Mrs. Charles: 10
Sia (pueblo): 58, 65, 73, 79
Sierra Azul: 77
Sierra Blanca: 136, 172
Sierra de San Antonio: 143
Sierra Negra: 77
Sierra Sacramento. *See* Sacramento Mountains
Skunk bush: 10, 27
Slavery: among Aztecs, 36; as practiced by Spanish, 36, 51, 56, 73; and French, 84; in Missouri, as

affecting Texas, 181
Sloth (prehistoric): 2
Smith, Wilson: 21
Smithers, W. D.: 14, 32
Snake herb: 22
Snake River: 169
Snakes: 6, 21-23
Snively Expedition: 131
Soap: 26
Sobrerete: 107
Socorro (pueblo): 60, 65
Sofias (Comanche chief): 147
Soledad. See La Soledad de los Janos
Soledad Creek: 147
Sonora, state of (Nueva Vizcaya): 49, 136
Sorel River: 129
Soto, Hernando de: 30, 48, 62
Sotol: 7, 11-12, 20, 21, 29
Sotol pit (mescal pit): 11-13, 20
South Carolina: 57, 120-130 *passim*
South Sea. See Gulf of California
South Spring (New Mexico): 100
Spanish: capture Mexico City, 30; occupy Cuba, 36; at war with French, 67; English-Dutch aid to, 67; retire from East Texas, 84; and Indian treaties, 91, 95, 96, 97, 136-137; at war with Northern Indians, 99; and American Revolution, 124, 125, 126, 128, 130, 139; fear U.S. aggression, 169; give Florida to U.S., 181
Spanish dagger: 22, 27. *See also* Yucca
Spinach (wild): 16, 19, 23
Squash: 43
Stamp Act: 115
Staten Island, New York: 121
Steam engine: 175
Stillwell, Hallie: 27
Stone Arabia, New York: 124
Stone, Charley: 24
Stony Point, New York: 124-125
Story, Dr. Dee Ann: 2
Sugar Act: 115-116
Sugar Eaters (Comanche band): 152
Sullivan, John: 125
Sumac: 8
Sumas (Indians): 50, 61, 63, 68, 72- 73, 77, 86
Susquehanna River: 125
Swedes: 55, 126

Talley Mountain: 162
Tamarón, Pedro: 98
Tamiques (Indians): 87
Tampico, Mexico: 39
Tanawas (Comanche band): 152
Tanimas (Comanche band): 152
Tanos (Indians): 50, 58, 59
Taos (pueblo): 47, 52, 58, 59, 62, 79, 95, 135
Taovayas (Indians): 97, 99, 104-105, 135, 138, 147
Tapalcomes (Indians): 94
Tarahumare (Indians): 14-15
Tarlton, Sir Banastre: 127
Tarreytown, New York: 114
Tasajillo. *See* Cactus
Tawakonis (Indians): 85, 104-105, 137, 147
Tecolote (Indians): 94
Tehua. *See* Tewa
Tehuacana, Texas: 137
Tejas (Indians): 56, 75, 82
Tejas (presidio): 87
Tenimama (Indians): 58
Tenimamar (Indians): 58
Tennessee: 168
Tequila: 21
Terán. *See* Rábago y Terán
Terlingua Creek: 43, 161, 162
Terlingua District: 31
Teroodan (Indians): 58
Terrenate (presidio): 108
Terreros, Father Ciraco: 95-96
Terreros, Pedro: 95
Tesuque (pueblo): 58, 65, 77
Tesvino (drink): 21
Tewa (Indians): 52, 58, 59, 65
Texas: first missions in, 55; Ysleta represents beginning of, 60; origin of name, 75; during American Revolution, 132
Thanksgiving Day: 54
Thomas, Mrs. Cullen F.: 64
Ticonderoga, New York: 120, 122, 127
Tiger (fang-toothed): 1

203

Tigua, Tiguex, Tiguez, Ti'wan, Tiwesh (Indians): 47, 49, 50, 51, 52, 61-62, 72
Tinaja Mountains: 161, 164, 166
Tinajas del Viento: 143
Tinicum Island: 55
Tlaloc: 36
Tlascaltec (Indians): 95
Tlaxcala: 37
Toboso grass: 20
Tobosos, (Indians): 20, 49
Toledo, José Alvares de: 177
Tomato: 25
Tonhen-t'a ka-i (Chihuahuans): 152
Tonkawas (Indians): 137, 139
Tornillo Creek: 28
Toronto. *See* York
Torres irrigation system: 88
Tortuga (Texas): 137
Toyah Lake: 50, 51, 98, 101
Tres Hermanos (Texas): 164
Trinity River: 95, 135
Tripes Hall: 129
Tuacana (Indians): 85
Tubac (presidio): 108
Tuberose (wild): 26
Tule. *See* Cattail
Tulipe (drink): 21
Tuna. *See* Cactus
Tunas Springs: 160
Turks: 67
Turtle (prehistoric): 2
Twisted Boy (Indians): 71

Ubates (province): 50
Ugalde, Juan: 139-147
Unadilla, New York: 128
University of Texas: O. W. Williams surveys for, 31
Upper Fort (New York): 128
Urrutia, Toribio de: 94
Utes (Indians): 81

Valle de José: 106
Valle de Ruiz: 108
Valle, Marín del: 101
Valley Forge, Pennsylvania: 123
Valverde (Spaniard): 85
Vaqueros (Indians): 52-53
Vargas, Diego de: 75, 77, 79, 81

Velas, Tomás: 100, 101
Velásquez, Diego: 38
Venereal diseases: 25
Vera Cruz, Mexico: 37, 38
Vermont: 122, 168
Vidaurre, Fermín: 93-94
Villasur (Spaniard): 85
Vincennes, Indiana: 124
Virginia: 117, 127, 175
Visitas: 98

Wagon trains: first in Texas, 52
Walter, Miss Gladys: 64
Wanderers (Comanche band): 152
War Hawks: 179
Warm Springs Apaches (Indians): 28
Warnock, Dr. Barton H.: 8, 25
War of 1812: 176-180
Washington, D.C.: 174, 178
Washington, George: 116, 120, 122, 123, 124, 130, 174
Wasps (Comanche band): 152
Wasson, Dr. Valentine P.: 15
Water hemlock: 24
Water potatoes: 16
Watercress: 16
Wax plant: 25-26, 30
Webster, Daniel: 179
Weches, Texas: 75
West Indies: 124, 128-129, 130
West Point, New York: 123, 124, 127
West Virginia: 122
Weymouth, George: 54
Wheeling, West Virginia: 122
White Plains, New York: 121
Whitehaven, England: 125
Whiting, William H. C.: 43
Whittlesey, Joseph: 131
Wichita River: 95
Wichitas (Indians): 147
Wilkinson, James: 177
Williams (American soldier): 127
Williams, Ezekiel: 173
Williams, Oscar Waldo: on Chisos Mountains, 5; on Indian paintings, 28; biographical sketch of, 31; on Cabeza de Vaca, 41, 43-44; on Jediondo camp site, 88; on Comanche raids, 156-157; on Osage

Orange, 162-164
Williams, Roger: 55
Williamsburg, Virginia: 114, 116
Willow: 8, 10
Willow Creek: 161
Willow Springs: 161
Wilmington, Delaware: 55
Wilmington, North Carolina: 130
Witchcraft: 58
Wolf: 2, 6, 47-48
Woods Hollow Creek: 162, 164
Wyoming Valley, Pennsylvania: 123

Xaeser (Indians): 58
Xaranames (Indians): 87
Xoman (Indians): 58
Xumanos (Indians): 52

Y Barbo, Gil: 138
Yamparicas, Yap Eaters, Yappathkas (Comanche band): 152, 171

Yorica (Indians): 58
York (Toronto): 177
Yorktown, Virginia: 129, 130
Ysandis (Indians): 92
Ysleta, Texas: 60, 86. *See also* Isleta del Sur
Yucca: 7, 9-10, 11, 26, 28, 35, 44. *See also* Spanish dagger
Yupes (Comanche band): 152

Zacatecas, Mexico: 63
Zaldívar Mendoza, Vicente de: 19, 52-53
Zapato Tuerto (Mescalero chief): 144-145
Zuñi (Indians): 46-47, 49, 53, 58, 61, 79
Zúñiga (mission). *See* Nuestra Señora del Espíritu Santo de Zúñiga
Zuñis Canyon: 53

JOE F. COMBS
5635 DUFF AVENUE
BEAUMONT, TEXAS 77706

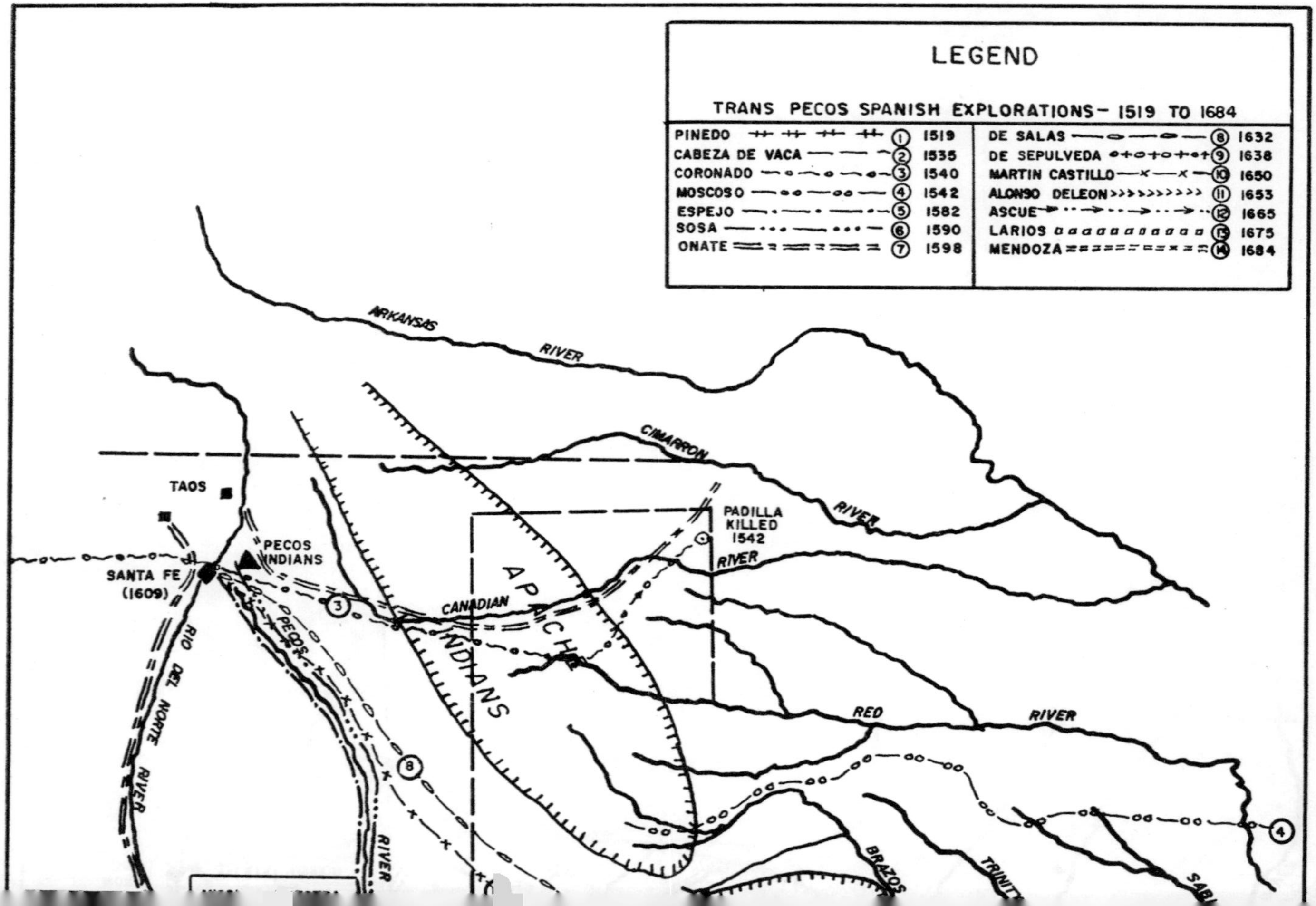
LEGEND
TRANS PECOS SPANISH EXPLORATIONS – 1519 TO 1684
PINEDO ① 1519
CABEZA DE VACA ② 1535
CORONADO ③ 1540
MOSCOSO ④ 1542
ESPEJO ⑤ 1582
SOSA ⑥ 1590
ONATE ⑦ 1598
DE SALAS ⑧ 1632
DE SEPULVEDA ⑨ 1638
MARTIN CASTILLO ⑩ 1650
ALONSO DELEON ⑪ 1653
ASCUE ⑫ 1665
LARIOS ⑬ 1675
MENDOZA ⑭ 1684
ARKANSAS RIVER
CIMARRON RIVER
TAOS
PECOS INDIANS
SANTA FE (1609)
PADILLA KILLED 1542
RIVER
CANADIAN
APACHE INDIANS
RIO DEL NORTE RIVER
PECOS
RIVER
RED RIVER
BRAZOS
TRINITY